CRIMINAL JUSTICE

MENTAL HEALTH AND THE

POLITICS OF RISK

Cavendish
Publishing
Limited

London • Sydney

CRIMINAL JUSTICE, MENTAL HEALTH AND THE POLITICS OF RISK

Edited by

Nicola S Gray, MSc, BSc, PhD
Senior Lecturer in Forensic Psychology,
Cardiff University and Consultant Clinical and Forensic Psychologist
at the South Wales Forensic Psychiatric Service at Caswell Clinic

Judith M Laing, LLB, PhD
Lecturer in Law, Cardiff University

Lesley Noaks, MSc (Econ), BSc (Econ), PhD
Lecturer in Criminology and Social Work, Cardiff University

Cavendish
Publishing
Limited

London • Sydney

First edition first published in Great Britain 2002 by
Cavendish Publishing Limited, The Glass House,
Wharton Street, London WC1X 9PX, United Kingdom
Telephone: + 44 (0)20 7278 8000   Facsimile: + 44 (0)20 7278 8080
Email: info@cavendishpublishing.com
Website: www.cavendishpublishing.com

Published in the United States by Cavendish Publishing
c/o International Specialized Book Services,
5824 NE Hassalo Street, Portland,
Oregon 97213-3644, USA

Published in Australia by Cavendish Publishing (Australia) Pty Ltd
45 Beach Street, Coogee, NSW 2034, Australia
Telephone: + 61 (2)9664 0909   Facsimile: +61 (2)9664 5420
Email: info@cavendishpublishing.com.au
Website: www.cavendishpublishing.com.au

British Library Cataloguing in Publication Data
Gray, Nicola
Criminal justice, mental health and the politics of risk
1 Mentally handicapped offenders 2 Criminal justice, administration of
I Title II Laing, Judith M III Noaks, Lesley
345'.0087

Library of Congress Cataloguing in Publication Data
Data available

ISBN 1 85941 640 3

3 5 7 9 10 8 6 4 2

Printed and bound in Great Britain

CONTRIBUTORS

Professor Nigel Eastman, MD, BSc (Econ), Barrister, FRC Psychology

Nigel Eastman is Professor of Law and Ethics in Psychiatry in the University of London and Head of Forensic Psychiatry at St George's Hospital Medical School. He is also a consultant forensic psychiatrist in the NHS. Professor Eastman is both a psychiatrist and lawyer and much of his academic research and writing centres on law and ethics as applied to all areas of psychiatric practice. Recently he co-chaired a Department of Health sponsored 'think tank' on mental health law reform, which was a precursor to the setting up by the Department of the Richardson Committee advising in detail on law reform, and published from it Eastman, N and Peay, J (eds), *Law Without Enforcement; Integrating Mental Health and Justice* (1999, Hart). He has also conducted major empirical studies relating to the operation of mental health law, as well as being the author of many scholarly papers on mental health law and ethics. Professor Eastman is Chairman of the Law Sub-Committee of the Royal College of Psychiatrists, and a longstanding member of the Mental Health and Disability Committee of the Law Society, and has spent much time involved in policy advisory work concerning the impact of law on mental health and services. In a different strand of his work he has conducted major empirical and policy research on services for mentally disordered offenders. Recently he gave evidence to the Parliamentary Home Affairs Select Committee on government proposals for individuals with 'dangerous and severe personality disorder' (DSPD) in relation both to new law and new services for those with DSPD.

Dr Philip Fennell, BA (Hons) Law (Kent), MPhil Law (Kent), PhD Law (Wales)

Philip Fennell is a Reader in Law in Cardiff Law School, Cardiff University, where he teaches Medical Law and European Community Law. He is a member of the Law Society's Mental Health and Disability Committee and was a member of the Mental Health Act Commission from 1983–89. He has published many articles on law and psychiatry. He is an editor of Butterworths Medico-Legal Reports, and is honorary legal adviser to Wales MIND. He also writes the Annual Review of Medical Law cases for the All England Law Reports. He is co-author of Gostin and Fennell, *Mental Health: Tribunal Procedure* (1992, Longman) and his book entitled *Treatment Without Consent: Law, Psychiatry and the Treatment of Mental Disorder since 1845* was published by Routledge in 1996. He has recently lectured on the Human Rights Act 1998 to the judiciary on behalf of the Judicial Studies Board.

Dr Nicola Gray, MSc Clinical Psychology (London), BSc (Hons) Psychology (London), PhD Psychology (London)

Nicola Gray is a Senior Lecturer in Psychology at Cardiff University where she teaches Forensic Psychology and Clinical Psychology to both undergraduates and Clinical Psychology trainees. Nicola holds a joint appointment between Cardiff University and the South Wales Forensic Psychiatric Service, where she is a Consultant Clinical and Forensic Psychologist. Her research has been mainly in the fields of cognitive function in people with schizophrenia and those with a predisposition for the illness (schizotypy); the development of cognitive tasks for the assessment of future risk of dangerousness in psychopathic offenders; offending outcome of mentally disordered patients from medium secure services; the incidence of post-traumatic stress disorder as a consequence of offending behaviour; and evaluating the effectiveness of processes underlying eye movement desensitisation and reprocessing (EMDR) in the treatment of PTSD (including those with personality disorder). She is the author of many scientific articles on both schizophrenia and forensic psychology.

Professor Robert Hare, BA, MA (Alberta), PhD (West Ontario)

Robert Hare is Emeritus Professor of Psychology, University of British Columbia, where he has taught and conducted research for some 35 years, and President of Darkstone Research Group Ltd, a forensic research and consulting firm. He has devoted most of his academic career to the investigation of psychopathy, its nature, assessment, and implications for mental health and criminal justice. He is the author of several books and many scientific articles on psychopathy, and is the developer of the Psychopathy Checklist – Revised (PCL-R) and its derivatives. He consults with law enforcement, including the FBI and the RCMP, and is a member of the Advisory Panel established by the English Prison Service to develop new programs for the treatment of psychopathic offenders. His current research on psychopathy includes its nature, assessment issues, developmental factors, neuroimaging, domestic violence, risk for recidivism and violence, and the development of new treatment and management strategies. In addition, he lectures widely on the use and misuse of the PCL-R in the criminal justice system. Among his recent awards are the 1999 Silver Medal of the Queen Sophia Center in Spain; the Canadian Psychological Association 2000 Award for Distinguished Applications of Psychology; the American Academy of Forensic Psychology 2001 Award for Distinguished Applications to the Field of Forensic Psychology; and the 2001 Isaac Ray Award presented by the American Psychiatric Association and the American Academy of Psychiatry and Law for Outstanding Contributions to Forensic Psychiatry and Psychiatric Jurisprudence.

Tom Horlick-Jones, BSc Mathematics and Theoretical Physics (Wales), MSc Mathematics and Theoretical Physics (Wales)

Tom Horlick-Jones is an experienced social researcher and policy analyst whose recent work has been concerned with ethnographic studies of risk-related practices associated with organisational risk management, risk perception and decision making. He is currently Senior Research Fellow at the Cardiff University School of Social Sciences and in the Department of Operational Research at the London School of Economics and Political Science. He contributed to the Royal Society's 1992 report, *Risk: Analysis, Perception and Management,* and his publications include *Natural Risk and Civil Protection* (1995, Spon).

Professor Barbara Hudson, BSc Economics (London), MA Sociology (Kent, Canterbury), PhD (Essex)

Barbara Hudson is a Professor at the Lancashire Law School, University of Central Lancashire. She teaches and researches within the fields of criminology, penology and sociology of law, with particular interests in the impact of penal strategies on the marginalised and disadvantaged. Publications include *Justice Through Punishment: A Critique of the 'Justice Model' of Corrections* (1987, Macmillan); *Penal Policy and Social Justice* (1993, Macmillan); *Racism and Criminology* (edited, with Dee Cook, 1993, Sage); *Understanding Justice: An introduction to Ideas, Perspectives and Controversies in Modern Penal Theory* (1996, Open University) and *Race, Crime and Justice* (edited, 1996, Dartmouth). She has also published many articles and chapters on subjects related to the general theme of 'justice and difference'. She is currently completing a new book, *Justice in the Risk Society* (Sage). This work is concerned with conflicts between logics of 'risk control' and 'doing justice' in penal strategies and the problem of how to do 'justice' to 'difference'. The book draws on recent developments in social and legal philosophy as well as on development in criminological theory and criminal justice practice, such as discursive ethics, and restorative justice.

Professor Hazel Kemshall, BA (Durham), MA (Birmingham), Dip Social Work (Birmingham), PhD (De Montfort)

Hazel Kemshall is Professor of Community and Criminal Justice at De Montfort University, UK, where she has research interests in risk assessment and management of offenders and implementing effective practice. She is the author of the Home Office risk training materials for probation officers, and the Scottish Office materials for social workers, and has numerous publications on risk including *Risk in Probation Practice* (1998, Ashgate). She is a member of the Home Office group on risk assessment tools for severe personality disorder, and has recently completed a literature review on risk assessment tools for violent and dangerous offenders (2000, Home Office). She was previously a probation officer, manager and trainer before entering academia. Her research interests include quality in service delivery, effective practice, and risk assessment and risk management. She has published extensively in these areas and has completed research for the Home Office, the Scottish Office and the Economic and Social Research Council.

Dr Judith Laing, LLB (Hons) (Leeds), PhD Law (Leeds)

Judith Laing is a Lecturer in Law at Cardiff Law School. Her areas of expertise are mental health law, medical law, criminal law and justice and she has published several articles in leading journals on these topics. Recent publications include 'Rights versus risk? Reform of the Mental Health Act 1983' (2000) 8(2) Med L Rev 210; 'Diversion of mentally disordered offenders: victim and offender perspectives' [1999] Crim L Rev 805; and 'An end to the lottery? The Fallon Report and personality disordered offenders' (1999) Journal of Mental Health Law 87. Her PhD was published in 1999 in book form by OUP, entitled *Care or Custody: Mentally Disordered Offenders in the Criminal Justice System*. She is Assistant Editor of the Medical Law Review and Recent Cases Editor of the Journal of Social Welfare and Family Law.

Dr Vivian Leacock, BA Politics (Glasgow), MA Criminology (Cantab), PhD Criminology (Cantab)

Vivian Leacock is a Senior Research Officer in the Scottish Executive Justice Department's Central Research Unit. She has recently completed her PhD on youth justice in England and Wales at the Department of Criminology, Keele University. Her PhD demonstrated that the history of youth justice is littered with struggle, contention and ambiguity and that its fragmented history can best be understood by theorising the co-existence of shifting political rationalities and their attendant penal rationalities. Her main thesis is that key concepts in youth justice have been and still are used to justify penal interventions (variously re-packaged and re-invented as 'reforms' and/or 'solutions') that constitute the individual as actively responsible for his/her offending behaviour and capable of self-regulation. Dr Leacock writes here in a personal capacity and outwith her employment at the Executive. The views expressed in her chapter are those of Dr Leacock and not those of the Scottish Executive (nor do they reflect government policy).

Professor Michael Levi, MA (Oxon), Dip Criminology (Cantab), PhD (Soton)

Michael Levi is Professor of Criminology and has taught at Cardiff University since 1975. His major contributions have been in the fields of white-collar crime and corruption, organised crime, money-laundering and violent crime. In addition to many articles in books and scholarly & professional journals, his books include *The Phantom Capitalists* (1981, Gower) and *Regulating Fraud:*

White-Collar Crime and the Criminal Process (1988, Routledge). His most recent book (with Andy Pithouse), *White-Collar Crime and its Victims*, on the impact of fraud on individual and institutional victims and responses to it, will be published by OUP in 2002. He is senior law enforcement policy adviser to Transparency International in Berlin and has served as a member of the UK Treasury's group of money-laundering experts and of the Cabinet Office Performance and Innovation Unit's Steering Committee on the Pursuit and Confiscation of the Proceeds of Crime. He has been involved as consultant on a very large number of research studies, some of them for internal governmental reviews and for the UN, EU and Council of Europe; some for governments (Home Office, Department of International Development, Department of Social Security); and others corporate, eg Ernst & Young corporate fraud surveys. He is currently conducting an ESRC-funded study under the Future Governance Research Initiative on the factors shaping the evolution of money laundering and corruption controls worldwide.

Anthony Maden, MB, BS (London), MRC Psychology (London), MD (London)

Tony Maden trained in psychiatry at the Bethlem and Maudsley Hospitals, where he worked as a senior lecturer and honorary consultant, before taking up a post as Professor of Forensic Psychiatry at Imperial College, London, in February 2000. His main interests are in risk management and needs assessment in mentally disordered offenders.

Professor Mike Maguire, MA Modern Languages (Oxford), B Litt Social Anthropology (Oxford)

Mike Maguire is Professor of Criminology and Criminal Justice at Cardiff University, Wales. He has conducted major research projects and published widely on burglary, victimisation, prisons, probation, parole and policing, and is currently involved in studies of targeted policing and prisoner resettlement under the Home Office Crime Reduction Programme. His main interests include penology, penal policy, regulation and accountability. He is a co-editor of *The Oxford Handbook of Criminology* and of *Punishment and Society*, and is a member of the Prison Service/Probation Service Joint Accreditation Panel.

Dr Lesley Noaks, MSc (Econ), BSc (Econ) (Wales), PhD Criminology (Wales), Dip Applied Social Studies (Wales)

Lesley Noaks is a Lecturer in Criminology and Social Work at Cardiff University. She has conducted research into criminology and criminal justice for the last 10 years, and her most recent projects include research for the Home Office in 1999 on Risk Assessment with Dangerous and Sex Offenders, and for the Nuffield Foundation in 1999 on Access to Justice for Remand Prisoners. She has a number of publications, including three jointly edited texts: Noaks, L, Levi, M and Maguire, M, *Contemporary Issues in Criminology* (1995, Wales UP); Dobash, R, Dobash, R and Noaks, L, *Gender and Crime* (1995, Wales UP); and Brookman, F, Noaks, L and Wincup, E, *Research Methods in Criminology* (1999, Ashgate).

Professor Richard Sparks, BA Social and Political Sciences, MPhil and Phd Criminology (Cantab)

Richard Sparks is Professor of Criminology at Keele University. His main research interests are in penal politics, the sociology of penal policy and institutions and criminology's relations with social and political theory. He has written or edited seven books including (with Tony Bottoms and Will Hay) *Prisons and the Problem of Order* (1996, OUP); (with Evi Girling and Ian Loader) *Crime and Social Change in Middle England* (2000, Routledge); (with Tim Hope, eds) *Crime, Risk and Insecurity* (2000, Routledge) and (with David Garland, eds) *Criminology and Social Theory* (2000, OUP). Sparks is Associate Editor of the British Journal of Criminology and Editor-in-Chief of *Punishment and Society*.

ACKNOWLEDGMENTS

The inspiration for this book came from the multi-disciplinary links that we forged at the Centre for Crime, Law and Justice at Cardiff University. We are very grateful for the administrative support given to us by Lesley-Anne Landeg. We would also like to thank the editorial staff at Cavendish Publishing Limited.

Nicola Gray
Judith Laing
Lesley Noaks
November 2001

CONTENTS

CHAPTER 1

RISK: THE PROFESSIONAL, THE INDIVIDUAL, SOCIETY AND THE LAW

Nicola Gray, Judith Laing and Lesley Noaks

Calculating and managing risks which nobody really knows has become one of our main preoccupations. That used to be a specialist job for actuaries, insurers and scientists. Now, we all have to engage in it, with whatever rusty tools we can lay our hands on – sometimes the calculator, sometimes the astrology column. [Beck in Franklin, 1998, p 12.]

1.1 INTRODUCTION – 'RISK SOCIETY'

A defining feature of contemporary criminal justice discourse has been the prominence of issues of risk. Risk as represented in criminal justice worlds has taken on a variety of guises. Risk 'talk' reveals a preoccupation both with those seen to pose a risk and those considered to be at risk. Linked to such preoccupations is a growing absorption with the legal, medical and psychological means by which we seek to manage risk. This text seeks to focus on all three of those elements and also consider the inter-relationships between them.

The body of theory which has defined us as a 'risk society' (Beck, 1992; Ericson and Haggerty, 1997) has pointed to the centrality of risk to social arrangements. Recent developments in criminal justice and mental health policy have been underpinned by the ways in which, as a 'risk society', we are increasingly motivated to invest in means to obviate the threat to ourselves from all forms of harm – personal, financial, emotional or physical. Identifiable high levels of anxiety in relation to crime provide an important backdrop to an increasing suspicion of the risks that others pose to personal security. Garland (1996) argues that individual households have adapted to high rates of crime with greater investment in physical security precautions and more security consciousness. Entwined with this has been more emotional investment in the 'war' against crime by the individual citizen. As a 'cultural phenomenon' crime control has become a pervasive feature of the lives of many individual citizens. Responses to crime have occurred both at the individual and at the more collective policy level and are reflected in a number of recent legislative changes outlined below. Consequent to such developments 'risk institutions and their communication systems have become an important basis of our society' (Ericson and Haggerty, 1997, p 11).

Sheptycki (1997, p 307) also argues that 'discourses of insecurity' and fear of crime are driving the growth in surveillance devices and procedures in many facets of late modern society. There is a related drive to create 'zones of risk suppression', which physically separate those who consider themselves at risk from those they judge to be a source of danger. While classically these occur in the gated communities of the USA, the thinking behind them increasingly permeates criminal justice philosophies and practices in the UK. Feeley and Simon (1992) identify the pre-eminence of thinking and working practices which seek to identify and classify sources of risk. Recent attention to sex offender registration schemes, and the promotion of standardised risk assessment tools, commonly for inclusion in pre-sentence reports, represent what they have termed the risk penology. In such climates, Shearing and Stenning (1987) argue that control and surveillance are 'pervasive'. Such control is 'consensual' with little evidence of, or need for, compulsion. Fear and a sense of danger serve to reinforce cleavages in society, emphasising division and a sense of the other. In the 'Risk Society' a significant proportion of citizens are more than willing to co-operate to support enhancement in the methods of surveillance. As crime has become increasingly salient for individual citizens they have become increasingly willing to co-operate in the expansion of control networks.

One of the main aims of this book is to analyse the relationship between theoretical models of risk and recent developments in criminal justice and mental health policy. Such developments are reviewed from psychological, psychiatric, legal and criminological perspectives. While the book is divided into sections linked to these elements a major focus of the text is with the interface between the disciplines. Such considerations become important in the face of changes currently being addressed on the boundaries of professional roles. Recent developments, including the recent legislative proposals on Dangerous and Severe Personality Disorder (DSPD), point to an increasing fusion of roles between key players in criminal justice and mental health spheres. This interplay between the key players is a major focus of several contributions to this book (Eastman, Fennell, Kemshall and Maguire).

The advent of government proposals to manage high-risk individuals (DSPD) and the consequences of these proposals for the individuals and professionals involved has been a major catalyst for this edited volume. The personality disordered have, over recent years, gained a more prominent profile with the emergence of a number of highly-publicised tragedies and killings, such as the murder of Megan and Lin Russell by Michael Stone, and the notorious paedophile, Sydney Cook, who has confessed his intention to continue to sexually offend against children. In the wake of such incidents, the government published a Consultation Paper, *Managing Dangerous People with Severe Personality Disorder – Proposals for Policy Development* (Home Office/Department of Health, 1999) in July 1999, to consider ways of introducing greater control over those who pose a significant risk to others. Its publication followed the announcement that powers would be established to indefinitely detain people with personality disorders who represent a danger to the public. The review process culminated in the government's White Paper on reforming mental health legislation, published in December 2000 (Home Office/Department of Health, 2000). The White Paper has emphasised the importance of managing risk and fully endorses the aim of public protection. It recommends a radical overhaul of the current mental health legislation and has proposed new criteria for compulsory commitment, which give authority to assess and detain all those who pose a significant risk of serious harm to others as a result of severe personality disorder. Both lawyers and psychiatrists (Crawford *et al*, 2001; Eastman, 1999; Gledhill, 2000; Laing, 1999) are highly critical of the proposals, perceiving them to be essentially public protection measures rather than progressive and enlightened mental health reforms. The government is making no excuses that the primary objective is risk management and public protection, and society's interests are being elevated above all others. However, it must not be forgotten that there are other competing interests at stake. It is of equal importance to consider the rights of the individual patient/offender and the interests of the criminal justice and mental health professionals involved, as well as the views and needs of society in general.

There are a number of significant features of this proposed legislation that make the existence of this book important. Foremost is the fact that the legislation proposes for the first time in the history of our criminal justice and mental health systems that individuals are to be indefinitely detained on the basis of 'risk'. Such developments directly put in jeopardy the civil liberties of these disordered individuals – those defined as the risky 'other'. Climates of fear and mistrust have historically created periods where the individual freedoms of the minority have been sacrificed to the anxieties and concerns of the majority. Such developments will require professional groups, faced with their extended roles, to question the ethics of what they are being required to do in order to address public insecurities. Politically it may not be popular to question the reliability of the risk assessment and management strategies that we have. Despite this, professionals in criminal justice, mental health and related fields will be required to manage a balancing of individual civil liberties and the greater good of society. Several of the contributors to this text (Fennell, Eastman, Hudson, Kemshall and Maguire, Leacock and Sparks) point to some of the ethical dilemmas that they will face in attempting to carefully balance the rights of those 'at risk' (victims and society) with the individual rights of the risky 'other'.

These ethical dilemmas are particularly acute for mental health professionals, who will be required to assess and manage the risky 'others' under the new DSPD proposals. From a psychiatric and psychological perspective, the main issues raised by the proposed legislation are (1) the profession's ability to reliably and validly diagnose 'severe personality disorder'; (2) its ability to accurately identify, assess and manage 'risk'; and (3) the ethics (professional and personal) of indefinitely and compulsorily detaining individuals purely on the basis of the risk that they pose and when they may not (yet) have committed a criminal offence. These issues will be discussed in Section One of this book – *Risk Assessment in Mental Health and Professional Responsibility*. The three contributors to this section (Eastman, Hare, Maden) are all internationally renowned clinicians and academics within forensic mental health (psychiatry and psychology), but, as you will see, they all hold widely differing views as to how these dilemmas should be resolved.

An important aspect of the proposed developments in relation to DSPD, and the relatively recent partnership requirements with regard to Dangerous and Sex Offenders (Crawford, 1997) is that their introduction requires a review of working relations between traditionally distinct professional groups. Following on from such legislative changes, groups such as psychiatrists, psychologists, police officers, probation officers and social workers find themselves having to review the boundaries of their role. As subsequent chapters will demonstrate (Eastman, Fennell, Kemshall and Maguire), professional roles are becoming increasingly diffuse and overlapping, as the mental health and criminal justice systems converge. This convergence will have major implications for the working practices of the different professions involved.

It will be crucial for the different disciplines involved to understand the concepts, professional ethics, methodologies, and practices of others. In the field of forensic mental health 'multi-disciplinary' is usually taken to mean the different health-related disciplines who, together, provide care for mentally disordered offenders (for example, mental health nursing, psychology, psychiatry, occupational therapy, social work). Because these disciplines work together (often on a daily basis) in the assessment, treatment and management of individuals with severe mental disorder and offending behaviour, they have developed an understanding and mutual respect for the philosophies and language, techniques and professional practices of each other. Unfortunately, the same might not be said to be true for the scientific and academic disciplines, however.

From a legal perspective, the need to balance the competing interests is crucial, as respect for individual rights and the protection of civil liberties are fundamental and gaining increasing prominence in light of the enactment of the Human Rights Act 1998 in October 2000. The Act has incorporated international human rights law directly into the United Kingdom legal system. This means that as well as protecting the public, any resulting legislation will also be required to emphasise and protect the rights of the detained individuals themselves. Specifically, under s 19 of the Act there is now an express obligation to ensure that any future legislation conforms with the European Convention on Human Rights (ECHR). With respect to the detention of dangerous people, any future legislation must comply with Article 5 of the Convention which safeguards against the arbitrary deprivation of liberty, especially Article 5(1)(e) which provides for the detention of 'persons of unsound mind, alcoholics, or drug addicts or vagrants'. In future, therefore, not only will courts be required to interpret any legislation in accordance with the Convention, but there is also this express obligation imposed on the government to ensure that any future legislation is compatible with it. In light of these obligations, contributors to Section Two of the book – *Risk Management and the Law: Balancing Individual Rights and Public Protection* (Fennell, Hudson) – assess the government's proposals from a human rights perspective. Their chapters focus on the role of the law and how it should ensure that rights and risks are carefully balanced to ensure compliance with the ECHR. It is also important to ensure that the procedures for assessing risk are robust and reliable in order that justice and due process is respected, and individual liberty is not deprived on the basis of inaccurate or exaggerated predictions of risk.

The pre-eminence of risk in our society cannot be understated – all sectors of society are preoccupied with notions of risk. Ericson and Haggerty in their attention to the role of the police in the 'risk society' point to an 'insatiable quest for more and better knowledge of risk', which can merely serve to reinforce pre-existing anxieties rather than counter them. Furedi in his text *Culture of Fear* (1997) also points to the prominence of notions of risk in how individuals organise their lives and evaluate their existence. He is not only concerned with crime related fear but rather with the proliferation of a whole range of anxieties, including fear about health and the environment. For him individuals increasingly live their lives through a prism of risk, adopting a range of risk limitation strategies, intended to enhance their risk aversion. Linked to this a risk management industry has emerged, which includes the various modes of classification and categorisation recently adopted in criminal justice spheres. Feeley and Simon (1992) propose that resort to the actuarial language of prediction is likely to be an ongoing process and will remain as a distinguishing characteristic of penal practice for the foreseeable future. With that in mind, several contributors highlight the prominence of risk assessment strategies and the use of actuarial data in predicting and managing risky behaviour in a number of different contexts. Kemshall and Maguire's chapter provides a pertinent review of how such approaches impact on multi-agency work with sexual and violent offenders. Eastman, Hare and Maden assess the efficacy of different risk management tools employed in psychology and psychiatry for identifying risk in disordered individuals; whereas Levi focuses on empirical data in identifying and regulating the risks of financial crime and Horlick-Jones uses the Notting Hill Carnival as an example of the importance of empirical work in effective risk management.

Traditionally mental health professionals, criminologists and lawyers have very little understanding of their respective roles, what their concepts and professional language mean, their scientific methodologies and techniques, or codes of conduct. Each discipline may also have very different perceptions of risk and different expectations about our ability to successfully identify, assess and manage risky behaviour. The proposed DSPD legislation will dramatically alter our working practices and require us to work much more closely together. Consequently there will be a need to develop new ways of working in harmony with each other. It is at this point that there is maximum opportunity for error, confusion, miscarriage of justice, and clinical catastrophe. Ignorance becomes dangerous and creates further risk. It is at these points in time that we need to develop our knowledge base and attempt to understand the working practices and philosophies of our colleagues in different disciplines. This is what this book aims to do. The three sections of this book each focus on different, yet overlapping, issues, each central to each discipline's (mental health, law, criminology) respective ability to balance all the competing interests and work effectively within the 'risk society' that we have become.

1.2 SECTION ONE: RISK ASSESSMENT IN MENTAL HEALTH AND PROFESSIONAL RESPONSIBILITY

Section One focuses upon our ability to predict future risk of offending in the individual and the different methodologies and scientific principles applied to this endeavour. This is very much the domain of psychologists and psychiatrists and these professionals attempt to assess, manage, control and treat 'risk' within the individual. Risk of reoffending can be assessed for any criminal behaviour, but most often applies to risk of serious violent and sexual offences.

In Chapter 1, Maden argues that the advances in the epidemiology of crime do not, and cannot, aid us in the risk assessment and risk management of the individual patient. To illustrate his point, Maden uses examples of epidemiological statistics, which demonstrate an association between certain ethnic groups and high, or low, rates of criminal behaviour. He argues that although these associations undoubtedly exist it would be wrong to base a risk assessment of any given individual purely on the basis of their ethnic origin. So too, argues Maden, would it be wrong to evaluate risk of dangerousness solely on the presence of mental illness or personality disorder, even though an association between these groups and criminal behaviour may exist. He cogently argues that population studies should not be applied directly to individuals and uses case examples to demonstrate that serious harm has been caused when this has been attempted. Maden also describes the advantages of learning lessons about individual clinical risk assessment and management from Inquiries after Homicide (statutory inquiries that occur if a mentally disordered person who has been in recent contact with psychiatric services kills somebody) and states that these lessons have never been identified from large scale actuarial risk studies. Importantly, not only do these Inquiries teach us important lessons about what the scientific risk assessment literature has not identified (and perhaps never can), but they also paint a picture not of clinicians using the best risk assessment tools and methods available and struggling to push the limits of these methodologies still further, but of failures of basic clinical care by individual clinicians and agencies. These failures are at the level of human error and occur both in terms of not taking sufficient account of the patient's history, poor evaluation of current mental state, discontinued treatment (by either poor diagnosis or poor compliance), not taking appropriate action early on in relapse, and poor communication both within and between agencies. Thus, Maden argues, it is not our poor ability at predicting risk in mentally disordered offenders that leads to tragedy but the inability of certain clinicians and agencies to follow simple rules of basic clinical care.

Hare's chapter describes the concept of psychopathy and its measurement. He describes psychopathy as 'a personality disorder defined by a cluster of interpersonal, affective, and lifestyle characteristics that results in serious negative consequences for society'. The validity of the construct of psychopathy is also discussed, specifically with regard to its ability to predict violent and sexual reoffending in male and female prisoners, adolescent offenders, mentally disordered offenders, and civil psychiatric patients. The evidence that psychopathy (as measured by the Psychopathy Checklist – Revised; PCL-R) can predict recidivism across all forensic populations is striking. It is now increasingly accepted by both forensic psychologists, clinical psychologists, psychiatrists and the legal profession that any assessment of future risk of violence should include an assessment of psychopathy using the PCL-R. Indeed, Hare goes so far as to state that the evidence that the PCL-R is the best identified predictor of violent reoffending to date is so strong that failure to conduct such an evaluation as part of a risk assessment on an individual may be unethical from a professional viewpoint.

The chapters by Maden and Hare illustrate the broad differences of opinion between the professions of psychiatry and psychology about how best to conduct risk assessment and management and the ethics of this endeavour. On the one hand Hare argues that it is 'unethical' and 'unprofessional' not to use assessments with proven predictive validity for assessing future risk of serious offending. On the other, Maden argues that such 'group' statistics offer little in the assessment of risk for the individual and indeed that it can be misleading and unethical to base such assessments on anything other than clinical observation. These markedly different opinions on the assessment of risk of future reoffending cut to the core of, and cast major doubts upon, the government's proposed legislation for DSPD, where assessment of risk is a central and essential component.

To add further fuel to the fire, both Maden and Hare only discuss risk assessment and risk management of people who have already offended. They do not address the issues involved in conducting individual risk assessments in people who have never previously been convicted. Presumably, this is because currently such assessments are a rare event. The validity of risk assessments of individuals who have not previously offended is to date an unknown quantity, both in terms of the predictive validity of risk assessment tools such as the PCL-R and in terms of individual clinical judgement of risk. Indeed, Hare discusses elsewhere that there are many people who meet criteria for psychopathy on the PCL-R but who never commit serious crime. Instead these people use their psychopathic personality to gain financial, personal or business advantage. If this is the case then how are clinicians going to be able to differentiate the 'dangerous' psychopaths from the 'industrial' psychopaths if both groups will show similarly high scores on the PCL-R? Presently, we do this by evaluating the presence or absence of known criminal behaviour. Both the current research literature and the experience of our clinicians has very little to say about how we might reliably and validly evaluate risk in someone who has never previously committed a serious criminal offence.

In Chapter 4, Eastman discusses the ethics and dangers of blurring the boundaries between the different professions, specifically law and psychiatry, and argues that the DSPD legislation would encourage mental health professionals to become agents of public protection. Eastman is a rare breed in that he is both a qualified consultant forensic psychiatrist and a barrister. He therefore understands more than most the interface between forensic mental health services and the law. He discusses the ethics and philosophies of the disciplines of psychiatry and the law and discusses how the pragmatic relationship between them might differ according to how strictly the legal profession applies the law and legal processes, and the psychiatric profession applies medical science. Eastman argues that it is important that the different professions adhere strictly to their social roles and that to move out of these roles (for example, by psychiatrists becoming agents of public protection) is not only professionally unethical but may bring about a 'disintegration' of that profession. Eastman further argues that 'Severe Personality Disorder' as described in the DSPD legislation is a policy-contrived group that does not map onto any diagnostic category. Thus there cannot be any scientific evidence for its existence: DSPD is an invented concept for use in policy and we cannot, therefore, validly identify it. Further, Eastman postulates that it is unclear as to whether we have any sophisticated measurement for the evaluation of future risk of dangerousness. He argues, therefore, that methodologies to address the two core concepts upon which DSPD legislation is based – Severe Personality Disorder and risk (of dangerousness) – are missing from our professional tool bag. Eastman goes on to warn against the dangers of policies of social control being based on 'invented' constructs without any methodology for their reliable and valid identification. Such an absence of validity of the concepts means that not only is research limited (how can we research what we cannot properly identify?) but that these constructs can be stretched and distorted to suit. Such distortions, in the name of public protection and public welfare, are a high price to pay in terms of both professional ethics, but perhaps more importantly, justice.

1.3 SECTION TWO: RISK MANAGEMENT AND THE LAW: BALANCING INDIVIDUAL RIGHTS AND PUBLIC PROTECTION

The need to promote justice is one of the main themes of Section Two, which focuses on some of the legal implications of risk assessment and management. Fennell's chapter, 'Radical risk management, mental health and criminal justice', explores how the government's pursuit of 'radical risk management' policies impacts upon the system of care of mentally disordered people. He examines the current mental health system as well as the government's recent proposals to reform the mental health legislation, placing particular emphasis upon the implications of the proposals to detain high-risk – DSPD – patients. In doing so, he argues that a 'convergence' is taking place between the values and legal structures of the hospital and penal systems, which has 'profound implications for the citizenship rights of mentally disordered people, and the nature of the doctor/patient relationship'.

He reinforces Eastman's reservations about the White Paper and maintains that it is a clear example of the government's increasingly protectionist stance – 'more reflective of criminal justice and risk management concerns than it is of traditional healthcare values'. He highlights the pressures placed on the professionals involved as a result of this shift, in particular, for health care practitioners, whose role is becoming increasingly blurred as the dividing line between care and control is eroded – 'increasingly psychiatrists are becoming involved in decision-making about risk in the penal system'. This has major implications for the practice of psychiatry as the proposals in the White Paper will 'encourage defensive medicine in the name of risk management'. In that sense, Fennell is in agreement with some of Eastman's conclusions and cautions against the dangers of blurring the boundaries of professional roles and responsibility.

Additionally, Fennell argues that the legal status of the mentally disordered as patients/prisoners is converging. The government's proposals also have severe consequences for mentally disordered patients, as the balance is moving towards risk management and away from patients' rights. Accordingly, Fennell also specifically considers the impact of the ECHR on the government's policies and analyses the relevant case law to demonstrate the need to strike a balance in order to protect individual rights and preserve the citizenship rights of people who suffer from mental disorder.

As the title of the next chapter by Hudson suggests, 'Balancing rights and risks: dilemmas of justice and difference', she shares many of Eastman and Fennell's concerns and is anxious to ensure that a balance is struck between 'reducing risk' and 'doing justice' as criminal justice objectives. She notes that 'there has been a significant shift from doing justice to controlling risk as the goal of law and order and penal strategies'. But she stresses how important it is to ensure that justice is not forgotten and that there is adequate protection of individual rights and due process safeguards built into the system: 'For risk society to be a society where justice sets limits to power, a vibrant culture of rights, and a non-repressive respect for difference, are pre-requisites.' She maintains that it is important to ensure that the demands of formal and substantive justice are met which means that we must apply the rules properly and also ensure that we make the right decisions. Hudson feels that we need to move away from risk management and crime control as the dominant themes of penal policy 'towards a renewal of justice'. She argues that *inter alia* the introduction of the Human Rights Act 1998 will be highly significant in this respect, as it will encourage the growth of a rights culture among the judiciary and this will provide a constraint on the pursuit of crime control goals.

Levi's chapter stands in contrast to the other contributors to this section as he considers how we police the 'risk society' in an entirely different sphere of criminal law and justice – the regulation of fraud and financial crime. Again, the goal here is to calculate and control 'risky' behaviour, albeit behaviour which causes a different type of harm – financial as opposed to personal/property. Common everyday examples of successful frauds include fake charities, fraudulent prices for goods on sale, fraudulent subscriptions and appliances/car repairs. Recent examples of financial crime on a much larger scale are the conviction of Ernest Saunders, the Chairman of Guinness, following the takeover of Distillers, and Robert Maxwell's fraudulent pensions scam. Levi maintains that financial risk regulation has an important political dimension as 'certain sorts of victim can do more harm to the party in power ... than others, and thereby may ascend the ranking of those deserving protection'. This political dimension is also evinced by the fact that, in the UK, the allocation of resources devoted to addressing the 'fear of financial crime' has, hitherto, been largely absent from political agendas. This is extremely unfortunate, as the statistics and surveys discussed in Levi's chapter demonstrate the devastating effects and huge financial losses incurred as a result of financial crime.

Levi explains how difficult it is for regulatory bodies such as the UK Financial Services Authority to reduce the risk of financial crime due to the unspecific nature of the 'forms of financial crime' and 'the sorts or classes of victim'. Their task is exacerbated by the 'problematic nature of the evidence on the extent and distribution of financial crime'. Levi argues that the 'at risk' estimates are distorted by the fact that in fraud cases, 'offenders can manipulate the victims' perceptions of "what happened" so that it may never even occur to them that they have been victimised improperly or criminally' in the first place. This reinforces the need to provide adequate protection to the victims of financial crime.

The international scale of financial crime is also a compounding factor. The rise in internet technology and widening of share ownership mean that the 'social spread of the population at risk increases', making it far more difficult to measure and manage those 'at risk'. As a result of such factors we are left feeling that there are limits to our ability to detect and control certain types of risky behaviour, a theme which also emerges from Maden's chapter on mentally disordered offenders.

1.4 SECTION THREE: RISK IN SOCIAL CONTEXTS

The final section begins with Horlick-Jones' chapter which traces the emerging and pervasive influence of risk-related language and technologies. He locates risk as a global phenomenon and points to a shift from a concern with the 'dangerous' to the 'risky'. He addresses the implications of such change for individuals bound up with such processes, including those individuals charged with monitoring the 'risky'. While acknowledging the major contribution of theorists in this area he also argues for the importance of empirical work and provides an example from the Notting Hill Carnival of risk management processes in action.

Kemshall and Maguire's chapter also uses empirical research on the implementation of risk assessment and risk management procedures by Public Protection Panels in England and Wales, to assess how far the evidence supports claims of a broad shift in modes of crime control from penal modernism towards a new 'risk penality' characteristic of the late (or post-) modern period. Such shifts reflect a categorisation of individuals on the basis of acts that they might commit rather than those for which they have been proven to be responsible. Their evidence points to a mixed and contradictory picture in which the dominant discourse around measures to deal with sexual and 'dangerous' offenders is in tune with this claim, but there are numerous aspects of agency culture and practice – for example, interest in the individual case, and (in contrast to current psychological practice) the valuing of professional judgement above actuarial tools – which reflect the continuing strength of the 'modernist' approach. There are however signs of a growing populist challenge to the modernist assumption that risk knowledge and management should be left to small groups of experts working in secret. Overall, perhaps the strongest evidence of a shift towards new penal forms lies in the emergence of new forms of partnership, driven by the logic of risk, and the significant dispersal of accountability which has accompanied their development.

Finally, Leacock and Sparks return to the theme of the contemporary significance accorded to risk while at the same time cautioning that we do not overlook its former role and influence. They warn against an over pre-occupation with risk as a new and emerging concept and the potential for a lack of awareness of the ongoing role it has played in policy developments and professional practice. While politicians, policy makers and professionals may now be more explicit about risk and require systems to manage it, it would be wrong to overlook risk as a key influential factor that has underpinned all of these areas in the past. Focusing on the area of youth justice, they trace how since 1990 the issue of risk has impacted on policy and its relationship with other key influences. Drawing on the theoretical literature they trace how a concern with risk intersected with other key factors in a 'complex, uneven and sharply politicised way' to emerge as youth justice policy. The significance of the politics of risk in the interrelated worlds of criminal justice and mental health is an important recurrent theme throughout the text.

SECTION ONE

RISK ASSESSMENT IN MENTAL HEALTH AND PROFESSIONAL RESPONSIBILITY

CHAPTER 2

RISK MANAGEMENT IN THE REAL WORLD

Anthony Maden

2.1 INTRODUCTION

Less that twenty years ago, the orthodox teaching was that there was no statistical association between schizophrenia and violence. Epidemiology showed this assumption to be invalid. For example, Swanson *et al* (1990) found self-reported violence over the last 12 months in 2% of the general public, increasing to 8% when there was a diagnosis of 'pure' schizophrenia and to 13% if that diagnosis was combined with substance misuse or personality disorder. There have been other studies since but the message is similar and it could be argued that this finding has had more impact on the practice of psychiatry in the UK than any other recent discovery. Once it is accepted that violent behaviour is sometimes a complication of a mental illness, or other form of mental disorder, then risk management becomes a priority.

Epidemiology has continued to contribute, with many studies of risk and prediction. The MacArthur Violence Risk Assessment Study, based on a sample of about 1,200 patients, has identified factors that predict violence (Appelbaum *et al*, 2000) and has attempted to incorporate them into a clinically useful tool (Monahan *et al*, 2000). Success has been limited and the present paper argues that our expectations of epidemiological or actuarial studies are unrealistic. There is inevitably a gap between studies of this type and clinical practice. That gap should be filled by studies of mechanism, which have not yet been done. Without an understanding of the causal links between psychiatric disorder and violence, at the level of the individual patient, actuarial studies may not help the clinician. Until such studies are carried out, it can be argued that the best accounts of practice in this area come from inquiries following homicide. This paper sets out the strengths and weaknesses of the actuarial work, then attempts to show how the homicide inquiries, unscientific as they are, should influence future research.

It must be emphasised that this chapter is not a criticism of epidemiology. If we turn to another branch of medicine, such as heart disease, it is obvious that epidemiology has most impact when combined with physiological, psychological, biochemical and pharmacological studies. The deficiency in psychiatry is in these areas, with epidemiology far ahead of the other lines of inquiry.

2.2 THEORETICAL LIMITATIONS OF STUDIES OF RISKS IN PSYCHIATRY

In some ways, risk is an ideal subject for research. It can be defined in terms of probability, so it invites statistical analyses of large-scale studies. Most of these studies have been done in the USA. They ask questions about the relationship between mental disorder and violence, and about the ability of psychiatrists to predict violence. In other respects, research on risk has been problematic. Science should proceed from observation to the design of experiments, but this is rarely possible when dealing with serious risk, so we are often stuck at the level of observation. We cannot easily proceed to testing hypotheses. Furthermore, even at the descriptive level, the large statistical studies have serious limitations, both theoretical and practical.

The main theoretical limitation of these studies arises from the fact that they make statements of probability about populations, when the clinician's interest is in the individual. The studies are modelled on the actuarial tables of the insurance industry. The successful insurer must be confident in making statements about the proportion of the population which is likely to die during a given period. He has no interest in predicting which individuals will die, nor does he have the ability to make such predictions. The priorities of the clinician are quite different, as they are dominated by the need to predict the behaviour of an individual patient. It is important to emphasise that this is a limitation in principle, and not just in practice. However much we refine our instruments, the problem remains. In order to illustrate this point, it is useful to turn to physical medicine. Despite the fact that the pathological processes are better understood, predictions of outcome in an individual are rarely simple. In many conditions, one-year or five-year survival rates have been worked out with some precision. It is possible to make an accurate estimate of the probability that the patient, with certain clinical characteristics, will survive for a given length of time. This still does not allow us to answer the crucial question, when will a particular patient die? A precise answer becomes possible only when the end is near, and the answer then derives from clinical observations rather than from actuarial figures. At that point, the doctor is identifying clinical signs that the process of dying is underway, rather than making a true prediction.

If prediction is a problem in physical medicine, it is bound to be much more so in psychiatry, where the understanding of pathological processes is less well developed. It is important to recognise that these limitations will not disappear as our epidemiological techniques improve. However good the actuarial data, it will still be impossible to use the information derived from it to predict accurately the behaviour of an individual. This limitation of epidemiology is emphasised because of the dangers associated with the crude application of population statistics to the individual. The following three examples illustrate some of these dangers.

(a) *Ethnic origin and crime*

In England and Wales, certain ethnic groups are over represented among prisoners and other populations of offenders. Some ethnic groups have low rates of offending, the classic example being the Japanese population of the USA. Many attempts have been made to explain these variations in offending rates, but the present argument requires only that such differences exist. Can one use such differences to draw conclusions about the criminality or otherwise of an individual, based only on his or her ethnic origin? The answer must be a resounding no, as any other response would amount to crude stereotyping at best, and racism at worst. Is it any more acceptable to use membership of other groups (the mentally ill or the personality disordered) as a basis for drawing conclusions about the likely criminality of an individual?

(b) *Conviction by mathematical error?*

In November 1999, a solicitor was convicted of smothering her two infant children. There was argument about the pathological evidence but a leading paediatrician stated that the chances of two cot deaths happening in one family were so small as to be insignificant (1 in 73 million). It was argued by a Director of Public Health (Watkins, 2000) that this evidence was based on a mathematical error. He had various grounds for his criticism, but one was that the Prosecution took the figure of 1 in 73 million (rather than 1 in 2.75 million) because the woman concerned was from an affluent family, and statistics show that cot death is less common in such families. Watkins describes the leap from this observation to the conclusion about an individual as an example of the ecological fallacy. Social class is a complex reality of interrelated circumstances, statistically summarised for use in population studies by selecting the one variable that performs best as an indicator. It is quite wrong to assume that any one individual has the attributes of the statistical group.

Watkins was very critical of the use of statistics in this case and argued strongly that the conviction was unsafe as a result of the incorrect expert evidence given to the court. He made a distinction between mathematical fact and opinion, and argued that there were factual errors in the evidence, which should not have been presented to the jury as if they were matters of opinion. It is, of course, reasonable to disagree over matters of opinion, whereas one would expect agreement on facts. These points are less relevant to the present argument, but this case stands as a good example of the problem of applying population studies directly to individuals. It illustrates also the fact that we are not dealing with an abstract problem, but with real, serious damage done to individuals.

(c) *Assessment and treatment of sex offenders*

It is common to see, in pre-trial reports, the assertion that sex offenders have always committed many more offences that they admit. This assertion is justified by research findings. It is applied directly to the individual in a challenging way, so that the person who maintains he has not committed further offences is regarded as being 'in denial', and adverse conclusions are drawn about him. These reports are often written by people who should know better, and it seems wrong that expert evidence is used in this way. There are many criticisms, including the fact that offenders of all types may commit more offences than are detected, or than they admit. This should come as no surprise to a court, so it is not clear why it is necessary to offer the above advice only in relation to sex offenders. The effect is to suggest that there is something different about this offender, compared with other offenders. A more serious objection is the fact that the inference is based on the same ecological fallacy referred to by Watkins. There is no basis for assuming that an individual must have all the characteristics of his or her class. It is extraordinary, and worrying, that professionals allow themselves to be drawn into this kind of prejudicial statement, in advance of the trial.

Similar attitudes pervade many approaches to the treatment of sex offenders. Treatment programmes are becoming rigid and, in some cases, dogmatic. If studies show that sex offenders have certain characteristics, then the individual offender is required to demonstrate these characteristics, or he is regarded as being dishonest. This criticism may be unfair to many treatment programmes that adopt an approach that is tailored to the individual. In addition, there are practical and economic considerations favouring rigid, packaged interventions, and it may be the case that treatment of this type is the only alternative to no treatment at all. Even so, there is debate among therapists about the limitations of a dogmatic insistence that individuals must be typical representatives of their class. On the statistical point alone, there can be no debate. It is simply incorrect.

Of course, it would be absurd to argue that statistical evidence should be ignored. It is quite proper that it should raise our awareness of associations, whose presence or absence in an individual can then be confirmed or disconfirmed by the appropriate investigations. It is a problem for those writing pre-trial reports, that some people will lie and will hide offences. Whilst recognising that this is a serious problem, we must also recognise and acknowledge that it is a problem that cannot be solved by statistics.

2.3 SUMMARY

These three examples illustrate the problems involved in generalising from statistical studies of populations, to draw conclusions about individuals. Returning to the field of mental disorder and violence, it appears that the research that has increased our understanding of the statistical associations between mental disorder and violence has not been of great assistance in the task of risk management in the individual. The main value of research to date has been in raising our awareness of the problem.

So far, the limitations described have been theoretical. They are particularly important, as they will not be solved by better statistical methods. There are also important practical limitations to many of the existing studies, which will be considered in the following section.

2.4 PRACTICAL LIMITATIONS OF STUDIES OF RISK IN PSYCHIATRY

The main problems are in the choice of variables to be measured, the focus on single events or interventions, and an unrealistic time frame. Each will be considered in turn.

(a) *Choice of variables*

Studies tend to measure only those variables that are easily measurable, such as demographic characteristics and previous convictions. It is more difficult to measure some of the factors that preoccupy clinicians, such as verbal threats, attitude, insight, compliance and early signs of relapse of mental illness.

(b) *The focus on single events*

Most studies tend to focus on a single intervention or event, such as discharge from hospital. In clinical practice, it would be better to regard the process of risk management as a series of decisions, some major but most minor, many of which are taken almost unconsciously. It is much more difficult to study these decisions in a systematic way.

(c) *Time scale*

Many studies use a time frame which may be unrealistic in terms of clinical practice. The need to acquire sufficient numbers for statistical analysis may mean that a study extends to events over several months, but it then becomes unrealistic to argue that the event caused the outcome. Some of these points can be illustrated by considering one of the definitive studies of risk in psychiatry. Lidz *et al* (1993) looked at 357 patients in whom emergency room psychiatrists predicted violence, along with 357 matched controls. Over a six-month follow-up period, violence was measured by self-report and collateral reports. It was found to have occurred in 53% of the predicted cases, and in 36% of the comparison group.

This is an important study, first for showing that violence was more common than many other studies had suggested, occurring in 45% of all cases. It also showed that clinicians did better than chance, even if they didn't do that much better. This is an excellent and influential study, but it has limitations. The most important is that it says nothing about treatment or its effect on outcome. This is particularly surprising to a clinician in the UK. Practice has come to be dominated by concern about violence and it is unthinkable that one would take no action, if violence appeared likely. The possibility of violence heads the list of pointers to psychiatric intervention. The view from this side of the Atlantic is that the USA is almost obsessed by litigation and, in these circumstances, it seems unbelievable that there would be no thought given to intervention in patients of this type. One assumes that the psychiatrists must have intervened in some way, and this leads to interesting possibilities. Are the results for the two groups rather similar because the 'predicted violent' group was treated, thereby reducing their actual level of violence, whereas the 'predicted non-violent' group was more likely to be left untreated, so that their actual levels of violence were higher than expected? Could the true message of this study be that treatment of psychiatric disorder works in reducing violence?

Of course, this is wild speculation. This study was not designed to answer the question I have posed, and it cannot answer it. This is no criticism of the authors, but it is reasonable to regard it as grounds for criticism of other researchers. In the eight years since that work was published, there has been little attention paid to this aspect, with few studies on the impact of treatment.

There is another major limitation of the study in relation to ordinary clinical practice. The six-month follow-up is too long for predictions based on a single assessment. This may be a reasonable time scale when looking at stable predictors of violence, such as demographic variables, but a time frame of six days, or even six hours, may be more appropriate for examining the effect of changes in mental state. After all, these were patients presenting to an emergency room, presumably at a point of crisis, often during an episode of acute illness.

It is not necessary to consider other studies in detail, as the main practical limitations have been mentioned. In contrast to the theoretical problems described above, the solutions in this case are achievable. Why should studies not focus on the series of small decisions that constitute risk management in psychiatry? It may be necessary to employ qualitative methods to supplement other data. The studies may need to be large and costly. Even so, there is no reason in principle why they should not be done. It is obvious that future research should improve on previous studies, but it should also be informed about the phenomenon by other sources of information. The following section will be concerned with the independent inquiries that are mandatory in England when a patient with recent psychiatric contact is responsible for a homicide.

2.5 UNTOWARD INCIDENT INQUIRIES

Most services carry out an untoward incident inquiry following acts of serious violence by one of their patients. It is difficult to use this information for other purposes. Most such inquiries are confidential, and there is great variability, both in deciding which incident should be investigated, and in deciding how the inquiry should be carried out.

Some of these problems, although not all, have been avoided by a peculiarly English institution: the homicide inquiry. It is a statutory requirement that an independent inquiry is held, whenever a homicide is committed by a current or recent patient of psychiatric services in England. These inquiries are subject to all the distortions of hindsight, and they remain variable in quality, but the best ones are excellent. They are a form of audit, and their value derives from two main sources. First, they deal with the reality of risk management in clinical practice. Second, they have the resources to present a detailed description of the management of an individual case.

Of course, homicide inquiries were never designed to be used as research tools. Even so, it is possible to derive useful information from them if one remains aware of their limitations. Inquiries may also carry important messages about clinicians' ability to predict violence. If psychiatrists' predictions are not much better than chance, as some actuarial studies suggest, then one would expect the inquiries to describe a catalogue of unpredictable violence. The dramatic event of a killing would not only take everyone by surprise, it would appear unpredictable even when the circumstances were re-examined after the event. In fact, it appears that this is often not the case. Many inquiries reveal a neglect of basic principles of clinical practice, rather than a service functioning well and being taken unawares by an unpredictable disaster. Petch and Bradley (1997) provide a more detailed review of inquiries, including some of their findings and shortcomings. The following account concentrates on a few cases, which have been selected to make particular points.

2.6 INQUIRY NO 1

A female patient (SC) killed her social worker and the subsequent inquiry (Department of Health and Social Security, 1988) led to the Royal College of Psychiatrists' (1991) guidelines on aftercare. A prominent feature of this case was rejection of a patient by mental health services on the mistaken grounds that the diagnosis was personality disorder rather than schizophrenia. There was a failure to respond adequately to earlier acts of violence.

Two major lessons appear to emerge from this inquiry. First, it is important to establish the correct diagnosis, so that the appropriate treatment can be given. Second, the consequences of getting the diagnosis wrong (which is bound to happen on occasion) may be less serious if treatment, rather than rejection, is the response to someone with personality disorder who is in regular contact with psychiatric services. This theme runs through several inquiries, many of which detail rejection by psychiatric services. It is also at the root of the current onslaught on psychiatry by politicians and the media. There are several unrealistic aspects to this onslaught, but it seems entirely reasonable that a publicly funded service should be designed to meet the needs of its clients, rather than rejecting those who do not fit certain narrow criteria. Of course, there is plenty of room for argument about how widespread the problem is within psychiatry as a whole, but the fact that it is a problem cannot be denied. The value of the homicide inquiries is illustrated immediately, as this issue has never been raised in the actuarial studies.

2.7 INQUIRY NO 2

Diagnostic confusion and lack of follow-up are also features of the Clunis Case (Ritchie *et al*, 1994), where previous episodes of illness were treated in isolation, rather than being integrated into an overall view of the case. The police had failed to act on complaints from the public, that this obviously mentally disordered man was brandishing a knife. This is another frequent theme of inquiries, that the police apply different rules when dealing with the mentally ill, without ensuring entry to services. The patient moved between different services, none of which made efforts to continue care after he left their area. Receiving services did not obtain full records of his previous history. The report was particularly critical of one health worker, never identified, who denied all knowledge of the patient when telephoned by a second hospital, where he had just presented. The implication in the report is that the health worker was lying, in order to avoid responsibility for a difficult patient. Again, one cannot find such issues in the research literature.

2.8 INQUIRY NO 3

The Falling Shadow (Blom-Cooper *et al*, 1995) describes a case in which incorrect diagnosis, based on a failure to consult previous records, led to the mistaken decision to discharge a patient from his restriction order. He had been placed on that order following a previous offence of serious violence. He had stolen a shotgun and attacked a woman, with whom he had become obsessed. The fact that no one was killed seems to have been due only to good fortune. The patient said later that the attack was planned, as part of an extended suicide. Doctors agreed on a diagnosis of schizophrenia and he was treated at Broadmoor Hospital, under a hospital order with restrictions. The restriction order was without limit of time, as there was nothing to indicate when his illness would get better, if ever. His mental state settled rapidly on medication, and he progressed to a conditional discharge, within five years of the original offence. Serious problems emerged in his outpatient care only when his consultant psychiatrist stopped his medication. That consultant rejected the diagnosis of schizophrenia, against all the evidence, and regarded the patient as suffering from a personality disorder. This view, which was at odds with all previous medical opinion, led a tribunal to grant the patient an absolute discharge.

The Responsible Medical Officer's opinion determined the outcome of the hearing, as there was no other medical evidence to set against it. The patient had refused to even see the tribunal doctor, alleging bias. Copious evidence of a disturbed mental state, in the hospital's medical and nursing notes, was not put before the tribunal. The authors argue that the correct course of action in such circumstances would have been not to proceed with the tribunal, as the patient was not consenting to an examination. In choosing to continue, disproportionate weight was given to a single medical opinion, which was later proven tragically wrong.

From this point, with no powers to impose community supervision, management was problematic. The inquiry catalogued numerous failures of communication, and failures of care. There was a specific failure to take account of the reports of relatives and other informants. Although these events carry important lessons, their link to the final tragedy is indirect. The killing took place during his seventh admission to a local hospital. He was a detained patient, but had unauthorised leaves from the hospital, during one of which he purchased a knife, with which he stabbed and killed a female occupational therapist. There is deserved criticism in the report of the fact that a detained patient was able to have unauthorised, unrecorded leaves from the hospital, and criticism of the fact that he was not searched on his return. This basic failure of care is the only one that could be linked directly to the final tragedy. The most horrifying aspect of the killing was its unpredictability. There had been no serious assaults for 15 years. There was no prior relationship between patient and victim. No interaction preceded the fatal assault. Two people had spoken to the patient in the hour before the killing, and neither detected a sense of threat or impending assault. The assault appears to have been the result of purely psychotic processes, and the delusional content was quite different from that which had been associated with his previous dangerous behaviour.

There is an important message here about the difference between predicting and preventing events. Even with the benefit of hindsight, it is difficult to see how this killing could have been predicted. Do we really expect to develop an instrument that can do a better job of prediction in these circumstances, when the hallmark of the illness may be unpredictability, and random events are so important in determining the final outcome? On the other hand, prevention was a simple matter of following the rules for writing reports for tribunals (take notice of the history), following the rules for looking after any patient (don't ignore the comments of relatives) and the rules for looking after detained patients (don't tolerate unauthorised absences, search patients when they return from any such absences).

2.9 INQUIRY NO 4

The Woodley Report described the killing of one patient by another in an East London Day Hospital. The inquiry was critical of many aspects of the offender-patient's care. He had been in prison for an earlier offence, despite the obvious presence of serious mental illness. As a result, he received no proper treatment for his psychosis. Another theme that runs through many inquiries is the failure of psychiatric care within prisons. When he was eventually admitted to a secure hospital, it was far away from his home area, and there was inadequate planning for his discharge. He did not receive proper treatment in the community. There was a basic failure to monitor his mental state, culminating in the killing, when he was floridly psychotic.

2.10 SUMMARY: ISSUES EMERGING FROM HOMICIDE INQUIRIES

Other common findings from inquiries include: poor record keeping; failures of communication, between agencies or between present and former carers; a narrow view of the diagnosis of schizophrenia, so that the history is ignored if delusions or hallucinations are not present at a single interview; and delay in intervening when relapse occurs, so that the patient becomes seriously unwell before anything is done. Of course, each case is different and caution is required before drawing general conclusions from particular cases. Even so, the inquiries do not reveal a picture of individuals struggling with the theoretical limits of risk assessment. In many cases, the risk was all too obvious, the problem being a failure to communicate that risk, or to take appropriate action.

2.11 DIRECTIONS FOR FUTURE RESEARCH

There is a need to devise large-scale studies, based around the treatment of mental disorder. The homicide inquiries, combined with previous research, provide a good indication of the measures that are likely to reduce violence. Violence must be used as an outcome measure in treatment studies, alongside more well established measures such as mental state and quality of life. The power of such a study would be increased by concentrating on individuals who present a higher risk of violence, and the existing literature provides the criteria by which such a group can be identified. In dealing with the details of treatment interventions, it may be necessary to incorporate qualitative methods, to supplement traditional quantitative approaches.

CHAPTER 3

PSYCHOPATHY AND RISK FOR RECIDIVISM AND VIOLENCE

Robert D Hare

Psychopathy is a personality disorder defined by a cluster of interpersonal, affective, and lifestyle characteristics that results in serious, negative consequences for society. Among the most devastating features of the disorder are a callous disregard for the rights of others and a propensity for predatory behaviour and violence. Following a brief discussion of the clinical concept of psychopathy and its assessment, I focus on the empirical literature on its association with crime and violence, the key role psychopathy plays in the new generation of risk assessment tools, and the implications of new research on the issue of its treatability.

3.1 INTRODUCTION

Aggression and violence are not unitary constructs. They take many forms and involve many levels of interpersonal and social complexity. The causes of violence at the interpersonal level are not the same as those that involve conflicts between groups or nations. However we define aggression and violence, they are the result of exceedingly complex interactions between genetic/biological factors and social/environmental factors. It is unlikely that we soon will have more than a rudimentary grasp of these interactions, given our penchant for investigating the two domains in isolation. Notwithstanding the importance of these interactions, we already know enough about the social and environmental correlates of individual and group violence to develop preventative strategies, given sufficient public pressure and political will. We know relatively little about the biological bases of human violence, in part because of the complexity of the problems but also because until recently we lacked the investigative tools needed to provide basic information about the workings of the human brain.

It is unlikely that we ever will have a unified theory of violence. However, I believe that we now can see the modest beginnings of what might be referred to as a 'mini-theory' of human predatory violence, based on the clinical and empirical research on psychopathy. It can be argued that the aggression and violence of the psychopath are instrumental, predatory, and cold-blooded, and owe more to the nature of the individual than to the social and environmental forces that help to drive most other types of violence. However, the issue addressed in this paper is the role played by psychopathy in the assessment of risk for criminal acts, particularly those that are violent.

3.2 THE ASSESSMENT OF RISK

Extensive discussions of the theories and methodologies of risk assessment are provided elsewhere (for example, see Hart, 1998; Monahan and Steadman, 1994; Quinsey *et al*, 1998). The latest generation of risk assessment instruments has largely dispelled the old legal and psychiatric myth that useful predictions cannot be made about criminal behaviour. Much of the recent debate has more to do with the relative effectiveness of actuarial instruments and structured clinical assessments. The former are empirically-derived sets of static (primarily criminal history, demographic) risk factors, and include the *Violent Risk Appraisal Guide* (VRAG; Quinsey *et al*, 1998), the *Rapid Risk for Sexual Offence Recidivism* (RRASOR; Hanson, 1997), and the *STATIC-2000* (Hanson and Thornton, 2000), instruments that improve considerably on unstructured clinical judgements or impressions. However, procedures that include *structured* clinical decisions based on specific criteria, are proving to be at least as good as purely actuarial scales. For example, the *HCR-20: Assessing Risk for Violence* (Webster, Douglas, Eaves and Hart, 1997) assesses 10 historical (H) variables, five clinical (C) variables, and five risk management (R) variables.

All decisions about risk are influenced by the quality of the information available, the reliability with which this information is coded, the base rate for outcome variables (for example, recidivism, violence), the nature of the population of offenders and patients used to derive the prediction schemes, and the problems associated with using group data to make decisions about individuals. Moreover, practical and legal issues such as the relative significance to the individual and to society of the likelihood of false positives, false negatives, and so forth, play an important role in determining how information about risk is used.

3.3 PSYCHOPATHY: THE CONCEPT

The modern conception of psychopathy is the result of several hundred years of clinical investigation and speculation by European and American psychiatrists and psychologists (see detailed accounts by Berrios, 1996; Millon, Simonsen, Birket-Smith and Davis, 1998; McCord and McCord, 1964; Pichot, 1978). As Millon *et al* (1998) put it, 'Psychopathy was the first personality disorder to be recognised in psychiatry. The concept has a long historical and clinical tradition, and in the last decade a growing body of research has supported its validity ...' (p 28). Although the aetiology, dynamics and conceptual boundaries of this personality disorder remain the subject of debate and research, there is a consistent clinical and empirical tradition concerning its core affective, interpersonal and behavioural attributes. On the interpersonal level, psychopaths are grandiose, arrogant, callous, dominant, superficial, and manipulative. Affectively, they are short-tempered, unable to form strong emotional bonds with others, and lacking in empathy, guilt or remorse. These interpersonal and affective features are associated with a socially deviant lifestyle that includes irresponsible and impulsive behaviour, and a tendency to ignore or violate social conventions and more.

Psychopathy cannot be understood solely, or even primarily, in terms of social and environmental forces and influences. It is likely that genetic factors contribute significantly to the formation of the personality traits and temperament considered essential to the disorder, although its lifelong expression is a product of complex interactions between biological / temperamental predispositions and social forces (Hare, 1998a; Livesley, 1998). Certainly, the traits and behaviours that define adult psychopathy begin to manifest themselves early in childhood, in some cases perhaps as a combination of two diagnostic categories, conduct disorder and attention deficit hyperactivity disorder (Frick, 1998; Lynam, 1996; McBride, 1998). The biological and environmental mechanisms responsible for the development and maintenance of psychopathy are not well understood, though subject to much speculation (see Hare, 1998a; Lykken, 1995; Mealey, 1995). Whether viewed as a mental disorder, a product of cerebral insult, an evolved 'cheater' strategy for passing on one's gene pool (Mealey, 1995), or simply as a variant of normal personality (Widiger, 1998), psychopathy clearly presents society with a serious problem, as the rest of this chapter will attest.

Although not all psychopaths come into formal contact with the criminal justice system (see Babiak, 1995; Hare, 1998b), their defining features clearly place them at high risk for crime and violence (Hare, Cooke and Hart, 1999). The problem, of course, is to identify these individuals as accurately as possible, particularly in situations where a diagnosis of psychopathy has serious implications for both the individual and society.

3.4 THE ASSESSMENT OF PSYCHOPATHY

The Psychopathy Checklist – Revised (PCL-R) and its derivatives

The Psychopathy Checklist – Revised (PCL-R) was designed to measure the clinical construct of psychopathy, not to assess risk for recidivism or violence. However, because of its demonstrated ability to predict recidivism, violence and treatment outcome, the PCL-R routinely is used in assessments of risks, either on its own or, more appropriately, as part of a battery of established risk factors (see below). Extensive descriptions of the development and psychometric properties of the PCL-R and its derivatives are available elsewhere (Cooke, Forth and Hare, 1998; Cooke and Michie, 1997; Cooke, Michie, Hart and Hare, 1999; Forth, Kosson and Hare, in press; Hare, 1991; Hare, Cooke and Hart, 1999; Hart, Cox and Hare, 1995) and only a brief outline is provided here.

The PCL-R is a clinical construct rating scale that uses a semi-structured interview, case history information, and specific scoring criteria to rate each of 20 items on a three-point scale (0, 1, 2) according to the extent to which it applies to a given individual (see Table 1). Total scores can range from 0 to 40 and reflect the degree to which the individual matches the prototypical psychopath. In North America a score of 30 typically is used as a diagnostic cut-off for research on psychopathy. However, in the United Kingdom, Sweden, and several other European countries a lower cut-off may be appropriate. For example, Cooke and Michie (1999) have used item response theory (IRT) analyses to show that a PCL-R score of 25 in Scotland appears to reflect the same level of the latent trait of psychopathy as does a score of 30 in North America. Similarly, cut-offs of 25 and 26 have proven useful in England and Sweden, respectively (see below). Total PCL-R scores are highly reliable when used with trained and experienced raters. The intraclass correlation (ICC) typically exceed .80 for a single rater (ICC1) and .90 for the average of two raters (ICC2). Internal consistency (alpha coefficients of .80+ and mean inter-item correlations of .20+) is also high.

Although developed primarily with data from male offenders and forensic patients, the psychometric properties of the PCL-R now are well established in a variety of other offender and patient populations, including females, substance abusers, and sex offenders (for example, Brown and Forth, 1997; Cooke et al, 1998; Hare, 1998a; Rice and Harris, 1997; McDermott et al, 2000; Porter et al, 2000; Salekin, Rogers and Sewell, 1997; Salekin, Rogers, Ustad and Sewell, 1998; Windle and Dumenci, 1999). Early indications are that the PCL-R has good cross-cultural generalisability (for example, Cooke, 1998; Gonçalves, 1999; Grann, Långström, Tengström and Stålenheim, 1998; Moltó, Poy and Torrubia, 2000; Pham, 1998).

Table 1: Items in the Hare Psychopathy Checklist – Revised (PCL-R)

Factor 1: Interpersonal/affective	Factor 2: Social deviance
1 Glibness/superficial charm	3 Need for stimulation/proneness to boredom
2 Grandiose sense of self worth	9 Parasitic lifestyle
4 Pathological lying	10 Poor behavioural controls
5 Conning/manipulative	12 Early behavioural problems
6 Lack of remorse or guilt	13 Lack of realistic, long-term goals
7 Shallow affect	14 Impulsivity
8 Callous/lack of empathy	15 Irresponsibility
16 Failure to accept responsibility for own actions	18 Juvenile delinquency
	19 Revocation of conditional release
* Additional items	
11 Promiscuous sexual behaviour	
17 Many short-term marital relationships	
20 Criminal versatility	

Note: From Hare (1991). The rater uses specific criteria, interview and file information to score each item on a 3-point scale (0, 1, 2).

*Items do not load on either factor.

A 12-item version of the PCL-R, the PCL:SV (Hart *et al*, 1995) was developed for use in the MacArthur Risk Assessment study (Steadman *et al*, 1999). It is conceptually and empirically related to the PCL-R (Hart *et al*, 1995; Cooke *et al*, 1999) and is used as a screen for psychopathy in forensic populations or as a stand-alone instrument for research with noncriminals, including civil psychiatric patients (as in the MacArthur study). There is rapidly accumulating evidence for the construct validity of PCL:SV, including its ability to predict aggression and violence in offenders and in both forensic and civil psychiatric patients (see below). The PCL:YV (Forth *et al*, in press) is an age-appropriate modification of the PCL-R intended for use with adolescents. It appears to have the same psychometric and predictive properties as its adult counterpart (for example, Brandt, Kennedy, Patrick and Curtin, 1997; Cruise, Rogers, Neumann and Sewell, 2000; Forth and

Burke, 1998; Forth, Hart and Hare, 1990; Gretton, McBride, O'Shaughnessy, Kumka and Hare, 2001; Toupin, Mercier, Déry, Côte and Hodgins, 1996).

3.5 FACTOR STRUCTURE

There is an extensive empirical literature indicating that in forensic populations the items in the PCL-R and PCL:SV measure a unitary construct formed by two correlated clusters or factors (for example, Cooke and Michie, 1999; Hare, 1991; Harpur, Hare and Hakstian, 1989; McDermott et al, 2000; Windle and Dumenci, 1999). Factor 1 reflects the interpersonal and affective components of the disorder, whereas Factor 2 is more closely allied with a socially deviant lifestyle. Cooke and his colleagues have used Item Response Theory (IRT) to investigate the discriminating properties of individual PCL-R and PCL:SV items. IRT provides information about the extent to which an item (or group of items) is discriminating of (relevant to) a given construct or trait, in this case, psychopathy. They found that the interpersonal and affective (Factor 1) items are more discriminating of the psychopathy construct than are the socially deviant (Factor 2) items (Cooke and Michie, 1997; Cooke et al, 1999, 2001).

On the basis of some recent IRT analyses of North American and European data sets, Cooke and Michie (2001) found that the 13 of the most discriminating PCL-R items defined a superordinate construct (psychopathy) made up of three correlated clusters or factors: interpersonal (four items), affective (four items), and lifestyle (five items). The first two factors represent a split of PCL-R Factor 1 into two parts, while the third factor is derived from PCL-R Factor 2. The remaining seven items primarily reflect antisocial and criminal behaviours, and may be less useful in assessing psychopathy in populations that are relatively homogeneous with respect to criminality. This 3-factor solution is theoretically and clinically appealing, and is consistent with the PCL-R manual's (Hare, 1991) breakdown of the attributes of psychopathy into interpersonal, affective, and behavioural/lifestyle components, as well as with the format and content of the Hare P-Scan (Hare and Hervé, 1999), a non-clinical tool for use by law enforcement, probation services, and correctional institutions.

Nevertheless, the reliability of the three individual factors is not very high, with the ICC_1, being around .60. The author is currently developing additional items in order to provide more reliable estimates of the three factors. Meanwhile, clinicians and researchers should continue to base their PCL-R assessments on all 20 items and on the original PCL-R factors. This is particularly important in light of recent evidence that the 2-factor solution remains viable and useful, not only for offenders (for example, McDermott et al, 2000) but for male, female, Caucasian, African-American, and Puerto-Rican alcoholic outpatients (Windle and Dumenci, 1999). Moreover,

McDermott *et al* (2000) have found that a single-factor solution is appropriate with substance-dependent populations in which chronic criminality is not pervasive. Finally, the seven items excluded from Cooke and Michie's (2001) solution play an important role in assessments of risk for recidivism and violence. They appear to reflect manifestations of the more central features of psychopathy. In effect, it appears that the IRT analyses have resulted in the original Factor 1 and Factor 2 each being split into two factors.

3.6 DSM-IV

The attributes measured by the PCL-R are similar in many respects to the diagnostic criteria for dyssocial personality disorder listed in the tenth revision of the *International Classification of Diseases and Related Disorders* (ICD-10; World Health Organisation, 1990). However, they differ in important ways from the criteria for antisocial personality disorder (APD) contained in the American Psychiatric Association's (1994) fourth revision of the *Diagnostic and Statistical Manual of Mental Disorders* (DSM-IV). The latter reflect the assumptions that it is difficult for clinicians to assess personality traits reliably, and that early onset delinquency is a cardinal symptom of the disorder (Robins, 1978). These assumptions account for the heavy emphasis on delinquent and antisocial behaviour in the criteria for APD (Hare and Hart, 1995; Rogers, Salekin, Sewell and Cruise, 2000; Widiger *et al*, 1996). In forensic populations the prevalence of APD is much higher (> 50%) than the prevalence of psychopathy (< 30%), resulting in an asymmetric association between the PCL-R and APD. In this respect, it is noteworthy that APD is strongly associated with PCL-R Factor 2 items, but only weakly associated with Factor 1 items. Most psychopaths meet the criteria for APD, but most of the offenders with APD are not psychopaths. Yet, as DSM-IV puts it, 'antisocial personality disorder has also been referred to as psychopathy ...' (p 645), effectively equating two different constructs. About this unfortunate and untenable position, Rogers *et al* (2000) had this to say: 'As noted by Hare (1998), DSM-IV does considerable disservice to diagnostic clarity in its equating of APD to psychopathy' (pp 236–37).

Recently, Quinsey, Harris, Rice and Cormier (1998) claimed that when the APD items are summed to provide a continuous score (symptom counts, rather than a categorical diagnosis) the correlation with PCL-R Total scores is 'in the .90s, indicating that the PCL-R and APD measure the same underlying construct, but that the dichotomous manner in which the APD diagnosis is arrived at wastes information' (p 83). However, these results apparently were contaminated by having rater the same score both the PCL-R and the APD items raters from the same archival file information. Quite a different picture emerges when the PCL-R and the APD items are scored, independently, from both file and interview data. Under these circumstances, the PCL-R correlates with APD symptom counts about the same as it does with APD diagnoses. For example, in a sample of 306 male offenders Hemphill and Hare (2000) found that APD symptom counts were correlated .65 with PCL-R Total scores, .44 with Factor 1 scores, and .68 with Factor 2 scores. In addition, conduct disorder symptom counts correlated .51, .44, and .68 with PCL-R Total, Factor 1, and Factor 2 scores, respectively. Adult symptom counts correlated .59, .46, and .48 with PCL-R Total, Factor 1, and Factor 2 scores, respectively. Much the same pattern of correlations has been obtained between DSM-IV conduct disorder symptom counts and PCL:YV Total, Factor 1, and Factor 2 scores (Brandt et al, 1997; Forth 1995; Toupin et al, 1996). The PCL-R and its derivatives do not measure the same construct as does APD.

3.7 PSYCHOPATHY AND CRIME

In the past few years there has been a dramatic change in the perceived and actual role played by psychopathy in the criminal justice system. Formerly, a prevailing view was that clinical diagnoses such as psychopathy were of little value in understanding and predicting criminal behaviours. However, even a cursory inspection of the features that define the disorder – callousness, impulsivity, egocentricity, grandiosity, irresponsibility, lack of empathy, guilt, or remorse, and so forth – indicates that psychopaths should be much more likely than other members of the general public to bend and break the rules and laws of society.

Although psychopathy is closely associated with antisocial and criminal behaviour, psychopaths are qualitatively different from others who routinely engage in criminal behaviour, different even from those whose criminal conduct is extremely serious and persistent. The typical criminal career is relatively short, but there are individuals who devote most of their adolescent and adult life to delinquent and criminal activities. Among these persistent offenders are psychopaths, who begin their antisocial and criminal activities at a relatively early age, and continue to engage in these activities throughout much of the lifespan. Many of these 'career' criminals become less grossly antisocial in middle age. About half of the criminal psychopaths we have studied show a relatively sharp reduction in criminality around age 35 or 40 (Hare, McPherson and Forth, 1988). This does not mean that they have given up crime completely, only that their level of general criminal activity has decreased to that of the average persistent offender. Moreover, this age-related decrease in crime may not apply to violent acts. The propensity for psychopaths to engage in violent and aggressive behaviour appears to decrease very little with age.

3.8 PSYCHOPATHY AND VIOLENCE

The importance of aggression and violence in psychopathic symptomatology has always been clear, and is well represented in the diagnostic criteria for dyssocial personality disorder (ICD-10) and psychopathy (PCL-R). Each set contains one criterion directly related to a history of irritability, hostility, and aggression, including overt physical violence. In addition, each set contains several criteria that are indirectly related to aggression or violence (for example, callousness, lack of remorse). The association between psychopathy and violence should not be surprising. Many of the characteristics important for inhibiting antisocial and violent behaviour – empathy, close emotional bonds, fear of punishment, guilt – are lacking or seriously deficient in psychopaths. Moreover, their egocentricity, grandiosity, sense of entitlement, impulsivity, general lack of behavioural inhibitions, and need for power and control, constitute what might be described as the perfect prescription for asocial, antisocial, and criminal acts. This would help to explain why psychopaths make up only about 1% of the general population but as much as a quarter of our prison populations. It also would explain why they find it so easy to victimise the vulnerable and to use intimidation and violence as tools to achieve power and control over others. As Silver, Mulvey and Monahan (1999) put it, 'Psychopathy's defining characteristics, such as impulsivity, criminal versatility, callousness, and lack of empathy or remorse make the conceptual link between violence and psychopathy straightforward' (p 244).

Many of the attitudes and behaviour of psychopaths have a predatory quality about them. Psychopaths apparently see others as little more than emotional, physical, and financial prey, and feel justified in their belief that the world is made up of 'givers and takers' and that they are 'natural born takers'. They are skilled at deception and manipulation (camouflage), stalking, and locating life's 'feeding grounds' and 'watering holes'. Moreover, their use of intimidation and violence tends to be cold-blooded and instrumental, and is more likely to be straightforward, uncomplicated, and businesslike ('a matter of process') than an expression of deep-seated distress or understandable precipitating factors. It lacks the emotional colouring that characterises the violence of most other individuals. The reactions of psychopaths to the damage they have inflicted are more likely to be cool indifference, a sense of power, pleasure, or smug satisfaction than regret or concern for what they have done. The ease with which psychopaths engage in violence has very real significance for society in general and for law enforcement personnel in particular. For example, a study by the Federal Bureau of Investigation (1992) found that almost half of the law enforcement officers who died in the line of duty were killed by individuals, mostly strangers, who closely matched the personality profile of the psychopath. And perhaps as many as 25–30% of persistent wife-batterers in court-mandated treatment programs may be psychopaths (Newlove, Hart, Dutton and Hare, 1992).

3.9 PSYCHOPATHY: RISK FOR RECIDIVISM AND VIOLENCE

Some criminologists argue that the most important thing criminals have in common is that they have been convicted of criminal acts, and that clinical constructs such as psychopathy are 'mythical' or of little value in helping to understand individual criminals (for example, Toch, 1998). A corollary of such a position is that two offenders with similar criminal and demographic backgrounds should pose much the same risk for reoffending, even though one is an egocentric, cold-blooded, and remorseless individual while the other is not. Logically, they should not present the same risk. And empirically, they do not, particularly with respect to violence. Indeed, the significance of psychopathy as a robust risk factor for recidivism in general, and for violence in particular, is now well established (see meta-analyses by Dolan and Doyle, 2000; Salekin, Rogers and Sewell, 1996; Hemphill, Hare and Wong, 1998). In their review, Salekin *et al* (1996) concluded that the ability of the PCL-R to predict violence was 'unparalleled' and 'unprecedented' in the literature on the assessment of dangerousness. They commented that this conclusion was based largely on work with white, Canadian offenders, but subsequent research indicates that their conclusions have considerable generality. In a more recent meta-analysis, Hemphill *et al* (1998) found that in the first year following release from prison psychopaths are three times more likely to reoffend, and four times more likely to violently reoffend, than are other offenders. The same pattern is found with white and African-American offenders in the United States (Hemphill, Newman and Hare, 2001).

Although a detailed account of psychopathy as a risk for recidivism and violence is beyond the scope of this chapter, some examples may be helpful. Unless otherwise indicated, the terms 'high' and 'low' PCL-R scores refer to scores at or near the upper cut-off of 30, and at or near the lower cut-off of 20, respectively. The term 'medium' PCL-R refers to scores between the upper and lower cut-offs.

3.10 ADULT OFFENDERS

In the first prospective study of its type (Hart, Kropp and Hare, 1988), the PCL-R was administered to 231 male offenders prior to their conditional release from a federal prison, and their progress in the community was followed for up to approximately four years or until 'failure', defined as a return to prison because of a new offence or a violation of the terms of the conditional release. Multiple regression analyses indicated that the PCL-R made a significant contribution to the prediction of failure, over and above the contribution made by relevant criminal-history and demographic variables. Because it is important to know when failure occurs, the data were subjected to survival analysis in which failure (recidivism, reoffending, or return to prison) was determined as a function of time following release. Within three years the percentage of offenders in the high, medium, and low PCL-R groups who had failed was approximately 80, 62, and 31, respectively. Similar results have been obtained by other investigators. For example, Hodgins, Cote, and Ross (1992) administered the French version of the PCL-R to 97 male offenders prior to their release on parole, and followed their progress for up to one year. Within one year about 60% of those with high PCL-R scores, 30% of those with medium scores, and about 10% of those with low scores, had failed. Serin and Amos (1995) administered the PCL-R to 299 male offenders and followed them for up to eight years. At the end of this period, about 80% of the high PCL-R group, 60% of the medium group, and 25% of the low group had reoffended or were back in prison. Results from a representative sample of 728 offenders in the English Prison Service indicate that the PCL-R is a relatively strong predictor of institutional misconduct, assaults on staff and inmates, and property damage (Hare, Clark, Grann and Thornton, 2000). Within two years following the release of 278 offenders, the reconviction rate for those with a PCL-R score above 25 was 82%, whereas the reconviction rate for those with a score of 25 or below was 40%.

The role of psychopathy in the prediction of violence is particularly impressive. When measured by the PCL-R or its derivatives, it frequently is the best predictor. Harris, Rice, and Quinsey (1993) found that the PCL-R was the single most important predictor of violent recidivism in a large sample of offenders released from a maximum security unit and a pre-trial assessment centre. In the Serin and Amos (1995) study, described above, the rate for violent reoffending was about 40% for the psychopaths but only about 10% for the non-psychopaths. Hemphill *et al* (2000) found that the violent recidivism rate for a sample of 930 white and 267 African-American offenders at 8 years post-release was about 23%, 16%, and 8% for offenders with high, medium, and low PCL-R scores, respectively. In the English Prison Service study described above (Hare *et al*, 2000), the reconviction rate for a violent offence was 38% for those with a PCL-R score of above 25, but only 3% for those with a score of 25 or less, a ratio of more than 12:1. A stepwise logistic regression analysis, with the PCL-R and a battery of established needs and risk factors as predictors, correctly classified 91% of the outcome, violent reconviction. Contrary to the position exemplified by Toch (1998), the only predictor to enter the equation was the PCL-R.

In a Swedish study, Grann, Längström, Tengström and Kullgren (1999) evaluated the relationship between the PCL-R and violent reoffending in a sample of 352 personality disordered offenders released into the community. They found that risk for violent recidivism during a follow-up period that averaged more than four years was about 65%, 48%, and 22% for those with high, medium, and low PCL-R scores, respectively. Grann *et al* (1999) also performed a receiver operating characteristic (ROC) analysis of the PCL-R and violent recidivism. The ROC curve is a plot of true positives (sensitivity) against false positives (1 minus specificity), and is independent of the base rate for violence. The Area Under the Curve (AUC; the-A area between the curve and the diagonal) represents the probability that a violent patient will have a higher PCL-R score than will a non-violent patient. The AUC was .67 within 6 months, .71 within one year, and .70 within five years following release. They concluded that the PCL-R was as valid a predictor of violent recidivism in Swedish forensic settings as it is in North American settings, a conclusion that held whether or not the offenders were born in Sweden, and even after other risk factors were taken into account.

Relatively little research has been conducted on psychopathy in adult female offenders. However, the available data indicate that, on average, about 10% of female offenders meet the PCL-R criteria for psychopathy (Hare, 2001). The recidivism rate for these offenders is considerably higher than it is for other female offenders. For example, in one study (Hemphill *et al*, 1999) about 62% of the female offenders with high PCL-R scores reoffended within one year of release, compared with less than 32% of those with medium scores, and 18% of those with low scores. Loucks and Zamble (2000) reported that the reconviction rate at five years post-release was 68% and 28% for female offenders with PCL-R scores above and below the median, respectively. Salekin *et al* (1998) reported that at 50 days following release from prison the recidivism rate for female psychopaths was almost seven times the rate for other female offenders. However, after 50 days the difference between the groups disappeared. The association between psychopathy and violence in adult female offenders has yet to be determined.

3.11 ADOLESCENT OFFENDERS

Psychopathy does not emerge unannounced in adulthood. The precursors are apparent at an early age, and the disorder can be measured reliably in adolescence with the PCL:YV (Forth and Burke, 1998; Forth *et al*, in press). The base rate of psychopathy is at least as high among adolescent offenders as among their adult counterparts. These adolescent psychopaths are at much higher risk for recidivism and violence than are other adolescent offenders. In one study, Gretton (1998) examined the predictive validity of the PCL:YV in a large sample of young offenders, age 12–18, who had been sent by the courts to a youth facility for pre-sentence psychological and psychiatric evaluation. In the 10-year follow-up period, the violent reoffence rate for offenders with high, medium, and low PCL:YV scores was approximately 80%, 68%, and 55%, respectively. Even when relevant demographic and criminal history variables were taken into account, the PCL:YV made a substantial and significant contribution to the prediction of violent offending. In fact, a history of violence was unrelated to subsequent violence among offenders with high or low PCL:YV scores. That is, offenders with no prior evidence of violence were just as likely to commit a violent offence during the follow-up period as were those with a history of violence.

Forth *et al* (1990) administered an early version of the PCL:YV to a sample of high-risk adolescent offenders in a maximum security facility. Forth (1995) reported that subsequent to their release into the community the psychopaths, then approaching early adulthood, committed almost four times as many violent crimes as did the other offenders. Toupin *et al* (1996) administered a French translation of the PCL-R (see Côté and Hodgins, 1996) to male adolescents receiving treatment in rehabilitation centres, day centres, or special educational programs. During a one-year follow-up period, PCL-R scores were significantly correlated with delinquency, aggressive behaviour, alcohol use, and number of aggressive conduct disorder symptoms. Similar results were obtained by Brandt *et al* (1997) with a sample of mostly African-American young offenders.

3.12 FORENSIC PSYCHIATRIC PATIENTS

The prevalence of psychopathy, as measured by the PCL-R or PCL:SV, is somewhat lower in forensic psychiatric populations in North America (about 10–15%) than it is in prison populations (about 15–25%). However, forensic patients who meet the PCL-R criteria for psychopathy or who have a significant number of psychopathic features are at much higher risk for recidivism and violence than are other forensic patients. For example, several studies have found that psychopathy is predictive of institutional aggression and violence in forensic psychiatric hospitals (Hill, Rogers and Bickford, 1996; Heilbrun *et al*, 1998). Rice and Harris (1992) found that scores on the PCL-R were as predictive of recidivism a sample of male not guilty-by-reason-of-insanity (NGRI) schizophrenics as in a sample of nonpsychotic offenders. Hart and Hare (1989) found that only a small minority of consecutive admissions to a forensic psychiatric hospital were psychopaths, but that many patients exhibited a significant number of PCL-R symptoms. Further, the PCL-R predicted recidivism rates in a five year follow-up period (Wintrup, 1994).

A recent Swedish study (Tengström, Grann, Långström and Kullgren, 2000) illustrates that there is a strong association between psychopathy and violence even in forensic patients with a history of violence. The sample in this study consisted of 202 violent psychotic offenders (most of whom had a diagnosis of schizophrenia) with a mean PCL-R score of 18.2 (sd = 7.5). Patients with a PCL-R score above 25 (22% of the sample) had a violent recidivism rate of 66% in the post-release follow-up period (which averaged 51 months), whereas those with a PCL-R score of 25 or below had a recidivism rate of 18%. A set of established risk factors for this population could not improve on the predictive power of the PCL-R. Moreover, PCL-R Factor 1 (interpersonal/affective features) was as predictive of violence as was Factor 2 (socially deviant lifestyle). An additional finding of note was a sharp increase in the likelihood of a violent offence shown by the psychopaths at about 48 months post-release. Apparently this coincided with the end of intensive community supervision, suggesting that tight supervision is a protective factor for psychopaths. An ROC analysis obtained an AUC of .75 for the PCL-R and violent recidivism within five years.

3.13 CIVIL PSYCHIATRIC PATIENTS

The relationship between psychopathy and the prediction of violence is not confined to prison and forensic psychiatric populations. Several recent studies clearly indicate that the PCL:SV is one of the strongest risk factors for violence in civil psychiatric patients. In one study, Douglas, Ogloff and Nicholls (1997) assessed post-release community violence in a sample of 167 male and 112 female patients who had been involuntarily committed to a civil psychiatric facility. Although very few of the patients had a score high enough to warrant a diagnosis of psychopathy, the PCL:SV nevertheless was highly predictive of violent behaviours and arrests for violent crimes. When the distribution of PCL:SV scores was split at the median (about 8 on a scale of 0–24), the odds ratio for an arrest for violent crime was about 10 times higher for patients above the median than it was for those below the median. The results of an ROC analysis of the PCL:SV and violent arrests yielded an AUC of .75.

In the MacArthur Foundation's Violence Risk Assessment Study, the most extensive and thorough study of its kind ever conducted, 134 potential predictors of violence in 939 patients were evaluated over a 20-week period following discharge from a civil psychiatric facility (Steadman et al, 1999). The single best predictor was the PCL:SV. The prevalence of post-discharge violence was 35.7% for patients with a PCL:SV score of 13 or more (out of a maximum of 24), but only 12.6% for patients with a PCL:SV score of less than 13. In presenting their results, the authors used a 'classification tree' approach in which a hierarchy of decisions is made about the risk posed by a given patient. In this scheme, the first decision is whether or not the patient has a PCL:SV score of 13 or more. Silver et al (1999) used a subsample of 293 of these patients to investigate the impact that neighbourhood factors have on individual risk factors for violence in discharged patients. Again, the single best predictor of violence was the PCL:SV; the odds that a patient with a PCL:SV score of 13 or more would commit a violent act were 5.3 times higher than were the odds that a patient with a score below 13 would commit such an act.

Although patients discharged into neighbourhoods with 'concentrated poverty' generally were at higher risk for violence than were those discharged into neighbourhoods with less poverty, the odds ratio for psychopathy associated with violence changed very little (from 5.3 to 4.8) when concentrated poverty was added to the equation.

3.14 SEXUAL VIOLENCE

The last few years have seen a sharp increase in public and professional attention paid to sex offenders, particularly those who commit a new offence following release from a treatment program or prison. It has long been recognised that psychopathic sex offenders present special problems for therapists and the criminal justice system. For example, the Kansas Sexually Violent Predator Act established procedures for the involuntary commitment of sexually violent predators, defined as 'any person who has been convicted of or charged with a sexually violent offence and who suffers from a mental abnormality or personality disorder which makes the person likely to engage in the predatory acts of sexual violence'. In a landmark decision (*Kansas v Hendricks*, June 1997), the United States Supreme Court upheld the constitutionality of such an involuntary commitment. As a result, many States are now introducing legislation that will allow for the civil commitment of dangerous sex offenders following their release from prison. Because most of these individuals will be psychopaths, Tucker (1999) has argued that the Supreme Court's decision will result in mixing the 'bad' with the 'mad', psychopathic criminals with psychiatric patients.

Several studies have investigated the prevalence of psychopathy among various types of sex offenders (for example, Brown and Forth, 1997; Miller, Geddings, Levenston, and Patrick, 1994; Porter *et al*, 2000; Quinsey, Rice and Harris, 1995). In general, the prevalence of psychopathy, as measured by the PCL-R, is much lower in child molesters than in rapists or 'mixed' offenders. For example, Porter *et al* (2000) obtained PCL-R scores for a sample of 228 sex offenders. They found that the percentage of each type of sex offender with a PCL-R score of 30 or above was as follows: extra-familial molesters, 6.3; incest offenders, 10.8; mixed molesters, 6.3; rapists, 35.9; mixed rapists/molesters, 64. The offences of psychopathic sex offenders are likely to be more violent or sadistic than are those of other sex offenders (Barbaree, Seto, Serin, Amos and Preston, 1994; Brown and Forth, 1997; Firestone,

Bradford, Greenberg and Larose, 1998; Miller *et al*, 1994; Serin, Malcolm, Khanna and Barbaree, 1994). In extreme cases – for example, among serial killers – comorbidity of psychopathy and sadistic personality is very high (Hare *et al*, 1999; Stone, 1998).

3.15 A DEADLY COMBINATION

Sex offenders generally are resistant to treatment, but it is the psychopaths among them who are most likely to recidivate early and often. Quinsey *et al* (1995) concluded that psychopathy functions as a general predictor of sexual and violent recidivism. They found that within six years of release from prison more than 80% of the psychopaths, but only about 20% of the non-psychopaths, had violently recidivated. Many, but not all, of their offences were sexual in nature. One of the most deadly combinations to emerge from the recent research on sex offenders is psychopathy coupled with evidence of deviant sexual arousal. In a recent follow-up of 1,340 sex offenders, Rice and Harris (1997) reported that the violent recidivism rate was about 90% for offenders with a PCL-R score of 25 or more, and about 50% for those with a PCL-R score of less than 25. In addition, however, they found that sexual recidivism (as opposed to violent recidivism in general) was strongly predicted by a combination of a high PCL-R score and phallometric evidence of deviant sexual arousal, defined as any phallometric test that indicated a preference for deviant stimuli, such as children, rape cues, or non-sexual violence cues. Thus, about 70% of those with a PCL-R score of 25 or more *and* evidence of deviant sexual arousal committed a sexual offence, compared with about 40% of all other groups. Recently, Serin, Mailloux and Malcolm (2001) obtained PCL-R scores and measures of deviant sexual arousal from a Canadian sample of 68 sex offenders released from a federal prison. Within four years of release, 70% of the offenders with a PCL-R score above the median for the sample and evidence of deviant sexual arousal had reoffended, compared with about 15% of those with a PCL-R score below the median and no evidence of deviant sexual arousal. Serin, Mailloux and Malcolm (2001) did not differentiate between sexual and non-sexual reoffending, perhaps because of the small sample they used. Harris and Hanson (1998) reported that offenders with a high PCL-R score and behavioural evidence of sexual deviance had committed more pre-index sexual offences, more kidnapping and forcible confinements, and more general (non-sexual) offences, and were more likely to violently recidivate than were other offenders.

The implications of psychopathy and deviant sexual arousal are just as serious among adolescent sex offenders as among their adult counterparts. Gretton *et al* (2001) tracked the criminal activities of 220 adolescent sex offenders released from a sex offender treatment facility. Their mean score on the PCL:YV was 21.7 (sd = 7.0). The reconviction rate for sexual offences in the first five years following release was about 30% for those with high PCL:YV scores and about 15% for those with low PCL:YV scores. However, the pattern for other types of offences was quite different. Thus, in the follow-up period half of the offenders committed another crime, and the rate of offending was more than three times as high in those with high PCL:YV scores than in those with low scores. The young offenders with high PCL:YV scores who also exhibited phallometric evidence of deviant sexual arousal were not at increased risk for sexual reoffending, but posed by far the highest risk of general reoffending; about 90% of these individuals committed at least one offence in the follow-up period. The difference between these results and those obtained by Rice and Harris (1997) with adult sex offenders is that the deadly combination was predictive of sexual violence in adults, whereas it was predictive of general offending, including violence, in adolescents. However, it is possible that as these adolescent offenders age, the combination of psychopathy and deviant sexual arousal will become less predictive of offending in general, and more predictive of sexual offending in particular. In any case, psychopathic sex offenders are more likely to be convicted of a non-sexual than a sexual offence (for example, Porter et al, 2000). Many of these individuals are not so much specialised sex offenders as they are general, versatile offenders. Their misbehaviour – sexual and otherwise – presumably is a reflection of a factor not specifically related to sexual behaviour. For the psychopaths, these factors no doubt include their personality structure, their predatory stance, and their readiness to take advantage of any opportunities that come their way. It may be more important to target the antisocial tendencies and behaviours of so called psychopathic sex offenders than it is to treat their sexual deviancy.

3.16 TREATMENT OF PSYCHOPATHS

There is little convincing scientific evidence that psychopaths respond favourably to treatment and intervention (see Dolan and Coid, 1993; Hare, 1998b; Losel, 1998; Suedfeld and Landon, 1978). This does not mean that their attitudes and behaviours are immutable, only that there have been no methodologically sound treatment or 'resocialisation' programs that have been shown to work with psychopaths.

Several empirical studies illustrate the point. For example, Ogloff, Wong and Greenwood (1990) reported that psychopaths, defined by a PCL-R score of at least 30, derived little benefit from a therapeutic community program designed to treat personality-disordered offenders. The psychopaths stayed in the program for a shorter time, were less motivated, and showed less clinical improvement than did other offenders. It might be argued that even though the psychopaths did not do well in this program, some residual benefits could conceivably show up following their release from prison. However, in a survival analysis Hemphill (1991) found that the estimated reconviction rate in the first year following release was twice as high for the psychopaths as for the other offenders. Rice, Harris and Cormier (1992) retrospectively scored the PCL-R from the institutional files of patients of a maximum security psychiatric facility. They defined psychopaths by a PCL-R score of 25 or more, and non-psychopaths by a score below 25. They then compared the violent recidivism rate of patients who had been treated in an intensive and lengthy therapeutic community program with patients who had not taken part in the program. For non-psychopaths, the violent recidivism rate of treated patients was half that of untreated patients. But the violent recidivism rate of treated psychopaths was about 50% higher than that of untreated psychopaths. Therapy apparently made the psychopaths worse. But why? The simple answer is that group therapy and insight-oriented programs may help psychopaths to develop better ways of manipulating, deceiving, and using people, but do little to help them to understand themselves. As a consequence, following release into the community they may be more likely than untreated psychopaths to continue to place themselves in situations where the potential for violence is high.

The findings by Rice et al (1992), though intriguing and suggestive, were based on retrospective research with a particular population of mentally disordered offenders, and with an unusual, complex, and highly controversial treatment program that included the use of LSD and nude-encounter therapy. These problems notwithstanding, there is recent evidence that psychopaths are not good candidates for traditional forms of prison treatment. Some recent findings from the English Prison Service (Hare et al, 2000) indicate that various short-term treatment programs have little effect on the post-release recidivism rates of offenders with low or medium PCL-R scores. However, these same programs appear to *increase* the post-release recidivism rates of offenders with high scores on the interpersonal/affective (PCL-R Factor 1) components of psychotherapy. Within two years following release from prison the reconviction rate for offenders with a high Factor 1 score (9 or more) was 85% if they had participated in a treatment program, but was 58.8% if they had not participated in a treatment program. Treatment had no effect on the reconviction rates of those with low Factor 1 scores. For them, the reconviction rate was, on average, about 30%. Similar findings were obtained when offenders with high educational and social needs were provided with educational upgrading and the development of social skills. However, an interesting difference was that offenders with low to moderate PCL-R Factor 1 scores seemed to derive considerable benefit from these programs, as reflected in a reduced reconviction rate.

Some indication of the psychopathy-related processes that might occur during institutional treatment programs is provided by a study conducted in an English prison. Hobson, Shine and Roberts (2000) administered the PCL-R to patients when they were admitted to the prison for treatment in a well-developed therapeutic community program. Their behaviour during treatment sessions and while on the wards was evaluated with specially designed checklists. High scores on the PCL-R were strongly predictive of disruptive behaviours during treatment sessions and on the wards three months and six months following admission to the prison. The effect was entirely due to the interpersonal and affective features of psychopathy (PCL-R Factor 1). The results clearly indicated that the psychopaths manipulated the system to satisfy their own need for power, control and prestige. They played 'head games' with other inmates and staff, continually tested the boundaries and looked for people and things to exploit, and showed no genuine interest in changing their own attitudes and behaviour. Nevertheless, they managed to manipulate and fool some staff into thinking their efforts were sincere and that they were making good progress.

The consequences of this manipulation of staff are likely to be reflected in reconviction rates. Seto and Barbaree (1999) divided 216 sex offenders into high and low PCL-R groups, and also into poor and good treatment groups based on therapist ratings of improvement shown during the course of treatment. These ratings were based on changes in the offender's expression of empathy for his victims, understanding of his offence cycle, and the quality of his relapse prevention plans. For the low PCL-R groups the therapists' ratings of treatment change were unrelated to post-release reoffence rates for general offences or for serious (sexual, violent) offences. In each case, reoffence rates were below 10% for general offences and 5% or less for serious offences. However, for the high PCL-R groups the ratings of treatment change were strongly related to reoffending. Thus, the reoffence rate for offenders in the high PCL-R group who had been placed in the poor treatment group (therapists thought they had not shown improvement during treatment) was about 12% for general offences and about 3% for serious offences. In sharp contrast, the reoffence rate for offenders in the high PCL-R group who had been placed in the good treatment group (therapists thought they had shown improvement during treatment) was about 28% for general offences and about 21% for serious offences. That is, offenders with many psychopathic features who convinced therapists that they had gained insight into their behaviour and had changed for the better actually reoffended at the highest rates. Indeed, their reoffence rate for serious (sexual and other violent) crimes was more than four times the rate shown by all other offenders.

In many respects, findings of this sort are understandable. Unlike most other offenders, psychopaths suffer little personal distress, see little wrong with their attitudes and behaviour, and seek treatment only when it is in their best interests to do so, such as when seeking probation or parole. It is therefore not surprising that they derive little benefit from traditional prison programs, particularly those aimed at the development of empathy, conscience, and interpersonal skills.

What should we do then? Do we simply keep them in prison until they are old enough to pose little risk to society? Do we ask psychopaths to participate in treatment programs that have little chance of success and that fool them and others into thinking that the exercise is worthwhile and of practical benefit to them? Rather than being discouraged, we should mount a concerted effort to develop innovative procedures designed specifically for psychopathic offenders. Losel (1998) has provided a thoughtful analysis of the issues involved in the treatment and management of psychopathic and other offenders, and has outlined in some detail the requirements for an effective program. An extensive set of program guidelines for development of a program specifically designed for psychopaths is now available (Wong and Hare, in press). In brief, we propose that relapse-prevention techniques should be integrated with elements of the best available cognitive-behavioural correctional programs. The program is less concerned with developing empathy and conscience or effecting changes in personality than with convincing participants that they alone are responsible for their behaviour, and that they can learn more prosocial ways of using their strengths and abilities to satisfy their needs and wants. It involves tight control and supervision, both in the institution and following release into the community, as well as comparisons with carefully selected groups of offenders treated in standard correctional programs. The experimental design would permit empirical evaluation of its treatment and intervention modules (what works and what does not work for particular individuals). That is, some modules or components might be effective with psychopaths but not with other offenders, and vice versa. Because correctional programs are constantly in danger of erosion because of changing institutional priorities, community concerns and political pressures, we proposed stringent safeguards for maintaining the integrity of the program.

3.17 CONCLUSIONS

There is a substantial amount of empirical evidence that psychopathy, as measured by the PCL-R and its derivatives, is a potent predictor of recidivism and violence in prison, forensic psychiatric, and civil psychiatric populations. Indeed, the PCL-R is one of the most generalisable of the risk factors identified thus far, and for this reason it is included in a variety of risk assessment procedures, both purely actuarial (for example, the VRAG; Quinsey et al, 1998) and structured clinical (for example, the HCR-20; Webster et al, 1997). Although psychopathy is not the only risk factor for recidivism and violence, it is too important to ignore, particularly with respect to violence. The situation may be summarised as follows (see Hart, 1998, pp 368–69):

1   Psychopathy should be considered in any assessment of violence. It is empirically related to future violence, is theoretically important in the explanation of violence, and is pragmatically relevant in making decisions about risk management. As Hart (1998, p 368) put it, 'Indeed, failure to consider psychopathy when conducting a risk assessment may be unreasonable (from a legal perspective) or unethical (from a professional perspective)'.

2   Psychopathy should be assessed with the PCL-R or its derivatives by qualified and trained personnel.

3   The presence of an extreme number of psychopathic features (for example, a PCL-R score that places the individual in the top 5% of offenders and patients) indicates that the individual is in a high risk group for future offending, particularly violence.

4   The absence of psychopathy does not compel a conclusion of low risk, particularly if the individual has expressed homicidal or suicidal ideation, or has a history of paedophilia or sexual sadism.

Author notes

Preparation of this chapter and some of the research described herein were supported by the Medical Research Council of Canada, the Social Sciences and Humanities Research Council of Canada, the British Columbia Health Research Foundation, the British Columbia Research Services Foundation, the Program of Research on Mental Health and the Law of the John D and Catherine T MacArthur Foundation, and the John Wacker Foundation. Portions of this presentation have been updated from material from Hare (2000) and Hare, Cooke and Hart (1999).

Address all correspondence to Robert D Hare, Department of Psychology, 2136 West Mall, University of British Columbia, Vancouver, British Columbia, Canada V6T I Z4.

THE ETHICS OF CLINICAL RISK ASSESSMENT AND MANAGEMENT: DEVELOPING LAW AND THE ROLE OF MENTAL HEALTH PROFESSIONALS

Nigel Eastman

'This is an opportunity of a lifetime.' What response does this form of offer tend to engender in you? Is it 'at last I shall be able to have what I have not had available to me all these years and after which I have, perhaps justifiably, hankered'? The optimistic and trusting response. Or is it 'opportunities of a lifetime are never what they seem, or are sold as, and so beware'? The suspicious and pessimistic, even cynical response.

These words of the hard sell vendor, perhaps most often heard in the open markets up and down our towns and cities rather than in the more sophisticated emporia in New Bond Street, were how the Deputy Home Secretary, Paul Boateng, chose to introduce the government's 'dangerous and severe personality disorder' (DSPD) proposals for new services and law at a conference in 1999 sponsored by Leicester University. To the hopeful researcher into personality disorder they were, perhaps, music to the academic ear, or at least encouragement that they could be assured of respectability within their institution in the next but one round of the Research Assessment Exercise. At last a government was taking personality disorder seriously and putting some money into it. But perhaps the words are reassuring only on their face. Their usual connotation suggests caution, even outright cynicism. Indeed, since most senior researchers are not only (necessarily) optimistic for their science but also (again necessarily) always at least *scientifically* skeptical, is it not likely that most, in welcoming the government's initiative, and money, would be quietly cynical; 'governments always have an eye on their own advantage and their reasons for this "opportunity of a lifetime" are likely to be *their* reasons, and not *mine*'. But perhaps the ultimate cynicism lies in one possible response to this insight of the researcher who is prepared to take the money, 'what matters is the money and the science, my reasons not the government's', since it is likely, perhaps consciously so, to cut the researcher off from a proper attempt to view the DSPD proposals in total, and in their broader context. After all, these are proposals not just for new research and services but also for new *law*, and new law that will be passed before a single research paper is published arising out of any new research funding. The law is to *precede* any research findings, suggestive at least that the attitude to the research, and certainly to any negative findings that might logically cut across, or counter-justify, the proposed new legal orders, may be 'so what?'.

This chapter, like the symposium which gave rise to this book, is not solely about risk arising from personality disorder but from mental disorder more broadly. Indeed, a review of government policy over the decade that was dominated by the 'Clunis factor' (Ritchie *et al*, 1994) makes it clear that it is fear of *all* the mentally disordered that has dominated mental health politics, and policy, in recent times. The 'ten point plan', supervision registers, supervised discharge orders, guidance on discharge and mandatory homicide inquiries which have all been driven by what Geoffrey Pearson has called a 'a moral panic' (1999) applied to all those to whom society attaches arithmetically irrational fear. Only with the last government's 'hybrid order' for those with legal 'psychopathic disorder', enacted as the 'hospital and limitation direction' in the Crime (Sentences) Act 1997, did that group come in for special policy consideration, and then mainly only because of concern about the 'shifting boundary' between illness and personality disorder, sometimes across time for the same offender, which was capable of resulting in loss of public safety by dint of a medical diagnostic decision. That is, it was the 'loss' of mental illness in the individual, leaving them 'only' with personality disorder, which was of concern. And the policy solution was to ensure that detention was based not on diagnosis, prognosis or any other medical concept or evidence, but upon penal sentence. Meanwhile the deserving and therapeutically ambivalent patient, or even clinician, could still 'have a therapeutic go', alongside public protection assured through a penal sentence.

But personality disorder *is* special. This is not the place to rehearse its 'specialness' comprehensively, but only in terms of its relevance to risk assessment and management, and then only in the restricted context of any implications that such 'specialness' may have for ethical, clinical, and research practice. Neither, incidentally, is this the place to rehearse arguments about how reliable and valid are both the identification of 'SPD' and the prediction of the 'D' part of 'DSPD'. The state of such science is the data upon which ethical analysis operates, that is, it is the substrate upon which the ethical calculus is made. It tells us how many misidentified, false positive, SPDs and how many false negative DSPD predictions there will have to be in order to effect how much public safety, but it does not tell us in what fashion it would be right ethically to construct the calculus. Indeed, ethical analysis itself only tells us what are the ethical *implications* of a particular choice, and not whether we should make that particular choice, or not.

So how *is* personality disorder to be seen as special in the context of ethical analysis *per se*? And how is it to be seen as special particularly in the context of an analysis of the ethics of risk assessment and management by mental health practitioners (not 'within mental health practice', because that would be to prejudge whether risk assessment and management of those who happen to be mentally disordered always amounts to 'mental health practice', of which more later)? Let me, for crude convenience, start by adopting, for the moment, the term 'psychopath' as a sort of discourse hybrid between psychiatry and law. A cross between 'anti-social' (American Psychiatric Association, 1994) or 'dissocial' (WHO, 1992) personality disorder and legal 'psychopathic disorder' (in s 1 of the Mental Health Act 1983). I want to suggest that it is the nature of 'psychopaths' which make them particularly suitable as a focus for the ethical analysis I intend to offer. And the analysis that I want to offer focuses on the developing social role of mental health practitioners in relation to public protection (a role about which much complaint is offered but where, through the passage of time and policy, and with changing generations of practitioners, there is a risk that the *reasons* for such initial complaint may be lost in the passing of one professional époque into the next).

Psychopaths offer a highly convenient ethical substrate essentially because of both their uncertain definition and so called 'treatability'. As I have written elsewhere with Jill Peay (1998, pp 93–94):

'Psychopaths' lie at the intersection between the so called 'mad' and 'bad'; that is, between those who clearly warrant treatment (the seriously mentally ill or handicapped) and those who should properly receive punishment. Psychopaths also reflect more general ambivalence towards mentally disordered offenders (MDOs) as a whole; namely, should we perceive their offending as wholly caused by their disorder, or does their disorder add some nuance to the particular way in which they offend, or are their disorder and offending merely coincidental? For psychiatrists and the caring agencies ambivalence about psychopaths is variously reflected in, and/or determined by, disagreement about whether the disorder(s) exist(s), what form(s) it takes, what treatment might be appropriate (never mind effective), how long it will take or, when treatment has occurred, whether it has been successful. As patients, psychopaths are not often self-evidently needy, nor do they routinely volunteer themselves as in distress.[1] Moreover, by comparison with mental illness or handicap, the focus of effect of the disorder is much more heavily on disadvantage or harm to others than to self (although it should be stressed that those with severe personality disorders have somewhat higher rates of self harm and suicide). Finally, psychopaths are thought to be peculiarly and inherently untouched by therapeutic or rehabilitative interventions, two of the commonly accepted diagnostic criteria for psychopathic personality disorder being a failure to learn from experience and a failure to show remorse.

---

1   People suffering from 'psychopathic disorder' are rarely subject to civil commitment, and the absolute number of formal admissions is very low. For the year ending 31 March 1996, only 63 'psychopathic' patients (out of a total of 9,520) were on s 3 orders (Department of Health, 1997). It is, of course, possible that a personality type with the characteristic of egocentric, uncaring ruthlessness is both a protective factor, where the person might otherwise be at risk of psychiatric intervention, and a recipe for entrepreneurial if not social success, thereby partially accounting for the infrequent appearance of psychopaths in conventional psychiatric populations.

It is their moral hybridness and both nosological and therapeutic uncertainty that determines the ethical specialness of psychopaths. Few but the die hard, and increasingly scientifically anachronistic, Szaszian would apply such a description as that which I have just given of psychopaths to people with schizophrenia, or even severe depressive illness. Psychopaths are the moral and scientific junctional case between the mad and the bad, between those warranting treatment and those demanding of punishment, or perhaps even preventive detention (again, of which more later, especially in terms of whether the *basis* for such preventive detention should properly be from mental health science or from an 'ordinary' criminal justice model).

Also, it is in relation to psychopaths that the use of mental health practitioners for social control or public protection is most 'isolated'. By that I do not mean that the practitioner is him/herself professionally isolated (although s/he may be so) but that, like a term in a set of equations, such a role is best seen, or viewed, when presented and written 'in terms of' psychopathy. Here it is, where there is *profound* uncertainty about definition and therapeutic effect, and even where the prediction of risk may be more problematic compared with mental illness, that the ethical nature and effect of what mental health practitioners do is best observed.

4.1 WELFARE AND JUSTICE, AND THEIR RELATION WITH THE SOCIAL ROLES OF MENTAL HEALTH PROFESSIONALS

But before turning to use of psychopaths as the model example for analysing the social role of mental health professionals, it is necessary to lay down some foundations in terms of what ethical principles underpin such roles. Very simply I want to suggest that the relevant principles are those of welfare and justice, since there is, I also want to suggest, something which inherently ethically separates the mental health practitioner from the policeman or the court, and that 'something' can best be expressed in terms of the distinction between *pursuing* welfare and *pursuing* justice. Psychiatry, for example, is inherently concerned, with welfare. Whilst legal agencies are concerned with justice and perhaps public protection, even though that may be expressed through welfare in terms of choosing to place the welfare of one person, or of society, above that of another individual (although Rawls (1971) seems to eschew this, see later, and an alternative approach is to restrict justice to procedural justice). And this distinction holds good whatever the actual behaviour of individual psychiatrists may be towards their patients, including, for example, in the way, in the aggregate, that they resource allocate between their patients.

Now let me ask you to consider the following argument (Eastman, 2000, pp 16–18):

Psychiatry and law can be seen as two disciplines strictly originating at poles of a continuum but operating sometimes elsewhere on it. At one pole is psychiatry as medical science, operating through strict adherence to a scientific model and directed solely at individual patient welfare.[2] At the opposite pole is law operating as a strict legal discourse, taking no account necessarily, for example, of any medically construed notion of patient welfare but concerning itself with justice and with due process.[3] Close to the latter pole, but somewhat towards the other pole, is the law as it operates in less of a strict 'legal discourse' like mode. An example of this is sentencing, where the rules are often more legally flexible than in relation to trial, and where there is the potential for consideration not only of just retribution but also of social deterrence, public welfare and even individual defendant welfare. Deterrence arises from a policy purpose of social control and individual welfare clearly moves the law towards the individual, and even potentially towards the therapeutic. In like fashion, psychiatry moves away from its polar position when it accepts, even if under protest,[4] a responsibility for social control, either in the interest of the individual patient, because the State has an interest in its citizens not harming themselves, or in the direct interest of the community.[5] In this mode of operation psychiatry may either/both loosen its scientific constructs or methods, in order to accommodate goals not inherently part of its strict science, or/and even breach its strict scientific rules so as, more crudely, to effect a social purpose. Finally the movement of law and psychiatry towards one another from each of their polar positions can cause them to meet in the middle, or even mutually to cross over the boundary between them. The latter can occur where, for example, law takes on an overtly mainly therapeutic purpose, substantially discarding much of its usual discourse strictures in order to do so. This is the stuff of extreme 'therapeutic jurisprudence' and can arise either through the way in which the law itself is framed or through the way in which it is operated ... as an illustration, if MHRTs operate more towards a patient and public welfare purpose than an individual justice purpose (Peay 1989) then they have at least met psychiatry in the middle of the spectrum and they may even have crossed over to the other side. Similarly, if psychiatry is operated with a heavy emphasis on social control then it is likely both to have to pull away from its own scientific discourse and even to cross over the boundary into domains which are more properly the concern of law

---

2 The public health model of medicine which pursues an aspect of public welfare is addressed later specifically in relation to the current government's proposals for 'dangerous severe personality disorder' (Home Office, 1999).

3 Of course law does itself sometimes purport to pursue welfare but it is open to question whether law and medicine construe the concept in the same way (see King and Piper, 1995). Also, it is arguable that the law's interest in welfare is a very general one (for example, as a utilitarian representation of the real purpose of abstract justice) and that it will never, or should never, choose the welfare of one individual over another where that conflicts with justice (see Rawls, 1971).

4 See the exchange between the then President of the Royal College of Psychiatrists and the Home Secretary on whether psychiatrists have a responsibility to detain untreatable 'psychopaths' for the public good (Kendall, 1998; Straw, 1998).

5 See Heginbotham and Elson (1999) for their description of 'communitarian politics' and its specific effect on the formation of public policy in relation to mental disorder.

than of medicine. Finally, and more theoretically, the 'mid point' of the spectrum may be seen as a strict divide where each discipline views the other just from their own side of the divide. This should include each discipline conducting an exercise in construct relations ... where the constructs, ways of thinking, and purposes of each side are seen through the eyes of the other. Failure to carry this out, particularly when a discipline is operating very close to the divide, is likely to result in unawareness on the part of practitioners that they have, indeed, crossed the Rubicon and trespassed into purposes which go beyond that which their science ethically 'allows'. That is, it is only through, at least, awareness of where he is operating on the spectrum and, better still, strong adherence to the principles and purposes of his own science, that the practitioner can avoid profound distortion of his social function. If the former requires vigilance which is beyond most practitioners on a day to day basis then that would suggest a high degree of ethical danger in operating 'too close to the divide'. Put another way, strict adherence to the practitioner's science is likely to be the best guarantee of ethical practice that remains within the proper confines of the discipline.[6] This applies not only to doctors who may stray into areas of social control at the expense of their proper medical function but also to lawyers or courts who may do their clients or defendants a disservice in terms of justice if they stray excessively towards matters therapeutic.

Also (Eastman, 2000, pp 18–19):

The latter assumes a natural relationship between the mode of operation and social purpose of a science and the definition of its ethical practice. To some, moving along the continuum from their own discipline towards the other is ethically acceptable, or even desirable. For the doctor, for example, it may be seen as ethically right to take on a social purpose of public protection, justified either by the paternalistic avoidance of the secondary harm to his patient who commits a crime that will arise through state punishment or as a valid 'public health psychiatry' activity *per se*.[7] Similarly, the lawyer may adopt an ethical responsibility for his client which is seen as transcending the duty to represent him to the best possible outcome in terms of justice and which addresses also his welfare ('never mind how long you are going to locked up in hospital, you will be getting treatment'). Depending upon the ethical perspective adopted, such 'crossings over' will be perceived properly either as productive cross fertilisation between the two disciplines or as mutual corruption. To adopt the former view is essentially to hold to a utilitarian ethical model. What really matters is the outcome; indeed, what matters is the outcome for all, based on an aggregate social calculation. To adopt the latter view is to hold to a more

---

6   This principle was well illustrated in an unpublished paper by John Wadham to the British Association of Mental Health and Law in relation to government proposals for a 'reviewable order' for those suffering from 'dangerous severe personality disorder' (London School of Economics, June 1999).

7   Again, see Eastman (1999) for a description of the distinction between true public health measures, where the patient himself can benefit from medical intervention and where it is strictly public health and not welfare which is at stake, and crude crime prevention, where psychiatry is used solely towards a public protection purpose, with no individual patient benefit, and even harm.

deontological model that emphasises principle rather than outcome; that is, it is seen as wrong to contravene the strict model of the discipline concerned because, ethically, process transcends outcome, either for the individual or for society. So, ...[there is] ethical conflict between perceiving psychiatry as oriented solely towards the welfare of the patient as against acknowledging it as an ethically valid means of social control and public welfare. This is matched by the contrasting of law as solely a means to justice and as a welfare seeking therapeutic tool. Finally, whichever position is adopted by each discipline will determine the extent to which there is collusion or conflict between them. The doctor who adopts a strong public or patient protection responsibility may tend to stretch his science in a legal context so as to achieve the best outcome (as he perceives it), irrespective of the law. The tribunal that is similarly minded will distort its own rules and process to the same end. That is, there will be collusion across the tribunal table. A meeting between a welfare oriented tribunal and a strict medical scientist may, by contrast, result in the tribunal experiencing difficulty in gaining its purpose because the doctor will not co-operate. Similarly, a tribunal wishing strictly to apply the law and legal process, in spite of the outcome, will tend to thwart the intentions of the welfare oriented doctor who wishes to use his science towards the end of patient or social advantage in spite of the law, if only because the medical member may properly return the medical evidence to strict medical science after the RMO has left the room. Ultimately, all this can be expressed in terms of the extent to which any incongruity of constructs between the two disciplines which flows naturally from their two sets of strictly defined purposes and methods is actually played out in the practical relationship between them. Alternatively, to what extent is such natural incongruity 'overcome' by cross fertilisation or mutual corruption?

This notion of cross-fertilisation as opposed to mutual corruption is crucial to the rest of what I want to argue. As has perhaps already become apparent (indeed it may already be known from other writings that I have offered) I hold that there is an important ethical protection in the notion of strictly defined science and social roles, and that to abandon adherence to them is to court the 'disintegration' of the very profession to which that role is usually properly ascribed. By this I do not mean that people will stop being psychiatrists (although there is much evidence that this is true, including because of corruption of the previous individual welfare role of the profession in favour of public protection) but that psychiatry will stop being 'psychiatry', and will certainly be at risk of no longer being part of 'medicine' as it is still defined (the same may apply to the definition of other mental health professions).

4.2 WELFARE VERSUS JUSTICE

I want now to return more specifically to risk assessment and management and specifically to its ethics in the context of the 'best focusing' example of psychopaths, addressing specifically the government's DSPD proposals as the extreme example of a trend in public policy development both for psychopaths and for all the mentally disordered and their 'care'. There are, I suggest, a number of important examples of shifts in the required, and/or at least requested social roles of psychiatry which go beyond DSPD (perhaps most notably s 2(2)(b) of the Criminal Justice Act 1991 which allows or requires a court to impose a 'longer than commensurate (or normal) sentence' where there is, for example, mental instability that is believed likely to contribute to continuing risk to the public beyond the tariff period since this requires psychiatrists to give evidence based on their 'science' but directed at an entirely public protective effect; involvement in any form of 'renewable sentence' such as was suggested by Fallon (1998) would have similar implications.

Now, consider this statement from Rawls, a not unknown jurisprudential writer on justice (1971, pp 11–13):

> Justice is the first virtue of social institutions, as truth is of systems of thought. A theory, however elegant and economical must be rejected or revised if it is untrue; likewise laws and institutions no matter how efficient and well arranged must be reformed or abolished if they are unjust. Each person possesses inviolability founded on justice that even the welfare of society as a whole cannot override.

I should start by making it clear that, personally, I adhere to Rawls' position, although I do not think that my argument from here on is dependent upon agreement, certainly not full agreement. So, even if we had, in relation to this awful term 'DSPD' (a policy concept not a scientific one), an efficient and a 'true' (as Rawls would put it), or valid (as we might do so), way of identifying this policy group (not diagnostic group), then I, personally, would still place welfare above justice. (Of course, the very idea of 'validly' identifying members of a policy contrived group called SPD is somewhat non-sensical, since validity is usually reserved for measuring things that actually 'exist'; members of this 'group' might *possibly* be identified reliably, if sufficient 'SPD practitioners' agreed sufficiently on an identification protocol, but that is very different from valid identification.)

But even if you do not agree with my suggested hegemony of justice over welfare, that is, even if you (thinking of course as a citizen and not a mental health professional, since it is not part specifically of your professional role to take a stance on welfare versus justice) *would* sometimes put public welfare above individual justice, you need still to be sufficiently sure of the 'truth' (validity) of systems of both diagnosis and risk assessment that, together, would bring an individual into the DSPD group, even to be able to pursue welfare, at the expense of justice.

Put even more weakly, even if we have *some* ability to diagnose personality disorder and its severity reliably and validly, in contributing to the legal determination of who comes within the DSPD group, are you confident that the level of ability is sufficient to override justice? That of course is to put the question in a form that requires an individual ethical response which, in one sense, cannot be validly contradicted, since we can all take our own view about the 'proper' balance between the risk of injustice against the securing of public welfare. However, posing the question in this stark way seems likely best to gain a frank professional, and public, debate about the DSPD proposals (or any other measures that can be reduced to this type of conflict). And ethics is only capable ultimately of exposing the ethical nature of any policy decision taken, and of specific legal measures pursued by society.

Suppose, for example, and drawing on a contribution to a similar debate made by Tony Bottoms 20 years ago (1982), that we knew that we could, on average, predict with one in three accuracy who will seriously offend, is that welfare achievement at the expense of locking up two (actually) non-serious future offenders an acceptable price in lost justice to pay for the welfare thereby gained? And here I refer to detaining someone not as punishment for what he has done but solely preventatively.

So that is the type of framework within which I want to place specific discussion of the DSPD proposals. Hence, even if you do not agree with me (and Rawls) that justice *is* (or at least should be) above welfare, we might agree at least on the ethical framework for deciding whether the welfare we might gain from the DSPD proposals (or any other public policy issue that boils down ethically to the same calculus) will be gained at too high a justice price, or not. And then, alongside this question still runs the further question of the proper, and ethical, definition of forensic mental health practice (of whatever discipline). That is, what place in all of this should we have, especially in relation to those individuals who are known initially, or about whom it might become known on initial assessment, that there is no welfare benefit *for them* in detention (aside from the avoidance of being detained after an offence that they might otherwise commit and, in relation to that 'benefit' the acceptance of it should perhaps obviously be with his/her consent).

4.3 MORE ON SOCIAL ROLES IN TERMS OF WELFARE AND JUSTICE

The law is predominantly concerned with justice. Assume for the moment that 'justice' amounts simply to 'being dealt with fairly'. This, as Tony Bottoms has observed, is to go further than 'being dealt with by a fair process', since fair processes can result in unfair results, that are no less unfair because they were arrived at fairly. The law is, of course, also often constructed in utilitarian terms towards achieving individual and public welfare, that is, the welfare of the citizens of the state; but not, according to Rawls, so as to take a view about the welfare of one citizen as against that of another in such a way as to inhibit justice to both. So, it is argued that the law is, or should be, interested in welfare but not at the expense of justice. As I have already suggested, by contrast mental health sciences are interested inherently in welfare, with no natural discourse concern with justice. However, law and mental health scientists can tend sometimes towards an overlapping of social roles. Hence, at the very least, psychiatrists effect justice, by offering evidence within the justice system, which 'facilitates' the operation of justice, or rather provides (properly unbiased) evidence on which the justice system then operates. But the psychiatrist can, if s/he so wishes, decide not merely to *effect* but to *affect* justice; that is to intend to influence the process and outcome of the justice system. This can occur, for example, by the way in which s/he interprets the law in clinical terms or whereby, on a range of reasonable clinical opinions that might be expressed (each potentially with different justice outcomes) s/he 'decides' to place his/her evidence at a particular point on the range. Indeed, the psychiatrist can stretch his/her science so far, and even with the clear *intention* of influencing the justice outcome, or public or patient outcome, that s/he ceases to operate what can reasonably be called 'psychiatry'. This can apply in civil courts, in tribunals, at trial in criminal courts and in relation to criminal disposal. So, psychiatrists can influence justice *per se* (for example, causing people to be locked up, even 'unfairly') and can also influence and achieve welfare in spite of the justice that should preclude the securing of such welfare. Indeed, as I have suggested, even lawyers can abandon justice for welfare ('never mind how long you will be locked up, you will be getting treatment to your benefit', again).

But whether or not it is ethical for clinicians to behave in that way, in relation to DSPD is it at all 'necessary'? The courts already have substantial protective sentences available to them to cover a range of criminal and defendant circumstances. And they can apply them using their own risk assessment basis, albeit always in the context of sentencing for an index offence. Aside from ss 37/41 'without limit of time' (given down in the knowledge that the legal definitions justifying discharge are so broadly drawn, and that other discharge 'rules' are written so with an eye on public protection, that public safety is well catered for), there is the mandatory life sentence for murder, the automatic life sentence for 'two strikes and out', the discretionary life sentence, s 2(2)(b) 'longer than normal sentences', the 'automatic life sentence' and finally the sentencing hybrid, the 'hospital and limitation direction'. Now this list clearly emphasises the range of sentences available to the courts specifically for the psychopath, including the psychopath who is deemed untreatable. So an obvious clue to the government's perceived problem lies in the fact that, on its own description, only 2% of those defendants that could attract a discretionary life sentence do so (Home Office and DoH, 1999). Indeed, Mr Boateng said as much to the Home Affairs Select Committee which investigated the DSPD proposals (House of Commons Home Affairs Select Committee, 2000). Perhaps that suggests close judicial reading of Rawls. So, is the government turning to psychiatrists and psychologists to achieve the welfare effect, over justice, that the courts will not effect? Otherwise, even on the government's own analysis, only the very few 'untreatable' psychopaths who do not have a current conviction or a current plus relevant list of past convictions, could not, if the courts so desired, be dealt with *by* the courts without reference to doctors. This is public policy, therefore, according to the 'sardine tin' principle; being determined to get that last little bit of welfare advantage out of the back of the tin, whatever the justice cost of so doing.

Returning more specifically to the proper roles of mental health professionals, clearly involvement in any civil or criminal justice process where the purpose, or perhaps one of the purposes, is therapeutic of the individual must be congruent with professional ethics. However, there has been developing in the last decade a new psychiatric jurisprudence. Part III of the 1983 Act updated a long tradition of welfare sentencing of mentally disordered offenders (MDOs). Doctors are merely required to inform the courts whether a particular MDO has a disorder in terms of the definitions used in both the civil part and Part III of the Act, whether it is 'of a nature or degree etc' and whether the other usual criteria for detention are met. Only by default then are doctors involved in penal sentencing, that is, when they do *not* recommend a medical disposal. Justice is also thereby at least partially respected by recognition of the MDO's disorder at sentencing, whereas the range of mental condition defences available at trial is highly, probably overly, restricted (Mackay, 1995). Once sentenced definitively to hospital, public welfare is dependent upon medical improvement of the condition which it is believed places the public at risk or upon continued detention because of lack of improvement. Hence the courts have no further role in achieving public safety than in their interpretation of the relevant discharge sections of the Act. If they adhere strictly to their science, doctors are similarly limited in their potential impact on public safety to describing the continuation of disorder as justifying continued detention under the Act. There is therefore a Rubicon crossed at sentencing where public welfare is thereafter dependent upon the definition of continuing disorder and of the pursuit of treatment. Indeed, it is the loss of any explicit and solely public protection directed legal mechanism unconnected with disorder and treatment which can draw doctors or courts into stretching their definitions within the Act in order somehow still to ensure public welfare. There is, in essence, little separation of public and private welfare. Indeed, public welfare is dependent either upon increased individual welfare (and discharge) or lack of increased individual welfare and continued detention.

What is at issue is therefore whether recent developments in sentencing law relevant to MDOs, as well as recent government sentencing proposals, can be seen as keeping to, or as moving away from, the tradition of welfare sentencing of MDOs. And if the latter, what are the implications both for the balance between welfare and justice and for the public protection role of doctors? Related to the latter question is the likely impact on the culture of forensic psychiatric services more broadly of new sentencing measures. Another related question is whether doctors may, under recently proposed DSPD provisions, be required sometimes to apply their science to wholly public protective objectives.

Such a shift in sentencing philosophy is suggested by the introduction of the 'hospital and limitation direction', which was presaged in the 1996 White Paper on *Sentencing* (Home Office, 1996), by s 2(2)(b), combined with s 4(1), of the Criminal Justice Act 1991 allowing the imposition of 'longer than normal (or commensurate) sentences', and by proposals for a 'reviewable order' for the dangerous severely personality disordered (Home Office, 1999). Extension of the mandatory life sentence to defendants found guilty of a second 'serious offence' in a way which includes within its terms mentally disordered offenders offers further evidence of the shift. This seems to represent a major English jurisprudential novelty that contradicts centuries of English sentencing practice based on a predominantly welfare approach to the mentally disordered. However, it is a novelty that also has major implications, both practical and ethical, for mental health clinicians and services. Mostly, these shifts involve the risk, sometimes certainty, that psychiatrists will be drawn into justice rather than welfare functions. Yet, the hospital and limitation direction can also be seen as potentially protective of professional integrity. Although it represents a shift away from welfare sentencing per se, the separation of the legal basis for detention from treatment that may occur during such treatment avoids the 'need' for any distortion of scientific constructs in evidence to tribunals, pursued in order to secure continuing public protection. Such a 'hybrid' solution may therefore have substantial advantages, especially in cases, such as with psychopaths, where there is profound uncertainty about both the definition of the 'disorder' and its 'treatability'. By contrast, the government's proposals for a civil DSPD order have exactly the opposite implications for professional ethics. Indeed, the Green Paper (DoH, 1999), by similarly removing the need for individual benefit from the required criteria for compulsion in relation to all forms of mental disorder to be included in a new Mental Health Act, not only seems to abolish any 'need' for special DSPD legislation but also signals even more obviously an intended *comprehensive* change in the social role of psychiatry. Even the most ardent critic of Szasz might wonder if he did not have a point in suggesting how the scientific looseness of psychiatric nosology left it open to be abused for social purposes little connected with the treatment of 'disease'.

In a related vein, and still concerning the different roles of doctors, breach of medical confidentiality by clinicians into the justice system can be seen as a 'narrow' bridge between their professional and citizen roles where the doctor has a right to breach (*W v Egdell* (1990)), or as a 'broad' bridge, where there is a duty to disclose information to non-health agencies. In either case disclosure is, of course, directed at a non-health related purpose. And there is evidence that both the broad and narrow bridges are themselves broadening. This too has implications for the ethics of practice where, as with some of the new sentencing measures, information gained under the cloak of a medical purpose is then applied to a societal purpose unconnected with patient welfare.

4.4 DSPD AS THE LEADING EDGE OF CHANGING PROFESSIONAL ROLES, AND AS THE FOCUS OF A PROFESSIONAL DEFENCE

Aubrey Lewis' caution in his seminal paper on psychopathy that the 'condition' represented 'a most elusive category (with) wavering confines' (Lewis, 1974) makes clear the dangers of policies of social control being based on constructs that can be stretched and distorted to suit. Yet DSPD is not even a 'real' construct. It is impossible to validate something that does not occur in the real world but which, unlike a psychiatric diagnosis (which is *open* to social abuse), does not even have the pretence of an exclusively real world core. True, it might be said that DSPD 'represents' psychiatric diagnoses but, as with any legal artifact which represents or reflects real world psychiatric constructs (as in the current Mental Health Act), the looser the real world constructs that an artifact represents the more open to abuse are both the artifact and that which it represents.

As I have already said, this is not the place to rehearse the arguments about reliability and validity in relation to diagnoses that might 'underpin' a finding of SPD or about the reliability of predicting D. But, restricting myself to the likely behaviour of those carrying out the operations, it seems almost certain that social pressure on mental health professionals to avoid 'false negatives' and the statistical 'base rate phenomenon' will result in widespread findings of 'false positives'. The fact that prediction involves substantially trying to predict the likely future 'environment' around the individual, since few are 'unconditionally dangerous', serves further to emphasise the profundity of the problem of prediction and the ethical implications for those making the predictions.

I have argued elsewhere that ethically a doctor's involvement in the criminal justice system can be defined in terms of the degree of proximity of his/her role to judicial punishment *per se*, or even the potential for punishment (Eastman and McInerny, 1997). Such proximity varies according to participation in the criminal justice stages of (1) investigation; (2) determination of fitness for trial; (3) determination of verdict; (4) sentencing; (5) assessment and treatment for fitness for punishment; (6) punishment *per se*; and (7) certification of completed punishment (the latter being applicable only to the death penalty). Differing degrees of proximity potentially determine differing ethical dilemma, both for individual clinicians and for corporate professional bodies. Also, participation can be seen in terms of not only the degree of proximity or remoteness from punishment but also the inevitability of punishment (whatever the actions of the doctor concerned) and whether there is *any* therapeutic purpose or aspect to the medical intervention contemplated. In the UK it is generally accepted individual professional practice to participate in stages 1–3, with the absence of any corporate proscription. Participation in stage 4, sentencing, is similarly accepted, albeit the Royal College statement in relation to the death penalty is silent on it.[8] College policy does, however, proscribe any involvement in stage 5 (again specifically where the punishment is death), as well as in stages 6 and 7.[9] However, acceptance of professional involvement in stage 4, sentencing, has arisen in the context of a welfare model of sentencing for the mentally disordered. Is such blanket acceptance now still ethical within the 'new psychiatric jurisprudence'?

Such a general approach to the ethics of clinician involvement, with stages distinguished by their degree of 'proximity' to punishment *per se*, is underpinned by drawing the distinction between the roles of 'doctor as doctor' and 'doctor as citizen'. However, whether that approach always offers an ethical escape from the problem of using medical knowledge for non-medical purposes is open to debate.

Applying this model to the DSPD proposals, where someone has been convicted of a *serious offence* the courts have available to them a range of 'non-medical' sentencing options, and psychiatric evidence to the court may either be unnecessary or merely add a 'nuance' to data considered by the

8   It is questionable whether acceptance is predicated on the (previously reasonable) assumption, given the sentencing welfare model, that medical participation will always be directed at advising the court about possible 'medical disposals'. If so then it may fail to recognise that, for example, s 2(2)(b) of the Criminal Justice Act 1991 infers participation where there can be no medical purpose to it. Indeed, it could be said that involvement in the latter process is even more ethically dubious than would be involvement in DSPD sentencing, since at least in the latter case there may be the possibility of therapeutic intervention of some sort.

9   It can be argued that medical participation in stages 5 and 6 could be inferred in the government's DSPD proposals if doctors were ever to be employed in facilities where some inmates received no (real, as opposed to spurious) therapeutic intervention from the doctors concerned. Only if such doctors were involved in 'reducing mental or physical distress' in some way might participation be justified, by analogy with reducing distress in the inmate on death row. However, it is even open to debate whether that is an ethical use of medical practice (again, see Eastman and McInerny, 1997).

court. And the data used by the court will be of the most reliable type, that is, known past behaviour objectively determined. Where the individual has, on the current occasion, been convicted of only a *minor offence* then, clearly, there could still be legislation which would allow retrospection to the previous totality of offending in the making of a reviewable sentence, as originally suggested in this country by Butler (1975) and repeated by Fallon (1998). Again, if society takes this route it has little to do with mental health professionals, unless, as suggested by Fallon, the 'entry ticket' into such special sentencing was a 'diagnosis' contributing to a legal concept like SPD. Then professional involvement is both crucial and potentially ethically problematic, especially if it were to extend to advising not only on the presence of the entry ticket but also on who, amongst those with histories of only minor offending, is likely to offend more seriously.

But what of the individual who is facing *no current conviction*? Again the 'past offences' approach could be taken but towards the making of a civil order. Here some of the ethical problems for the mental health practitioner are somewhat similar, but the psychiatric role is, legally, bound ultimately to be very different. In terms of the European Convention on Human Rights there would be a requirement of 'objective medical evidence' demonstrating 'unsoundness of mind' in order for there to be any valid legal basis at all for preventive detention. And the less the evidence of actual offending behaviour in the past the greater must be the reliance in choosing preventive detainees upon the identification and description of psychopathology as predicting of future offending. This suggests possible unethical practice, either/both because of the highly uncertain reliability and validity base of predicting future behaviour in that way or/and, where it is known, or becomes known through assessment, because such a practice would involve the application of welfare based mental health sciences to an entirely non personal related purpose, namely public protection. Indeed, the Home Affairs Select Committee seemed to recognise just how much of a general (not just professional) ethical problem such legislation presents by its quite extra-ordinary recommendation that any Act passed should be subject to a 'sunset clause' and regular parliamentary scrutiny, seen in this époque only in relation to anti-terrorist detention law (Home Affairs Select Committee 2000). It also suggested that the law should allow detention of the un-convicted only where 'it is almost certain that they will commit a very serious offence'. The obvious un-workability of such a legal criterion makes clear the unacceptability of the proposals. Indeed, if such wording were included in the enabling Act then no orders for the unconvicted could ever be made, assuming expert witnesses did not perjure themselves, or their science.

But am I *right* to suggest that it is unethical for doctors, for example, to apply their skills towards a social purpose wholly unconnected to the benefit of the individual 'patient'? Is there not a proper field of public health psychiatry?[10]

Responsibilities on clinicians going beyond, and even conflicting with, the interests of the individual patient are not unique to mental health care. There are infectious diseases that have long been legally notifiable on the basis for removing individual liberty. However, there seems to be a clear distinction between responsibilities for public health which relate to the potential for harm to the public arising directly from disease and responsibility for controlling attacks by patients which are either not solely, or even directly, attributable to mental disease. Indeed, although the 1983 Act clearly allows doctors to recommend detention of the mentally disordered for the protection of others, this is only reflected in one of the tertiary criteria for detention; it is necessary first to determine that the person has a mental disorder of a nature or degree that makes it appropriate for them to be admitted to hospital for medical treatment before public protection becomes a legal issue. Beyond these precise subtleties, however, it seems clear that public expectations and political rhetoric moved in the 1990s to a new and much higher level as regards the required public protective role of psychiatrists. This is most starkly typified by provisions which emphasise a public protective function of psychiatrists in the criminal justice system itself. However, if it is assumed for the moment that, in the absence of criminal conviction, the only possible ethical justification for public protection psychiatry arises from the public health model, it may assist to consider specifically the example of DSPDs currently convicted of no offence and who may be subject to a renewable civil order.

Section 37 of the Public Health (Control of Diseases) Act 1984 allows the detention of persons suffering from a notifiable disease, where they pose a serious risk of infection to others (tuberculosis is the most common basis for a section 37 order, indeed it is hardly used at all for other conditions; see Coker, 1999). However, some important distinctions can be drawn in relation to possible measures to protect the public from DSPD individuals. That is, there are crucial distinctions between the valid exercise of public health psychiatry and crude crime prevention or social control (Eastman, 1999). First, the reliability of predicting rates of infection in members of the public is likely to be far higher than the equivalent risk assessment applied to those with DSPD. Second, there is almost invariably a high level of validity and reliability of diagnosis of the infectious condition itself, not at all matched in either the medical diagnosis of anti-social personality disorder or its legal translation into SPD. Third, there is usually (admittedly not always) effective treatment offered to the infected person themselves so that not all the welfare benefits accrue to members of the public. In this regard the then

---

10   Graham Thornicroft has indicated that, as a research 'community psychiatrist', he is unhappy with the term 'public health psychiatry' being used to refer to any notion beyond that of (essentially) psychiatric epidemiology (personal communication).

Home Secretary argues that there are, in any event, many doctors who properly and ethically care for many people with untreatable conditions and that not to do so is not only inhumane but therapeutically nihilistic (Straw, 1998). It follows, he says, that psychiatrists should adopt the same position vis à vis DSPD. Indeed, he has offered substantial research and service funding to that end (Straw, 1999). However, there is perhaps one important response. If civil liberties are to be removed on the basis of newly developed science (of assessment and treatment) then that new science should precede the new law and not the reverse. To plan otherwise is analogous with having created the Human Fertilisation and Embryology Authority before the first in vitro fertilisation had been achieved. There is also a risk, of course, that Treasury constraints will result in detentions based on new law, which achieves the public welfare objective, not then being followed by funding aimed at more reliable assessment and at rehabilitation by way of risk reduction. Finally, there is a clear distinction between public health and public welfare, and to equate the two is almost entirely to abolish any boundary around what activities are truly 'medical'.[11]

In addition, however, harm from DSPD arises from voluntary and intended behaviour on the part of the person. That is, for harm to occur there has to be a decision on the part of the DSPD individual. Indeed, this is the basis for it being so much more difficult to predict behaviour than infection. Only where infection requires an active decision on the part of the infected person to expose the other to the risk of infection (as, for example, with HIV) can the analogy with DSPD be said to hold in any measure. In fact, the virus then becomes a weapon which the person happens to have and which can be used against others.

However, the limits of the public health model as an ethical justification are most clearly emphasised by the fact that health benefit is embedded within the model, and 'public health' is a far narrower concept than 'public welfare'. Hence, merely to say that there will be improved public welfare from medical involvement in a legal measure does not imply valid involvement in public health improvement. DSPD measures are not to do with health but with safety. This is so even though medical injuries can arise through lack of safety. To define health so as to equate it with welfare, for example because attacks can result in victim injuries requiring medical attention, is to place almost no limit on what is a health matter. And that is especially so if psychological health (of victims) is included within the model. So, the DSPD proposals are directed not at public health but at public welfare. They represent, therefore, a form of Public Protection Act, not a Public Mental Health Act.

---

11 Interestingly, in a speech to a conference at Leicester University, 'Squaring the circle', October 1999 (at which the author also spoke), Paul Boateng, Minister of State at the Home Office, repeatedly referred to 'public safety and welfare' as the objectives of the proposed legislation, never to 'public health'.

All this said, even corporate medical ethics are altering at least in the same direction as social expectations and government policy. Although the imperatives of 'doing good and avoiding doing harm' (with the latter usually taking precedence over the former) are embodied in the Hippocratic Oath ('I will prescribe regimen for the good of my patients according to my ability and my judgement and never do harm to anyone'), one suggested new (draft) Hippocratic Oath clearly includes a notion of a duty towards the public (Hurwitz and Richardson, 1997). Also, increasingly the General Medical Council (GMC) defined ethical rights of doctors in this regard are developing into duties, for example, in relation to the breaching confidence to the DVLA regarding irresponsible epileptics (GMC, 1995, at Appendix, pp 11–12). Hence, generally the 'broad bridge' is becoming broader, or the 'membrane' more permeable. This may make individual mental health care directed substantially at public protection less alien to psychiatrists. However, that is to raise a far broader question of the extent to which medical ethics should be robust against social and political pressure or responsive to it.

4.5 CONCLUSION

In evidence to the Home Affairs Select Committee (2000), I, perhaps incautiously, suggested that it was a failure of the government to get the judges to 'roll over', so as to use the sentencing options available to them more widely for purposes of public protection, that had, at least partly, caused them to turn to mental health professionals. As I put it, 'If we can't get the judges to roll over then let's get the shrinks to roll over'. But is there not an entirely proper reason that the judges are intransigent? And should psychiatrists 'fill the public welfare gap', that little bit of the sardine tin contents that is so elusive, by applying psychiatry spuriously, or applying spurious psychiatry?

Perhaps the reason that the judges adopt the position they do is that they, at least, do hold to Rawls' assertion. That is, justice is above even public welfare. It is, or should be, certainly 'above' politics, even if it is so called 'communitarian politics', or, differently interpreted, the hegemony of the majority exercised in the pursuit of 'the good life in a good (and safe) society'. And is not sardine tin public policy driven by arithmetically irrational moral panic (Pearson, 1998)? Extending the analogy, is it worth the justice cost implied to get that last bit of welfare fish out of the corner of the sardine tin when you cannot quite open the lid far enough even properly to see what is there? Finally, sardine tins are, of course, themselves very sharp, and therefore dangerous, especially if you are determined to extract from them that last morsel of fish!

SECTION TWO

RISK MANAGEMENT AND THE LAW: BALANCING INDIVIDUAL RIGHTS AND PUBLIC PROTECTION

CHAPTER 5

RADICAL RISK MANAGEMENT, MENTAL HEALTH AND CRIMINAL JUSTICE

Philip Fennell

5.1 INTRODUCTION

This essay examines the contradictory philosophies and policies at play in the system of care of mentally disordered people, and the impact of the case law of the European Court of Human Rights on that system. It argues that a convergence is taking place between the values and legal structures of the hospital system on the one hand and the penal system on the other, a convergence with profound implications for the citizenship rights of mentally disordered people, and the nature of the doctor/patient relationship. The essay traces how pursuit by the Government of radical risk management policies within the constraints of European Convention case law has affected and will continue to affect the legal framework of compulsory care for mentally disordered people, how it has altered the balance between therapy, retribution, and social defence, and, finally, how it has affected the nature of the relationship between clinicians and patients.

I shall examine current Government proposals to reform the Mental Health Act 1983 in the context of other reforms and proposed reforms of the penal system. The Government's two volume White Paper (*Reforming the Mental Health Act: Part I The New Legal Framework* and *Part II High Risk Patients* (Home Office, 2000a, b)) heralds a radical departure in mental health legislation. The Government claims that it forms the basis of modern mental health legislation and, in the modern jargon, is an example of 'joined up government'. The proposals are jointly issued by the Department of Health, which is in charge of the system of psychiatric care, and the Home Office, which has charge of the penal policy, criminal justice policy, and the supervision of mentally disordered patients who are subject to Home Office restrictions on discharge on grounds of dangerousness. As we shall see, the joined up Government approach is more reflective of criminal justice and risk management concerns than it is of traditional healthcare values. The current proposals represent a reaction to increasing concerns about the risks to self and others, but mainly to others, posed by mentally disordered people. I argue that these proposals herald a further convergence between the mental health and criminal justice systems, with profound implications for the citizenship rights of mentally disordered people.

Convergence is driven by the Government's desire to be able to manage risk through preventive detention. In the penal system it is marked by a strong move away from the notion of just deserts and proportionality between offence and sentence toward greater use of so called protective (that is, indeterminate) sentencing, once the province of the psychiatric system. In the psychiatric system convergence is marked by such developments as the broadening of powers to detain on grounds of risk to other people and the erosion of patients' rights to confidentiality of medical information by the introduction of duties to share information about patients thought to be high risk.

Since before the Lunacy Act 1890 a prime concern of mental health legislation has been the protection of patients from wrongful or unduly prolonged use of powers to detain and treat compulsorily. The Mental Health Act 1959 introduced the Mental Health Review Tribunal (MHRT) to provide review of the lawfulness of and continued need for detention. The Mental Health Act 1983, partly prompted the adverse ruling of the European Court of Human Rights in *X v United Kingdom*[1] increased the frequency with which patients could apply for discharge, gave them rights to second opinions if treated compulsorily, and added to those due process rights a welfare entitlement by giving patients subject to long term powers of detention a right to after-care following discharge.

That concern for rights in the sense of due process rights and latterly patient entitlement to treatment has been replaced by a concern for human rights in a much broader sense. This embraces not only the rights of patients to protection against arbitrary use of State therapeutic power (the due process rights under Arts 5–7 of the Convention and the right of sanctity of the person under the right of respect for privacy in Art 8), but also the human rights of victims or potential victims of mentally disordered people to protection of their right to life under Art 2 and to protection against inhuman and degrading treatment under Art 3. In this essay I shall examine these developments, which I shall characterise as policies of radical risk management, against the wider political background and in the light of the coming into force of the Human Rights Act 1998.

---

1   (1981) 4 EHRR 188.

5.2 RADICAL RISK MANAGEMENT

The social control of so called 'risky populations' has always been a goal of criminal justice policy,[2] but lately it has become an increasingly overt preoccupation.[3] Since the early 1990s mentally disordered people in general, let alone those who have committed criminal offences, are increasingly portrayed as a risky population. A steady procession of inquiries into homicides by former psychiatric in-patients has increased the association in the public mind between mental disorder and dangerousness, leading to increasing demands for protection from crime particularly crimes committed by mentally disordered people, although a survey of homicides since the 1950s shows that homicides by mentally disordered people have not increased (Taylor and Gunn, 1999). This in turn has resulted in a role re-definition whereby risk management has assumed increasing centrality in the role of psychiatrists and other mental health professionals, and philosophies of risk management now permeate decision-making in both the psychiatric system and the penal system.

Risk management may be defined as the identification, assessment, elimination or reduction of the possibility of incurring misfortune (Castel, 1991). As Nikolas Rose has put it, risk management 'operates through transforming professional subjectivity':

> It is the individual professional who has to make the assessment and management of risk their central professional obligation They have to assess the individual client in terms of the riskiness they represent, to allocate each to a risk level, to put in place the appropriate administrative arrangements for the management of the individual in the light of the requirement to minimise risk and to take responsibility, indeed blame – if an untoward incident occurs. It appears that it is no longer good enough to say that behaviour is difficult to predict and 'accidents will happen'. Every unwelcome incident may be seen as a failure of professional expertise: someone must be held accountable [Rose, 1997].

Ulrich Beck has written of the transition from industrial society to what he describes as the risk society, speaking of a 'calculus of risks', where

> protection by insurance liability, laws and the like promise the impossible: events that have not yet occurred become the object of current action – prevention, compensation or precautionary after-care. The 'invention' of the calculus of risk lies in making the incalculable calculable. In this way a norm system of rules for social accountability compensation and precautions, always

---

2   See, for example, Kellow Chesney's discussion of the Victorian preoccupation with 'the dangerous classes'.

3   The most obvious example being the Government's proposals in relation to *Dangerous People with Severe Personality Disorder*, discussed below.

very controversial in its details, creates present security in the face of an open uncertain future [Beck, 1992].

Beck also writes of the 'technocratic authoritarianism' which can result where the presence of the technology to manage risk creates a political expectation that it will be used, whatever the consequences in terms of expense or interference with other fundamental values. An example of this kind of expectation is the Government's statement in the *High Risk Patients* Volume of the White Paper that:

> There is no single answer to the problem of dangerousness. No society can ever be completely free of the risk of serious harm. But where there are deficiencies in the provision of specialist services, as in the case of dangerous people with severe personality disorder (DSPD), the public rightly expects the Government to take action [Home Office, 2000b, para 1.8].

The action which the Government proposes is to remove 'weaknesses' in the law. This involves broadening immensely the scope of the concept of detainable mental disorder, broadening the powers of psychiatric detention under civil powers, rendering mental health professionals accountable for their decisions not to implement compulsory care, and allowing detention of personality disordered offenders as long as there are treatments which can manage the behaviours consequent upon the disorder, even if they cannot treat the core disorder. As the Government put it:

> This approach will provide the unambiguous authority to detain individuals who would fall within the DSPD group where appropriate interventions are offered to tackle the individual's high-risk behaviour. In all cases treatment will be delivered in an appropriate therapeutic environment [Home Office, 2000b, para 3.7].

These proposals entail the further expansion of powers of preventive detention, the ultimate risk management mechanism of both the penal and the psychiatric system to protect society from dangerous offenders. Both the penal and the psychiatric system provide for detention in different levels of security. In both sectors great reliance is placed on strategies of 'graduated relaxation of security'. Patients and prisoners who start in high security are gradually tested in conditions of lesser security before release to the community through probation or supervised after-care. Both sectors concern themselves with the management of risk to the public, and risk management becomes more difficult once a patient or prisoner leaves detention and is made subject to community supervision.

In 1990, the inherently parlous nature of risk management in community settings was revealed by the inquiry into the killing of a social worker, Isabel Schwarz, by a psychiatric patient (Home Office, 1988). Later that year the Department of Health issued a circular to health and social services authorities promoting a Care Programme Approach (CPA) for mentally ill people who have been referred to specialist mental health services (Department of Health, 1990). This requires needs assessments, a written care plan based on the needs assessment, a key worker whose task is to ensure that the services are delivered and received, and regular review. The CPA applies to all patients receiving care from the specialist psychiatric services, whether or not they have been in hospital (Department of Health, 1996). In December 1992 Jonathan Zito, a young musician barely three months married, was killed by Christopher Clunis, a paranoid schizophrenic with a long history of violence. Clunis had been released from hospital three months before the attack. An inquiry was instituted by the health authorities concerned, which reported in February 1994, identifying a woeful catalogue of failure to provide adequate care for Clunis, that there had been no after-care plan, and that the authorities had failed to manage or oversee provision of health and social services for him (Ritchie *et al*, 1994). Since 1994 a prime focus of public concern has been on homicides by people who have been psychiatric in-patients, a focus maintained by the fact that Health Authorities are required to institute an inquiry chaired by an independent person every time such a homicide occurs (Department of Health, 1995). There have been many inquiries into incidents involving former in-patients, most notably *The Falling Shadow* (Blom-Cooper *et al*, 1995), and *The Case of Jason Mitchell: Report of the Independent Panel of Inquiry* (Blom-Cooper *et al*, 1996). Following the Clunis affair the Mental Health (Patients in the Community) Act 1995 added provisions (ss 25A-J) to the 1983 Act to allow for supervised after-care of non-restricted patients subject to long term detention.

In 1994 new *Guidance on Discharge of Mentally Disordered People and their Continued Care in the Community*[4] was published, and this laid unprecedented emphasis on risk assessment. Also in 1994 guidance was issued requiring purchasing health authorities to include terms in their contracts with provider bodies that providers would maintain a supervision register for patients felt to pose a risk to self or to others.[5] Current guidance is found in the Department of Health 'Policy Booklet' entitled *Effective Care Co-ordination in Mental Health Services: Modernising the Care Programme Approach*. This re-emphasises the Government's commitment to the Care Programme Approach and renames key workers who will henceforth be

---

4   HSG (94)27 LASSL (94)4.
5   HSG (94)5.

know as care co-ordinators. The Mental Health National Service Framework sets a standard which requires that those on the CPA should be able to access services 24 hours a day, 365 days a year. The Modernised Care Programme Approach abolishes supervision registers. However, the Policy makes it clear that supervision registers would be otiose given the 'Information Requirements' which it stipulates, and the guidance given on information sharing between health, social services and criminal justice agencies.

The information requirements are that local service providers are to 'ensure that a system is in place to collect data on all service users, including total numbers in contact with services and the numbers whose care is managed through enhanced and standard CPA'. The CPA is to be subject to local audit, which 'should move away from a focus on simply numbers and more towards assessing the quality of CPA implementation, including the quality of care plans, the attainment of treatment goals and, particularly for those with multiple needs, the effectiveness of inter-agency working' (DoH, 1999a, paras 29–30).

Paragraphs 45–49 are entitled 'The CPA, the Criminal Justice System and Information Sharing'. The following advice is offered where a service user is 'not in formal contact with the criminal justice system' (that is, has not been charged) but 'is assessed as being a potential risk to others':

> Careful liaison with the police to manage the risk is necessary. In this context it is important to note that the common law duty of confidence requires that, in the absence of a statutory requirement to share information provided in confidence, such information should only be shared with the informed consent of the individual. This duty is not absolute and can be over-ridden if the holder of the information can justify disclosure as being in the public interest (including a risk to public safety).

These 'information requirements' are to be further strengthened, and confidentiality further eroded by the proposal in the Mental Health Act White Paper to introduce a new statutory duty covering 'the disclosure of information about patients suffering from mental disorder between health and social services agencies and other agencies, for example housing and criminal justice agencies, where it can be justified. This will include cases where there is a significant risk of serious harm to others' (Home Office, 2000b, para 5.2).

The Sex Offenders Act 1997 puts a duty on the police to monitor those offenders who are on the sex offender register, and Multi-Agency Risk Panels or Public Protection Panels have been set up to meet these requirements. The White Paper reports that 'Many panels have subsequently extended their remit to respond to the risks posed by other potentially dangerous offenders in their communities and a range of other agencies are now involved in local arrangements, led by police and probation services' (Home Office, 2000b, para 5.4). The Criminal Justice and Court Services Act

2000 places a statutory duty on police and probation services to establish arrangements for the assessment and management of risks posed by relevant sexual or violent offenders in the community and to monitor those arrangements. The duty extends to patients who have been detained on a hospital order as well as those sentenced to imprisonment, so that information will have to be shared with police when violent or sex offenders are discharged from hospital.

The purpose of these provisions is to bridge the information barriers between health and social services with their emphasis on individualistic health and social care values such as confidentiality, and the police, whose primary task is risk management. This necessarily entails the incorporation of the police into what previously were health and social care decisions. As we shall also see, criminal justice agencies (police, probation the prisons and the courts) will be given a new entitlement to request a Mental Health Act assessment and will be entitled to written reasons if compulsory powers are not used.

The right of privacy under Art 8 of the European Convention allows for exceptions to the confidentiality of medical records if it is in accordance with law and necessary in a democratic society for the prevention of crime, for health, or for the protection of the rights of others. Given the breadth of these exceptions, it is unlikely that the new statutory duty of disclosure would fall foul of Art 8, provided that those making decisions to share information without the consent of the subject observe the requirement to restrict this to a need to know basis, and to bear in mind the principle of proportionality, that the method chosen to achieve the protection of the public interest does not go beyond what is strictly necessary for that purpose. The provisions on information sharing are a classic example of risk management values justifying exceptions to the medical principle of confidentiality. It also shows a desire to limit clinical discretion by imposing a duty to share information, and it also opens up the possibility of an action for breach of that statutory duty, if a person suffers damage as a result.

5.3 HUMAN RIGHTS

Detention, or the power to detain indefinitely, is the bedrock of risk management because the authorities can use recall to detention as the safety net for risk management in the community. A significant policy aim of the Home Office is to facilitate risk management by three main legal expedients: (a) extendable detention where a mentally disordered offender presents a serious risk to the public; (b) continued control over offenders who are discharged into the community; and (c) easy recall to detention in hospital or prison of those whose conduct in the community gives rise to concern.

The main countervailing force to these developments is individual rights, particularly those conferred by Arts 3 and 5–8 of the European Convention on Human Rights (ECHR). The Human Rights Act 1998 requires all public authorities (including courts and tribunals) to act compatibly with Convention rights, and requires ministers introducing legislation to certify to Parliament that the relevant Bill is compatible with Convention Rights.

Article 5 of the ECHR provides the grounds on which States may lawfully deprive a person of their liberty. Deprivation of liberty basically means detention. Article 5(1) is an exhaustive list of six grounds on which the State may detain an individual in the public interest. Article 5(1)(a) permits the lawful detention of a person after conviction by a competent court. Article 5(1)(b) permits the lawful arrest or detention of a person for non-compliance with the lawful order of a court, or in order to secure the fulfilment of any obligation imposed by law. Article 5(1)(c) authorises lawful arrest or detention of a person effected for the purpose of bringing him before the competent legal authority on reasonable suspicion of having committed an offence or where it is reasonably considered necessary to prevent his committing an offence or fleeing having done so. Article 5(1)(d) allows the detention of minors by lawful order for the purpose of educational supervision or his lawful detention for the purpose of bringing him before the competent legal authority. Article 5(1)(e) authorises the lawful detention of persons for the prevention of the spreading of infectious diseases, of persons of unsound mind, alcoholics or drug addicts and vagrants. Article 5(1)(f) allows lawful arrest or detention of a person to prevent his effecting an unauthorised entry into the country or a person against whom action is being taken with a view to extradition or deportation. All of these, with the exception of the provision for minors, require the person to have been convicted or to be reasonably suspected of criminal behaviour.

If detention is taking place under Art 5(1)(a) following conviction by a competent court of an offence punishable by law by imprisonment, the full safeguards required by Art 6(2) and (3) for criminal trials must be present, including the right not to be compelled to give evidence against oneself. In *E v Norway* (1997) extendable preventive detention of an offender on grounds of dangerousness was held to be lawful under the Convention as long as the extension is necessary and is carried out in accordance with a procedure prescribed by law. E was described as 'mentally incapacitated' and was detained under a Norwegian law allowing for preventive detention if the offender had an impaired mental capacity and posed a serious risk. E satisfied both criteria. His preventive detention was not renewed within the time limits Nevertheless his detention was held not to infringe either Art 5(1)(a) or (c). The detention was lawful because there was a link between the conviction and the prolongation of sentence on grounds of dangerousness.

The court acknowledged that 'After the passage of time the link between the initial conviction and the prolongation may become less strong and may eventually be broken where the prolongation no longer has any connection with the objectives of the initial decision or was based on an unreasonable assessment'. Moreover, Art 5(4) required that there be continuing review of dangerousness before a court or tribunal with the power to order release.

Article 5(1)(c) allows detention for the prevention of crime, but the European Court of Human Rights has held that this provision is 'not adapted to a policy of general prevention directed against an individual or category of individuals who, like Mafiosi, present a danger on account of their continuing propensity to crime – it does no more than afford the Contracting States a means of preventing a *concrete and specific offence'* (*Guzzardi v Italy*, 2 October 1980). Furthermore, the Strasbourg Court has held in *E v Norway* that 'as a rule Art 5(1)(c) does not provide justification for re-detention or continued detention of a person who has served a sentence where there is a suspicion that he or she might commit a further similar offence'. The position was different in *E v Norway*, where security measures imposed following conviction of a criminal offence were not renewed in time and the person was held for a short period pending bringing them to court.

Article 5(1)(e) authorises the lawful detention of persons for the prevention of the spreading of infectious diseases, of persons of unsound mind, alcoholics or drug addicts and vagrants. There is no need for conviction of criminal offence or other wrongdoing. The full Art 6(2) and (3) criminal trial safeguards do not apply. Although the Strasbourg Court has developed a number of substantive and procedural guarantees analogous to Art 6, Art 5(1)(e) is nevertheless a trap door out of the full protection of Art 6 and it is difficult to disagree with Wachenfeld's assessment that 'The Convention drafters grouped together the unhealthy outcasts of society, throwing together widely divergent categories of persons as if they were all infected by a disease from which society has to be protected' (1992, p 128).

Although the rights under Art 5(1)(e) are less than under Art 6, the ECHR has nevertheless improved the legal rights of mentally disordered people in many respects. Article 5 of the European Convention allows 'lawful' detention on grounds of unsoundness of mind. To be lawful detention must not be arbitrary. Detention is not arbitrary if it is in conformity with the procedural and substantive requirements of domestic law and is carried out for the purpose allowed by the Convention. In *Winterwerp v the Netherlands*[6] the European Court of Human Rights laid down three conditions of lawful psychiatric detention. The government must be able to show by reliable evidence before a competent authority that (a) a true mental disorder has been established by objective medical

---

6   (1979) 2 EHRR 387.

expertise; and (b) the mental disorder is of a kind or degree warranting compulsory confinement; and (c) if detention is to be prolonged the government must be able to show that the continued confinement is based on the persistence of the disorder.

Since the *Winterwerp* ruling, the Strasbourg Court has further improved due process safeguards, requiring the right to review of detention before a tribunal with the power to order (as opposed to recommend) discharge (established in *X v United Kingdom*[7]). It has also provided protection against arbitrary recall to hospital (as in *James Kay v United Kingdom*[8]), and has moved towards creating positive rights to after-care for patients who no longer meet the legal criteria for psychiatric detention (as in *Stanley Johnson v United Kingdom*[9]).

Interference with liberty where there is no detention, such as compulsory treatment, a requirement to attend for treatment, or a requirement to allow professionals access to the person's home, fall to be examined under Art 8 which guarantees respect for privacy, home and family life, and requires that any interference be proportionate, be authorised by law and be necessary in a democratic society for the prevention of crime or disorder, to uphold the rights of others, or to protect health.

Set against these patients' rights are the rights of victims and their relatives following the decision of the European Court of Human Rights in *Osman v United Kingdom*. Here the Court held that the State's positive duty to protect the right to life under Art 2 would be breached if 'the authorities knew or ought to have known at the time of the existence of a real and immediate risk to the life of identified individual or individuals from the criminal acts of a third party, and failed to take action within the scope of their powers which, judged reasonably, might have been expected to avoid that risk'.[10] The authorities referred to need not necessarily be the police. There is no reason why it should not apply to the psychiatric authorities. Moreover, the Court further held in *Osman* that it was a breach of the right of access to a court in determination of civil rights and obligations under Art 6 to have a blanket rule debarring relatives of victims or their surviving relatives from suing the police for negligence in the investigation of crime. There is clear potential for conflict between these rights, in that the efficient discharge of the State's duty to protect potential victims (effective risk management, if you like) might well be impeded by effective protections for patients' due process rights.

---

7   (1981) 4 EHRR 188.
8   (1994) 40 BMLR 20.
9   (1997) 40 BMLR 1.
10   (1998) 29 EHRR 245 at 305.

This developing Strasbourg jurisprudence on detention on grounds of unsoundness of mind (Art 5(1)(e)), detention following conviction of a criminal offence (Art 5(1)(a)), detention for the prevention of crime (Art 5(1)(c)), and on the rights of victims under Art 2 and Art 3 has led to more subtle responses by the Home Office in terms of its desire to manage the risk posed by mentally disordered people and by offenders. Policy goals in relation to preventive detention may therefore be pursued in the name of 'Convention compliance'. The Government can point to the fact that it has to balance the rights to protection against arbitrary use of State therapeutic power against the rights of potential victims to protection against homicide and inhuman and degrading treatment. As the White Paper puts it, 'New legislation will balance the rights of the patient who is undergoing compulsory care and treatment with the right of the public to be protected from serious harm' (Home Office, 2000b, para 1.4). Furthermore the Government can argue that it is within their 'margin of appreciation' to decide how these competing rights are to be weighed in the balance. These policies are bringing about a convergence between the penal system and the hospital system, a convergence which manifests itself in a number of ways. At one time the great advantage of psychiatric detention over imprisonment was that it allowed for potentially indefinite detention. Life sentences have now become possible in relation to an increasing range of offences, with offenders not being released until they are deemed no longer to pose a risk. Increasingly psychological treatment programmes are used in the prison system for personality disordered offenders subject to discretionary life sentences, and offenders released from prison are subject to supervision and recall. The advantage of imprisonment over a hospital order was that the offender could be required to serve a minimum period in detention, whereas someone who is a patient would be entitled to discharge once they were no longer mentally disordered to the extent that they require detention. The hybrid order introduced by the Crime Sentences Act 1997 and the Government's Proposals for Dangerous People with Severe Personality Disorder both sought to ensure that personality disordered offenders serve a period of detention proportionate to the gravity of their offence, and the White Paper proposes extending this to patients with any mental disorder including mental illness. Juridically, the Government has realised that for Convention purposes it is easier to achieve its policy goals allowing for indeterminate detention whilst at the same ensuring that the offender serves a minimum period of detention proportionate to the seriousness of the crime if mentally disordered offenders have the legal status of prisoners first and patients second.

5.4 PRISONERS AND PATIENTS:
CONVERGING LEGAL STATUS?

The prison population is more than 60,000. In 1991 Gunn *et al* carried out a study of 5% of the male prison population and found that 1% were diagnosed schizophrenic, and 10% personality disordered (74% of whom required psychiatric treatment) (Gunn *et al*, 1991). Although the growth of forensic psychiatry as a specialism has been dramatic, from two consultants in 1962 to 70 consultants in 1992 (Home Office, 1992, para 2.8), the capacity of the health service to absorb mentally disordered offenders is limited. On 31 March 2000 there were 12,900 patients detained in hospital, of whom 1,305 were detained in high security hospitals, 10,200 in other NHS hospitals, and 1,400 in private mental nursing homes. The number of court admissions increased from 1,500 in 1988–89 to 2,110 by 1994–5, but then fell back to 1,900 in 1998–99 and more steeply to 1,600 in 1999–2000 (DoH, 2000, para 3.9). Whilst the penal system has the capacity to absorb large numbers of offenders, the ability of the health service to do so is limited by three main constraints: the lack of facilities, the reluctance of the psychiatric profession to become involved in treating those whom they do not believe are likely to respond to treatment, and competing demands for health and social services budgets.

For Convention purposes, offenders detained under the Mental Health Act system of hospital orders and restriction orders are patients detained on grounds of unsoundness of mind. Until the ruling of the European Court of Human Rights in *X v United Kingdom*,[11] the Home Secretary, a Government minister, retained control over the discharge of restriction order patients. Restricted patients could have their cases referred to a Mental Health Review Tribunal, which could advise the Home Secretary on suitability for discharge, but the Home Secretary was not bound by their advice. The European Court of Human Rights held that Art 5(4) entitles everyone detained on grounds of unsoundness of mind to seek review of the lawfulness of their detention before a court or tribunal. In order to be a competent court for the purposes of the Art 5(4), the Mental Health Review Tribunal had to be given the power to discharge restricted patients if the conditions which justified the initial detention were no longer met. The judicial body had to have the final say regardless of the minister's view.

In order for a psychiatric detention to remain lawful for the purposes of Art 5 there must be objective medical evidence of unsoundness of mind of a kind or degree warranting confinement. The most disturbing aspect of the ruling in *X v United Kingdom* from the Home Office's point of view was the

---

11   (1981) 4 EHRR 188.

possibility that an offender who was given a hospital order with restrictions for a serious offence would be entitled to seek discharge before a Mental Health Review Tribunal after only six months in hospital, and might be discharged after a comparatively short period of detention if the unsoundness of mind which originally justified the detention was no longer present. Offenders committing crimes meriting 10 or 15 years in prison might be found no longer to be mentally disordered to a degree warranting detention shortly after admission, and might then be discharged after only a few months' detention.

Mental disorder has a very broad meaning under the Mental Health Act 1983, including mental illness, psychopathic disorder, mental impairment and severe mental impairment. An offender who is mentally disordered may be detained in prison or in hospital. Which route they follow, therapeutic or penal, depends on whether they are identified, by psychiatrists willing to treat them, as being mentally disordered within the meaning of the 1983 Act. In the case of patients with mental impairment or psychopathic disorder, the doctors must consider that medical treatment is likely to alleviate or prevent deterioration in their condition (in short that they are treatable). Section 37 of the 1983 Act allows for the detention of mentally disordered offenders in hospital under hospital orders. It is important to recognise that the system of hospital orders requires no causal connection between the mental disorder and the offence. The only relevant considerations are the offender's mental condition at the time of sentencing. Detention may be prolonged by the psychiatrist in charge of the patient's treatment, the responsible medical officer, who may furnish a report to the hospital managers 'renewing' the authority after six months and thereafter at annual intervals. Hospital order patients may be discharged to the community subject to 'supervised discharge' under ss 25A–25J of the Mental Health Act 1983.

If an offender is given a hospital order and the Crown Court feels it necessary to impose restrictions on discharge because of the need to protect the public from serious harm, it may impose a restriction order. Restrictions may be imposed for a prescribed period, or without limit of time. This has the effect of requiring the leave of the Home Secretary via the Home Office Mental Health Unit before the patient can be granted leave, transferred to another hospital, or discharged. At the end of 1995 there were 2,482 mentally disordered offenders detained in hospital subject to Home Office restrictions on discharge, more than in any of the previous 10 years.[12] Restriction order patients may be subject to conditional discharge, which means that they

---

12 One difficulty in assessing the scale of the use of therapeutic disposals is that the Home Office issues statistics of mentally disordered offenders which are collected by calendar year and which cover mainly restricted patients. Meanwhile, the Department of Health collects statistics by financial year of all admissions to psychiatric hospitals, including those of the many offenders admitted without restrictions.

remain liable to recall to hospital at any time during the currency of the restriction order.

From a risk management point of view, therapeutic detention of offenders under the Mental Health Act has the advantage that it is potentially indefinite. It can extend until the offender is deemed well enough to leave hospital. The Mental Health Act offers the possibility of extending detention beyond the duration of whatever prison sentence is proportionate to the gravity of the offence. But after *X v United Kingdom*, detention under the Mental Health Act could not guarantee that the offender would spend a minimum period in detention. Worse still, it opened up the possibility that people with psychopathic disorder would have to be discharged if they were no longer treatable, even if they still posed a risk to the public.

The legal status of prisoner means that for Convention purposes a person is detained following conviction of a criminal offence (Art 5(1)(a)), and in these cases it is possible to stipulate a minimum period to be served in detention which is proportionate to the gravity of the offence. In *Thynne Wilson and Gunnell v United Kingdom*[13] the European Court held that in the case of discretionary life prisoners it was allowable for a criminal court to impose a minimum tariff period of detention to reflect the gravity of the offence and the culpability of the offender, and for detention to be extended beyond that period if the prisoner remained dangerous. To comply with Art 5, the sentencing court must specify the amount of the sentence attributable to the gravity of the offence and the culpability of the offender (the tariff period). After this, the basis of detention is continued dangerousness, which is susceptible to change with the passage of time. Because of this, as soon as the offender enters the protective part of the sentence Art 5(4) is engaged. This requires that the prisoner must have the right to seek review of the continuing need for his detention and to challenge the view that he remains dangerous before a court or tribunal with the power to order release.

Section 34 of the Criminal Justice Act 1991 was enacted to take the consequences of the *Thynne* ruling.[14] Certain offences carry a discretionary life sentence, where the dangerousness and instability of the offender are the determining factors. The 1991 Act entitles discretionary life prisoners to have their cases referred to the Parole Board once the tariff part of the sentence has been served. The Board can direct release if satisfied that the prisoner is not likely to be dangerous, regardless of the views of the Home Secretary.

Whilst a hospital patient has the right under the Mental Health Act to seek review of detention after the first six months of detention, a life prisoner has to wait until the tariff period has expired before becoming entitled to review. The tariff period is the part of the sentence which reflects

---

13   Series A, No 190, Judgment of 25 October 1990.

14   See now Crime (Sentences) Act 1997, s 28.

the gravity of the offence. The legal status of prisoner has always had advantages over that of patient if the goals of policy are to ensure that an offender will be detained for a minimum period commensurate with the gravity of the offence and the level of blameworthiness. Following *Thynne* it was clear that the Convention represented no obstacle to extending detention beyond the tariff period on grounds of dangerousness, as long as there were opportunities for review. The possibility of indefinite detention on grounds of dangerousness, which used to be the advantage of patient status from the risk management point of view, was now available in relation to prisoners.

Offenders initially sent to prison on a determinate sentence may be transferred to psychiatric hospital with a restriction direction at any time during the sentence of imprisonment. If they recover from their mental disorder before the expiry of their sentence, the Home Secretary decides whether they should be discharged or returned to prison to serve out the sentence. Where the sentence of a transferred prisoner expires whilst he is in hospital, he may be kept in detention and his detention may be renewed by the doctor if the patient is mentally disordered and detention is necessary. This means that transfer to hospital can be, and is, used at the end of a sentence to extend a patient's detention if he or she is thought to be mentally disordered and to pose a risk. From time to time concerns have been raised about the fairness of transfers close to the end of sentence, in terms of proportionality between the time spent in detention and the gravity of the index offence (Grounds, 1990, 1991).

There are three provisions in English law for protective sentencing: life imprisonment, protective sentencing under ss 1(2)(b) and 2(2)(b) (longer than normal) of the Criminal Justice Act 1991, and the new procedures for mandatory minimum sentences in the Crime (Sentences) Act 1997, whereby conviction of a second serious offence attracts a mandatory life sentence.[15]

The Crime (Sentences) Act 1997 introduced two protective sentencing provisions of relevance. Section 2 provides that a second serious sexual or violent offence will attract a mandatory life sentence unless there are exceptional circumstances relating to either of the offences or to the offender. This means that release on life licence will depend on an assessment that the prisoner is no longer dangerous, and if released the person will be subject to the supervision of a Multi-Agency Risk Panel, which can refer him for mental health assessment or return him to prison if he becomes dangerous again.

---

15   The offences defined as serious include the following: (a) serious offences involving harm to the person (attempted murder, soliciting murder, conspiracy or incitement to murder, manslaughter, wounding or causing grievous bodily harm with intent); (b) serious sexual offences (rape, attempted rape, intercourse with a girl under 13); and (c) offences involving firearms.

The key step in the 1997 Act with regard to the process of convergence between the penal and psychiatric legal regimes is the hospital direction whereby a mentally disordered offender may be given a sentence of imprisonment coupled with an immediate direction to hospital, resulting in the offender being returned to prison in the event of the mental disorder being successfully treated before the expiry of the prison sentence. Under this sentencing power, the mentally disordered offender is given a prison sentence which is calculated in accordance with normal sentencing principles, but is directed to hospital in the first instance. If he recovers prior to the expiry of the sentence, he will be remitted to prison to serve the remaining sentence. This avoids the problem of the Mental Health Review Tribunals discharging patients 'early', because if the offender is no longer mentally disordered, the Home Secretary has the ultimate say in whether he returns to prison. In 1999–2000 there were two recorded uses of this section (DoH, 2000, para 4.14). At present these orders are only available in relation to people with a diagnosis of psychopathic disorder. The White Paper proposes that they should be available in relation to any offender with any mental disorder, defined as 'Any disability or disorder or mind or brain, whether permanent or temporary which results in an impairment or disturbance of mental functioning'. 'In this way,' proclaims the White Paper, 'the Court will retain the option of combining criminal justice tariff with an order for care and treatment under the mental health legislation' (Home Office, 2000b, para 4.10).

The protective sentencing provisions in relation to discretionary lifers and protective determinate sentencing are characterised by wide discretion and an absence of precise criteria in relation to instability or the need for protection. Henham has observed that 'the present protective provisions militate unfairly against mentally disordered offenders who are more likely to be adjudged dangerous because they are more likely to commit violent or sexual harm within the meaning of the Act' (Henham, 1996, p 444). Be that as it may, the experience with protective sentencing shows that it is applied predominantly to one class of offenders, those with personality disorders who are viewed as unlikely to respond to psychiatric intervention, so called 'untreatable psychopaths'. An offender whose crime resulted from mental illness will probably benefit from a reduction of any determinate term of imprisonment imposed, but a personality disordered offender will probably have his mental disorder taken into account to increase his sentence. Only if the personality disorder is regarded as treatable will the offender be admitted to hospital. The problem facing the Government is that the judiciary have not taken up these protective sentencing options with the desired vigour, and there are significant numbers of offenders with a diagnosis of personality disorder currently in prison on determinate sentences. The discretion vested in the psychiatric profession to decline to detain psychopathically disordered offenders by the treatability requirement, means that the Government cannot be confident that they would be detainable under mental health legislation.

5.5 PERSONALITY DISORDER: TREATMENT OR PREVENTIVE DETENTION

All the recent major legal developments in relation to mentally disordered offenders result from the conundrum posed by personality disordered offenders. The concern of the Home Office is that the protective sentencing powers outlined above are being insufficiently used by the judiciary, and that offenders who pose a high risk on account of personality disorder will receive determinate sentences. This means that the personality disordered offender will have to be released at the end of sentence, regardless of the risk to the public, unless he is transferred to hospital before it expires. He can only be transferred on grounds of psychopathic disorder if that disorder is deemed treatable. The Consultation document on Severe Personality Disorder Home Office/DoH, 1999) summarises the difficulty from a risk management point of view in these terms:

> All offenders on whom the courts have passed fixed term prison sentences have to be released from custody at some point. The vast majority serving one or more years in prison are subject to some form of supervision following release. But once the compulsory period of supervision in the community ends there is no mandatory provision to continue supervision even though the individual may continue to present a risk. Probation officers may refer clients about whom they have continuing concerns to other agencies but there is no certainty that this will result in the risk being reduced [para 18].

These worries lay behind the proposals of the Fallon Committee for reviewable sentences for dangerous personality disordered offenders (DoH, 1999b), and have led to the Government's proposals for management of this group by allowing for their indefinite detention on grounds of risk. In *E v Norway* the European Court of Human Rights held that it is lawful under the Convention to extend the period of detention on grounds of dangerousness, as long as the extension is necessary and is carried out in accordance with a procedure prescribed by law.[16] In that case the patient was detained under a Norwegian law allowing for preventive detention if the offender had an impaired mental capacity and posed a serious risk. E satisfied both criteria. His preventive detention was lawful under Art 5(1)(e) (unsoundness of mind), but Art 5(4) required that he be given access to periodic review of his continued impaired capacity and dangerousness before a court with power

---

16 *E v Norway* (1990) Series A, Vol 181.

of discharge. The proposals for personality disorder raise contentious ethical issues about the boundary between therapy and preventive detention. Whilst there is consensus among psychiatrists that drug therapy and ECT are effective in treating mental illness, no such consensus exists about the treatment of personality disorder, or even what severe personality disorder is.

Although advances in the treatment of personality disorder have been pioneered in the special hospital and secure unit sectors of the hospital system, many personality-disordered offenders have been 'treated' in the prison system. The most disruptive are detained in Close Supervision Centres. Some are in vulnerable prisoner units or on pre-release sex offender treatment programmes. Some are benefiting from therapeutic communities in prisons, and others are in Grendon Underwood Prison, which is run on therapeutic community lines. Nevertheless the Government's conclusion is that most dangerous offenders with severe personality disorders receive little consistent or long term help with their disorders either while they are in prison or on release (Home Office/DoH, 1999, para 17).

Even though mental illness and personality disorder are often the result of an abusive upbringing, and both in different ways cause the same level of pain to the sufferer, there is undoubtedly a moral hierarchy of mental disorder. In crude terms the mentally ill are seen as the 'afflicted mad or the deserving mad', whilst people with psychopathic or personality disorder are seen as the 'bad mad or the undeserving mad'. The principal reason is the disruptive and often highly manipulative behaviour exhibited by people with personality disorders.

The concept of psychopathic disorder was introduced in the Mental Health Act 1959, an Act which is said to reflect therapeutic optimism about the treatment of personality disorder.[17] But it was optimism tempered with a degree of realism. Psychopathy was defined as 'a persistent disorder or disability of mind which results in abnormally aggressive or seriously irresponsible conduct on the part of the patient and requires or is susceptible to hospital treatment'. So there was a 'treatability' test in the 1959 Act, albeit less elaborate than the current 'medical treatment for mental disorder is likely to alleviate or prevent deterioration in the patient's condition'. Both reflect hesitancy in authorising detention on a purely medical condition whose precise boundaries are unknown, and where there was little science about effective therapies. Under the 1959 Act there was also an age limit, reflecting contemporary perception that it was necessary to tackle psychopathy while the patient was still young to have any prospect of

---

17 The Home Office and Department of Health Discussion Document (1999) refers to the 'enthusiasm and optimism dating from the 1940s and 1950s for treating people with personality disorder having given way over the past 15 years to greater realism as it has become apparent that outcomes relating to reduction in risk, improvements in quality of life, and social integration remain uncertain'.

success. A person classified psychopathically disordered could not be compulsorily admitted under the power to admit for treatment if they were over the age of 21.[18] If they were admitted before the age of 21, their detention could be renewed until they were 25, but no further unless they were either dangerous to themselves or to others,[19] or they had committed a criminal offence.

The contributions of the psychiatrist and medical Members of Parliament who spoke in the debates express reservations, which might be expressed differently today, but they persist within contemporary psychiatry (Cope, 1993; Lewis, 1974; Collins, 1991). Dr Bennett MP referred to the requirement in the definition of psychopathy that the patient's condition must require or be susceptible to hospital treatment – and remarked that so far as he could make out the treatment was 'custodial'. 'Perhaps,' he continued, 'the treatment intended for the psychopath is simply ageing in custody, in which case it seems unnecessary to commit him to hospital.'[20] Dr Bennett also referred to the disruptive influence of psychopaths in hospitals. 'No hospital can stand more than one or two psychopaths in the whole hospital, let alone in one ward. The whole place becomes a bear garden. They put the other chaps up to tricks and they are frightfully clever at finding out bright ideas for perhaps the duller members of the community or the more disturbed ones.'[21] Indeed many who spoke advocated the development of separate specialist units for psychopaths on these very grounds.[22] The 1983 Act abolished the age limits and introduced a new treatability test that medical treatment must be likely to alleviate or prevent deterioration in the patient's condition. Hence the question became one of pure clinical judgment for psychiatrists.

One of the hopes expressed during the debates on the 1959 Act was that the introduction of psychopathy into the legislation would enable this group to be identified and worked with and for the medical science to develop effective treatment interventions. Kenneth Robinson MP welcomed the fact that 'at last the nettle had been grasped':

> The Bill makes a great stride forward, in that it enables patients to be placed for the first time in a category. Hitherto we have been thinking and talking of psychopaths as a kind of spectrum of behaviour disorders, a word meaning different things to different psychiatrists. Now at any rate we have a definition

---

18 Mental Health Act 1959, s 26.

19 *Ibid*, s 44.

20 *Hansard* HC Debs, Series 5, Vol 598, cols 783–84, 26 January 1959.

21 *Ibid*.

22 Dr Bennett MP argued for the establishment of some special sort of accommodation and Mr Iremonger MP advocated the establishment of small pilot units for the treatment of the intelligent psychopath. *Hansard* HC Debs, Series 5, Vol 605, cols 423, 432, 6 May 1959.

of a certain kind which will enable a certain amount of isolation and categorisation to take place. That will facilitate, and for the first time make possible social and clinical research into these cases.[23]

This hope has not been realised, and 40 years later the same nettle falls to be grasped. The Government's proposals for dangerous people with severe personality disorders express the view that 'psychiatrists are poorly equipped by training' to deal with this group, and 'most psychiatrists are reluctant to recommend that dangerous people with severe personality disorder should be admitted to hospital unless they also suffer from mental illness'.

5.6 REFORMING THE MENTAL HEALTH ACT 1983: THE WHITE PAPER PROPOSALS

In October 1998 the Government appointed an expert 'scoping group' to consider the reform of the Mental Health Act 1983. Paul Boateng, then Under Secretary of State for Health, addressed the group on their appointment, emphasising that individual patients had a responsibility to comply with their agreed programmes of care: 'Non-compliance can no longer be an option when appropriate care in appropriate settings is in place ... [T]his is not negotiable.' The minister then went on to say this:

> We are not talking about forcibly administering treatment over the individual's kitchen table. The new arrangements should only require treatment in an appropriate clinical setting and therefore may need powers for compulsory conveyance ... Your delivery of this central objective will be critical to the whole process of reform [DoH, 1999c, p 142].

The Richardson Committee Report was based on a number of principles, most notably those of non-discrimination, patient autonomy and reciprocity, the last connoting entitlement to a service in return for the imposition of community powers. A key issue in relation to non-discrimination was whether the imposition of detention and treatment without consent should be based on incapacity, as it is under common law in relation to citizens in general. The Richardson Committee proposed that instead of having separate community treatment and detention powers, there should be a single care and treatment order, which would permit compulsory powers in the community as well as detention in hospital. Compulsion would be based on the presence of mental disorder broadly defined and the presence of risk to self or to others. In keeping with its principle of non-discrimination, the Richardson Committee sought to apply a general medical law model and

---

23 *Hansard* HC Debs, Series 5, Vol 605, col 434, 6 May 1959.

bring the test closer to the common law, by requiring a higher level of risk if compulsory powers were to be used in relation to patients with capacity than for those who were incapable.

The Government published simultaneously with the Richardson Committee Report a Green Paper, *Reform of the Mental Health Act: Proposals for Consultation* (1999) which has since been followed in December 2000 by a two volume White Paper *Reforming the Mental Health Act.* There are three principal policy goals. They are: (1) to introduce more effective compulsory community powers than guardianship or supervised discharge to ensure that patients in the community are subject to an effective undertaking to carry on with medication; (2) to ensure that dangerous severely personality disordered patients can be subject to detention in the mental health system; and (3) to ensure ownership and transparency of decision-making by mental health professionals, in other words, to require them to give reasons for not implementing compulsory powers. Although some of the Richardson proposals have been taken up in the White Paper, such as broadening the definition of 'mental disorder', and authorisation of compulsory detention or treatment on a long term basis by the Mental Health Tribunal, the emphasis of the White Paper is much more on risk management than on the Richardson principles of autonomy and non-discrimination.

The White Paper proclaims that it will provide modern legislation which reflects 'a markedly different landscape' to that which faced the drafters of the Mental Health Act 1983. A new broad definition of 'mental disorder' is proposed, covering 'any disorder of mind or brain, whether permanent or temporary, which results in an impairment or disturbance of mental functioning'. This is intended to ensure that the presence or absence of any particular condition does not limit the discretion of clinicians to consider whether a patient with mental disorder should be treated under compulsory powers (Home Office, 2000a, para 3.3). The aim behind this is to encourage the detention of people with a personality disorder, whether or not they are treatable. The new legislation will require that there be a treatment plan if compulsory powers are to be imposed, but where there is a risk to other people, that plan can be directed at 'managing behaviours consequent upon the disorder and not necessarily at the core disorder itself'.

Currently people with a diagnosis of psychopathic disorder or mental impairment can only be detained if they are 'treatable' in the sense that 'medical treatment for mental disorder is likely to alleviate or prevent deterioration in their condition'. In *Reid v Secretary of State for Scotland* (1998) the House of Lords held that a person could be treatable if he was receiving anger management in a structured environment, as this was preventing deterioration in his condition, which would surely occur if he were released from secure hospital and committed an offence. Despite this legally broad definition of 'treatability', few psychopaths are admitted and treated under the current legislation. The new definition will make it clear that personality disorder is included, and that a treatment plan directed at managing the behaviours consequent upon the disorder will be enough to justify Mental Health Act compulsion. The Government also plans to abolish the current exclusion that no one shall be treated as suffering from mental disorder by reason only of sexual deviancy, addiction to alcohol or drugs. This, if followed through, will lead to a significant increase in the number of people potentially subject to compulsion.

The White Paper proposes that in future there should be a single pathway to compulsion, the care and treatment order, which will authorise compulsory treatment in hospital or in the community. Decision-making will be divided into three stages (Home Office, 2000a, para 3.10). Stage 1 is the initial decision to begin assessment and initial treatment of a patient under compulsory powers. This will be carried out by doctors and other mental health professionals, and will be very similar to the current procedures for admission for assessment. A reasonable request from a patient, a patient's carer or GP or from criminal justice agencies puts a duty on the relevant Trust to arrange a preliminary examination (Home Office, 2000a, para 3.29). Under the current legislation, where there is a request for an assessment from the nearest relative, the approved social worker making the assessment must give written reasons if compulsory powers are not used.[24] The proposals regarding ownership of psychiatric decision-making suggest that this will appear in the new legislation, and will be a significant pressure towards defensive medicine. If a person who has been assessed as not needing detention subsequently commits an offence, the reasons for not detaining will have to be given. At present the treatability criterion covers the discretion to decline. But under the new arrangements, if the person is suffering from a disturbance or disorder of mind or brain which results in a disturbance of mental functioning, and if their behaviour can be managed in a structured environment, it is difficult to see any reason why they should not be detained.

Assessment will be carried out by two doctors and a social worker or 'other approved mental health professional', perhaps heralding the introduction of community psychiatric nurse applicants alongside approved social workers. Two preliminary conditions have to be met before compulsory powers can be implemented. First, the patient must be suffering from a mental disorder that is sufficiently serious to warrant further assessment or urgent treatment by specialist mental health services. Secondly, without such intervention the patient must be likely to be at risk of serious harm, including deterioration in health, or to pose a significant risk of serious harm to other people. These are similar criteria to those for admission under the power to admit for assessment under the current Act.

---

24 Mental Health Act 1983, s 13(4).

Once the preliminary examination is complete, and there is a decision to assess and treat under compulsory powers, the mental health professional/social worker will co-ordinate the next steps, registering the decision with the trust within seven days. The period of assessment and treatment starts on the decision being registered. The legislation will allow assessment and preliminary treatment to take place in the community if detention in hospital is not a necessary prerequisite of assessment and treatment. The patient will have a fast track right of appeal to the Mental Health Tribunal similar to that enjoyed currently by patients detained for up to 28 days' assessment.

Stage 2 is formal assessment and treatment under compulsory powers for up to 28 days, the equivalent of detention under the current s 2 of the 1983 Act. Three criteria must be met. No treatment other than urgent treatment can take place without the consent of the patient until a written care plan has been drawn up. Unless there are exceptional circumstances that care plan must be drawn up according to a standard pro-forma within three days of the decision being registered. After the treatment plan is drawn up, in order for compulsory powers to be justified, the clinical supervisor will have to be of the opinion that the conditions for a care and treatment order are met. After 28 days, continuing use of compulsory powers can only be by way of a care and treatment order, which must be authorised by an independent decision-making body – the new Mental Health Tribunal.

Stage 3 is the care and treatment order. Three conditions must be satisfied. First, the patient must be diagnosed as suffering from a mental disorder. Secondly, the mental disorder must be of a nature or degree warranting specialist care and treatment. This may be because care and treatment is necessary in the best interests of the patient and/or because without it there is a significant risk of serious harm to other people. Thirdly, and finally, a plan of care and treatment must be available to address the mental disorder. In cases where the use of compulsory powers arises in the patient's own best interests that plan must be anticipated to be of direct therapeutic benefit to the individual concerned. In cases where compulsory powers are sought mainly because of the risk the patient poses to others, the plan must be considered necessary directly to treat the underlying mental disorder and/or to manage behaviours arising from the disorder (Home Office, 2000a, para 3.38).

The tribunal will be able to make a first care and treatment order for up to six months; renewable for six months, and subsequently for up to 12 months at a time. The care and treatment order will authorise the care and treatment specified in a care plan recommended by the clinical team.

Part II of the White Paper deals with high risk patients, a group characterised primarily by the risk which they pose to others. It includes both those detained under civil powers and offenders who have been given a mental health disposal by a criminal court (Home Office, 2000b, para 1.3).

This part of the White Paper sets the mental health reforms in the context of the other criminal justice measures being taken for public protection. These include legislative measures requiring sex offenders to register with the police on leaving prison under the Sex Offenders Act 1997, sex offender orders under the Crime and Disorder Act 1998 and automatic life sentences for second serious violent or sexual offence (Crime (Sentences) Act 1997). The Government has also introduced an 'early warning system' to alert the Home Office to the imminent release of potentially dangerous violent or sexual offenders and enable the risk management arrangements for those offenders to be monitored.

Proposed public protection measures include 'strengthening the effectiveness' of child protection law, putting police and probation service risk management strategies on a statutory basis to improve standards, preventing sex or violent offenders against children from working with them on release, and, finally, tagging as condition of licence (Home Office, 2000b, para 1.8)·

A prime focus of the High Risk Volume is on managing dangerous people with severe personality disorder. The Government's proposals in relation to dangerous people with severe personality disorder (DSPD) are basically designed to provide authority for the detention of people who are DSPD on the basis of the risk they present, and if necessary, for that detention to be indefinite (Home Office/DoH, 1999, p 13). In order to ensure that these changes comply with the European Convention on Human Rights, detention would be based on evidence from an intensive specialist assessment, and would be subject to a process of appeal and regular review. If a defendant who is DSPD is before the courts on remand or following conviction, the court will be able to refer for specialist assessment any individual where there is evidence of mental disorder from preliminary psychiatric reports and evidence from the police or probation service of risk to the public.

In the case of individuals not currently before the courts, prisoners, offenders under statutory supervision, and others, referral for specialist assessment will be made in what the Government calls 'civil proceedings' and will be subject to appeal. The main target group is probably prisoners who are due to come out of prison after a determinate sentence and who present a significant risk. Referral will be on the basis of prior psychiatric reports together with evidence of probable risk. Evidence of risk will be presented to a Mental Health Tribunal through reports from the police, probation or prison service. In time, such evidence is likely to come from the local multi-agency public protection panels and risk panels which have been set up around the country, as part of the overall management of risky populations.

In 1999 the Government put forward two options. Both rely on the development of 'new, more rigorous, procedures for assessing risk associated with presence of severe personality disorder'. Under each option the specific aim is ensure that the arrangements for detention and management focus on reducing these risks. Both options involve closing off the option of the hospital order for a DSPD offender. Hospital orders will be reserved for mentally ill and mentally impaired people. This would avoid the problem that Mental Health Review Tribunals are obliged to discharge psychopathically disordered patients if they consider that medical treatment for their disorder is unlikely to alleviate or prevent deterioration in the patient's condition.

In terms of powers for the criminal courts, Option A would have encouraged greater use of the discretionary life sentence, by improving the quality of information available to the courts and extending its availability to a wider range of offences, and providing new powers for remand and specialist assessment. Legislation would be 'strengthened' to ensure that prisoners identified as DSPD would not be released at the end of their sentence. For non-offender patients the 'treatability' requirement for detention and renewal of detention would be removed, and new powers would be introduced for compulsory supervision and recall of DSPD individuals following discharge from detention.

In terms of service provision, services would be provided within the prison and hospital system including the creation of better specialist facilities and better procedures for assessment and court reporting. Specialist facilities would be established within the prison and health services (potentially including independent sector providers), but drawing such facilities closer together, for example by ring fencing funding and setting up one central agency to commission services for DSPD individuals in both the prison service and the health service.

Option B involves the creation of new institutions, neither hospital nor prison, 'a third way'. A new specialist service would be set up, separate from, but with close links to, the prison service. These specialist units would be 50 beds with 8–12 to a ward. Option B involves powers for the indeterminate detention of DSPD people in both criminal and civil proceedings. Those detained under the new orders would be managed in facilities run separately from prison and health service provision. The location for detention would be based on the risk that the person presented and their therapeutic needs, rather than whether they had been convicted of an offence. The White Paper states that the Government has not taken a final decision on how services will best be provided long term, but they will bring forward legislative changes that will be required whether Option A or B is chosen. The new framework will provide for the detention of DSPD in a therapeutic environment for as long as they pose a risk to others as a result of mental disorder (Home Office, 2000b, para2.12).

The proposals will work in the following way. If there was evidence that an offender was suffering from a severe personality disorder and as a consequence presented a serious risk to the public, the offender could be remanded for assessment in a specialist facility. The disposal would be subject to appeal and periodic review. A DSPD direction could be attached to any sentence passed by the higher courts, except mandatory life sentences which are fixed by law (analogous to the existing procedures for making a hospital direction under s 45A of the Mental Health Act 1983). The effect of a DSPD direction would be that the offender would be detained in a specialist facility until such time as they were no longer considered to present a serious risk on the grounds of their disorder. At that point they would be released into the community or returned to prison to serve the remainder of their sentence. Release to the community would be subject to formal supervision and, as necessary, compliance with specified conditions. A person who had been detained on a DSPD direction would be liable to recall for further assessment. Sentenced prisoners, including those subject to mandatory life sentences, could be referred for consideration of making a DSPD order at any time during their term of imprisonment. Such an order would be made under the non-offender procedures and would result in the transfer of the individual from prison to specialist facilities.

The 'civil' DSPD order would be made by the Mental Health Tribunal under the non-offender provisions of the legislation. It would be subject to appeal and periodic review. The order would be available on the basis of evidence that the individual was suffering from a severe personality disorder and as a consequence of the disorder presented a serious risk to the public. A DSPD order could only be made following a period of compulsory assessment in a specialist facility, a process lasting 12 weeks. The effect of an order would be that the individual would be detained in a specialist facility until such time as they were no longer considered to present a serious risk on grounds of their disorder and could (subject to any necessary supervision) be released safely into the community; but there would be provision for transfer elsewhere for treatment for other mental disorders if necessary. A person who had been detained on a DSPD order would remain liable to recall to detention for further assessment.

These proposals effectively replace treatment with risk management. The treatability test will disappear for personality disorder to be replaced by risk assessment and risk management. Rigorous, robust, etc methods of assessment and management are necessary to achieve 'Convention compliance' because the only ground on which people who have not committed any offence, or who are coming out of prison after a determinate sentence, will be on grounds of 'unsoundness of mind' (Art 5(1)(e)). This means there must be objective evidence of unsoundness of mind which goes beyond mere deviance from society's norms. The international diagnostic manuals of mental disorder are replete with categories of personality disorder, so this requirement will be not be difficult to satisfy. The only further requirement is that stipulated by the European Court of Human Rights in *Aerts v Belgium*[25] that, where the sole basis of detention is unsoundness of mind (Art 5(1)(e)), there had to be some relationship between the ground of permitted deprivation of liberty relied on and the place and conditions of detention. In principle, the detention of a person as a mental health patient would only be lawful for the purposes of Art 5(1)(e) if effected in a hospital, clinic, or other appropriate institution.

The question with the third way institutions is whether they are genuinely offering therapy which has some prospect of reducing the risk to a level where the DPSD person can be released, or is the primary purpose to achieve a form of indefinite preventive detention. Undoubtedly, if there were a humane environment and if some scientific therapeutic efforts were being made there would be no risk of the *Aerts* principle being contravened, although we should remember that the Convention rights are a floor, not a ceiling. This is what makes the development of the necessary science to offer effective therapy a pressing imperative.

In institutional and professional terms, the effects of these changes may be far-reaching. Currently, each detained patient must have a responsible medical officer who is the person with legal responsibility and ultimate power in relation to their care and treatment. That person must be a doctor. Under the new legislation the responsible medical officer will be replaced by the clinical supervisor, who could, and in the case of personality disorder most probably would, be a psychologist.

5.7 CONCLUSION

Foucault has written evocatively of the development and refinement of a 'carceral network' where deviancy and delinquency can be controlled through the development not just of penal institutions but other institutions aimed at cure and reformation, and the development of surveillance mechanisms in the community (Foucault, 1977). The hallmark of these developments is that risky individuals who pose a threat to the social fabric can be detained and monitored, and that legal mechanisms exist to move them from one set of institutions to another with relative ease if the risk management dictates. The proposed arrangements for DSPD individuals represent the apotheosis of the cross fertilisation of risk management and therapeutic strategies between the penal and the psychiatric systems which I have described as a convergence. They would allow the indefinite detention usually associated with the psychiatric system, but without the requirement

---

25   Judgment of European Court of Human Rights, 30 July 1998.

of treatability beyond the stipulation that behaviour consequent upon the disorder can be managed. In other words, risk management becomes treatment.

The convergence of the penal and the psychiatric systems continues apace, and the ethical dilemma is if and where a boundary line can be drawn between therapy and preventive detention or 'growing old in custody'. Jeremy Bentham's Panopticon, the model upon which both the penitentiary and the asylum system were based, enabled a large number of inmates to be supervised with relative ease from a central point. The new system into which we are moving is increasingly characterised by controls exercised from an institutional base, where patients can be detained if necessary, and where they can be brought by force by specialist teams of paramedics for compulsory treatment. Those posing a risk will be tracked in the community. Supervisors in the community will assume responsibility for ensuring that patients receive community care.

What are the likely consequences of the convergence I have described in terms of the relationship between therapist and patient? Increasingly psychiatrists are becoming involved in decision-making about risk in the penal system, whether sitting as medical members of the various panels of the Parole Board, or giving expert evidence on risk before those panels. The Modernised Care Programme Approach suggests a significant role for the police in what has traditionally been health and social care decision-making about risk management and community care. The ethics of health care are based around the primacy of therapy (*primum non nocere*) key notions such as respect for autonomy, informed consent and confidentiality. The ethics of criminal justice and risk management afford primacy to deterrence, retributivism, social protection, selective incapacitation and recognition of the rights of victims. The erosion of the boundaries between the medical world with its values and the criminal justice system with its own very different concerns results in the concept of confidentiality being redefined to accommodate the information sharing requirements of effective risk management. Most notably, however, the proposals will greatly limit therapeutic discretion, the discretion not to disclose medical secrets, and the discretion not to detain being significant examples. It has always been a principle of the psychiatric system that a psychiatrist cannot be legally required to accept a patient under his care and custody. This principle remains, but where there is risk, it will be uncomfortable for the mental health professionals under the new proposals if they have to give reasons for not taking compulsory powers. The proposals are designed to encourage defensive medicine in the name of risk management. Just as there is a calculus of risk, so too there is a calculus of rights. The liberty rights of the mentally disordered person have to be balanced against the right to life and protection against inhuman and degrading treatment enjoyed by potential victims, reflected in expedients such as the right of victims and their families to make representations to the Mental Health Tribunal considering the patient's discharge. At the moment the balance is moving towards risk management and away from patients' rights.

This all has consequences in terms of the citizenship rights of mentally disordered patients. The Richardson Committee tried to promote principles of non-discrimination by bringing the regime of powers regarding mentally disordered people as close as possible to the common law powers to treat people with mental incapacity without their consent. In short they tried to use general medical law as their starting point. The current proposals take criminal justice models of risk management as their starting point. As such their philosophy bears many of the hallmarks of late 19th century thinking about the status of mentally disordered people. In 1890 the authors of Pope's *Treatise on the Law and Practice of Lunacy* said this:

> Possessed of physical force without a regulating mind, and subject to the natural instincts untutored by discipline and uncontrolled by fear or punishment, some classes of the insane threaten continual danger to those with whom they are brought in contact ...

> So far as they are irrational, the insane, though in the state are not of the state. On the other hand, though not of the state, the insane are yet in the state. Hence the state has relations with them, though not those which it has with its citizens proper [p xiv].

The tenor of these proposals is that people with a mental disorder are not citizens proper in a number of senses. First, they may be detained on grounds of risk on the basis of a very broad concept of mental disorder. Secondly, the proposals are stigmatising in drawing a constant association between mental disorder, risk and criminality, and in subjecting mentally disordered people to regimes of surveillance and liability to detention which are outside the framework of the criminal law, but which are based on criminal justice and penal models rather than general medical law.

CHAPTER 6

BALANCING RIGHTS AND RISKS: DILEMMAS OF JUSTICE AND DIFFERENCE

Barbara Hudson

6.1 INTRODUCTION – JUSTICE IN THE RISK SOCIETY

Like other contributors to this volume, I am concerned about the balance between 'reducing risk' and 'doing justice' as criminal justice objectives. In my own recent work, and in my engagement with criminal justice agencies such as the probation service, I have expressed the anxiety that 'justice' is something of an endangered concept in the UK, USA, and other similar societies (Hudson, 2000). Apart from a few members of the judiciary, legal theorists, philosophers, and some human rights specialists and civil libertarians, our societies seem to be losing sight of the importance of justice as a regulative ideal.

My anxiety, in brief, is that in current criminal justice policy and practice developments, and in the wider politics of law and order, 'justice' is either being forgotten altogether, relegated to a minor concern, or its meaning is becoming distorted. This anxiety leads me to raise an additional question which takes us a little way outside the traditional framing of the debate, which has generally been conducted in Packer's (1969) terms of the balance between crime control objectives and due process safeguards. My additional question is whether our established theories and institutions of justice are adequate to withstand the challenges of the politics of risk and safety. This question leads me to look at emerging theories of justice which may be more in balance with contemporary attitudes to risk and the powers they legitimate.

We can see lack of commitment to justice very clearly in policies to do with crime and punishment. Mandatory sentencing laws in particular and the reduction of judicial discretion in general diminish the scope for substantive justice in criminal justice proceedings; we also find lack of concern for justice in the absence of substantial opposition to altering the implications of maintaining silence in police interviewing, and to altering the rules of disclosure of evidence because it is thought that too many 'guilty' people are being acquitted by the courts.

'Justice' is now very much less important than 'risk' as a preoccupation of criminal justice/law and order policy; the politics of safety have overwhelmed attachment to justice in the institutions of late-modern democratic polities. If someone, or some category of persons, is categorised as a risk to public safety, there seems to remain scarcely any sense that they are nonetheless owed justice. The vocabulary of justice is almost entirely absent from current debates about sexual offending (in particular); about safety in public spaces; and about penal treatment of those deemed at risk of re-offending. Proliferation of crime prevention techniques such as CCTV, for example, show how easily risk to the law-abiding public 'trumps' justice not only to offenders, but also to others who may come into various contemporary categories of suspicion.

'Justice', in popular and political discourse, seems now to be synonymous with 'punishment'. When victims, or the public generally, talk of wanting justice, or being denied justice, what is meant is a demand for an offender, or offenders, to be punished, or to be punished more severely.

For those, myself included, who seek to identify some quality of justice, which is not simply retribution – or vengeance – the quest for an adequate definition is difficult and inconclusive. The jurist Hans Kelsen comments on the elusiveness of an answer to the question of what is meant by 'justice', saying that down the ages, the most illustrious of minds have failed to find a definitive answer to the question 'what is justice', but have only been able to improve the cogency with which the question is posed (Kelsen, 1996, p 183).

Most discussions of justice discuss the rules and social institutions necessary to secure justice, rather than attempting any definition of justice itself. Kelsen himself describes it as a 'social happiness'. He explains that he cannot say universally what this happiness involves, he can only say what it is for him. For him, 'justice is that social order under whose protection the search for truth can prosper'. '"My" justice,' he says, 'is the justice of freedom, the justice of peace, the justice of democracy – the justice of tolerance' (Kelsen, 1996, p 206). This relativistic, almost-definition is compatible with that of John Stuart Mill, for whom 'Justice is a name for certain classes of moral rules, which concern the essentials of human well-being more nearly, and are therefore of more absolute obligation, than any other rules for the guidance of life' (Mill, 1996, p 173).

Kelsen's almost-definition is also compatible with my own preferred perspective, which is American criminologist and moral philosopher Jeffrey Reiman's theory of *justice as reason's answer to subjugation* (Reiman, 1990). While I might not agree with all Reiman's arguments, and while I approach both the necessity of an ideal of justice and the requirements of that ideal from a somewhat different direction, the essentials of his conclusion that the principles of justice are the principles which are necessary to defend humans living in societies against oppression, are ones that I share, and which underpin this paper.

Whatever their differences of wording, nuance and emphasis, approaches to justice generally refer to two different elements: a quantitative element and a qualitative element; distributive justice, and treatment which meets the requirements of the person being dealt with, treatment which meets the moral claims of the concrete Other. The first requires dealing with people fairly in relation to other people; the second requires dealing with people decently in relation to their own needs, beliefs and desires. These two different principles of justice are often known as *justice as fairness* and *justice as alterity*, and they are more or less equivalent to the principles termed *formal* and *substantive* justice in law. The formal elements of law involve applying legal rules consistently, and therefore if carried out fulfil the requirements of justice as fairness; substantive justice involves making the right decisions, providing the right remedy, for the particular case, and thus corresponds with the principle of justice as alterity.

These two components of justice are in some tension with each other, and the history of penal change reflects shifting balances between them. In the so called rehabilitation era, substantive justice was emphasised to the detriment of formal justice; in the 1980s the formal elements, justice as fairness, were brought back to the centre, with substantive concerns relegated to very secondary status. As Bottoms has described, over-emphasis on formal elements comes to look as though criminal justice is concerned only with internal, managerial objectives, and has lost adherence to any external referent (Bottoms, 1995). A rebalancing after the 1980s was almost inevitable, therefore. As we have seen on both sides of the Atlantic, however, the predominant substantive referent of criminal justice in the 1990s has come to be risk, rather than 'justice'.

Before looking at the possibilities offered by emerging approaches to justice, I will review some of the current perspectives on 'risk'. My purpose here is not to demonstrate or describe the growing influence of 'risk' considerations in criminal justice. These developments have been well documented elsewhere (Cohen, 1985; Feeley and Simon, 1994; Garland, 1996, 1997; O'Malley, 1992, 1996). My purpose is, rather, to discuss the implications of this engagement with risk for justice, in both theory and practice. I will mention one or two examples of this 'risk orientation', chosen because they are very obviously in tension with the ideal of justice. Although my review of developments is highly selective, I do not believe that the examples are unrepresentative; I do believe that there has been a significant shift from *doing justice* to *controlling risk* as the goal of law and order and penal strategies.

Much of the discussion of risk-oriented responses to crime has drawn on the so called 'governmentality' perspective, which in turn derives much of its conceptual framework from the later work of Foucault (Gordon, 1991; Miller and Rose, 1990; Rose, 1996; Rose and Miller, 1992). This literature focuses on the project of governance in the age of regulation by norm, and fits well with many aspects of current trends in crime control and penal policy, so that descriptions of 'new' or 'managerialist' penology draw on many of the same concepts and examples as the governmentality writings (Cohen, 1994; Feeley and Simon, 1994). Although this perspective is helpful for understanding many aspects of contemporary penal strategies, the fit is not complete. For example, the emergence of private and community strategies for dealing with crime has not displaced state apparatuses, as in spheres such as health and welfare, but rather the new responses to crime have augmented the old, and have led to demands for more rather than less state activism (Hudson, 1998a). Furthermore, the governmentality perspective, as Garland has pointed out, neglects important expressive elements in punishment (Garland, 1997), and it also leaves unexamined the cultural contexts in which penal strategies develop (Garland, 1999).

This literature, and the work of Foucault on which it draws, also omits to balance the description and analysis of governmental powers and technologies legitimated by reference to the provision of security, with consideration of the Enlightenment theories of justice and of political legitimacy which were developed to set limits to governance. In Foucault's works, and in the works deriving from them, governmental power is granted an overwhelming puissance, uninhibited by considerations of justice. Although, therefore, he gives us warnings of the totalitarian possibilities of power, Foucault provides little indication of the principles and institutions that need either to be preserved or to be initiated if Western liberal democracies are not to become full-blown totalitarian carceral archipelagos (Hudson, 1996; Walzer, 1986).

It is, in fact, in the works of writers sympathetic to, or fully fledged-members of, the post-modern perspective who have paid most attention to theories and practices of justice. Although this approach is often accused of being nihilistic, apolitical, or at least relativist, prominent post-modernists such as Bauman (1989, 1993), Derrida (1990) and Lyotard (1984) are amongst those who have argued the importance and urgency of developing new formulations of 'justice' which can meet the philosophical challenges, social conditions and existential lacunae of late modern 'risk society'.

My argument is that, if risk management is a legitimate goal of governance, it needs to be framed and limited by respect for the ideal of justice; if governmental power in relation to the risk of crime is enhanced, it needs to be balanced by correspondingly strengthened commitment to justice as regulative limit. I therefore discuss some developments that have potential for providing surfaces of emergence for another rebalancing, a shift of the pendulum back towards justice. By far the most important of these is the growing significance of the European Convention on Human Rights, which has now been inscribed into domestic law by virtue of the Human Rights Act 1998. Therefore there is the possibility that it could turn from pious but empty words to a real influence on institutions and practices.

My main theoretical concern is to bring a focus on rights together with the literature on difference. The paper therefore ends with a look at the relational theory of rights found in some, mainly US, legal scholarship (Minow, 1990), and the idea of 'legal guaranteeism' put forward, albeit sketchily as yet, by some European critical criminologists (Cohen, 1998; Pitch, 1995; Van Swaaningen, 1997).

6.2 RISK AND PENAL POLICY IN THE 1990s

Developments in penal policy in England and Wales since 1993, in common with the US and much of the developed world, show increasing harshness, combined with increasing preoccupation with the idea of risk. The resulting practices are aptly described by Garland as *punitive segregation*, combined with *penal marking*:

> Punitive segregation – lengthy sentence terms in no frills prisons, and a marked, monitored existence for those who are eventually released – is increasingly the penal strategy of choice [Garland, 1999 p 8].

This strategy combines, Garland explains, a functional, instrumental logic which is focused on managing the risk of crime, and an expressive logic which makes clear that punishing is a blaming, stigmatising ritual which allows the public to vent feelings of vengeance on wrongdoers (Sarat, 1997).

It is easy to see that penal policy developments reflect a change in the balance between the principles of proportionality and risk management. In the late 1980s and in the Criminal Justice Act 1991, proportionality was by far the dominant principle, with risk the exceptional approach; in the later 1990s, risk became more and more the main idea in criminal justice. The CJA 1991 prescribed proportionality to be the overwhelming consideration in most cases. It provided for two kinds of exception to proportionality. Section 1(2)(b) allowed for custody to be imposed where seriousness of the current offence does not warrant, and s 2(2)(b) allowed for custodial terms longer than warranted by the offence – in both cases this was to be allowed only if necessary to protect the public from serious harm. As the decade progressed, risk became a more prominent theme, with more indeterminate life sentences, so that parole or conditional release subject to risk assessment replaced the automatic release associated with determinate sentences.

Community penalties, too, have become more attuned to the idea of risk. In the 1980s, the probation service saw itself as a provider of 'alternatives to custody' for offences of intermediate seriousness. Its objectives and its procedures were oriented to intervening according to levels of seriousness – services introduced 'gravity of offending' scales to help them with their recommendations to court, and the social background inquiry was replaced with the justice-model pre-sentence report. Assessing seriousness and responding to it were the operational parameters for probation. Day centres, community service and other community penalties were also geared to providing a graduated community response to seriousness. This approach was codified in the CJA 1991, according to which community penalties were to incorporate degrees of restriction of liberty, and community sentences were to be imposed such that the amount of restriction of liberty reflected the seriousness of the offence. As the 1990s progressed, community penalties too became not just concerned with, but dominated by, the idea of risk. Assessing 'risk of re-offending' has displaced assessing 'gravity of offence', and the probation service now describes its objectives in terms of 'risk management' (Roberts and Domurad, 1995).

An interesting question is 'which risks, what harm' the newly risk-dominated criminal justice system is targeted at. In 1991 the understanding was that departures from proportionality were only justified to protect the public from 'serious harm' – danger, as commonly understood. Section 31(3) of the CJA 1991 defines 'serious harm' as 'death or serious injury'. By 1996, the objective of risk management as defined in the white paper *Protecting the Public: The Government's Strategy on Crime in England and Wales*, was to protect the public from 'dangerous and persistent criminals' (Home Office, 1996).

Persistent offending (especially young persistent offenders) had been the theme of one of the main 'moral panics' of the mid-1990s. The existence of young offenders with extensive criminal records ('rat boy' in Newcastle upon Tyne, 'one boy crime wave' in Nottingham, Sunderland and elsewhere) as well as 'bail bandits' – people offending whilst on bail – were luridly reported in the tabloid press (Williams, 1993). Such stories meshed with the popularity in police and policy circles of the belief that much crime is the result of a small number of offenders. As Simon (1996) points out, the two great contributions of criminology to penal policy in the 1990s have been victim surveys and research to identify persistent offenders. Victim surveys have constituted crime rates as objects of knowledge, and thereby objects of policy intervention, whilst persistent offender profiling has provided a prime tactic for tackling high crime rates. 'Punitive segregation' of persistent offenders thus becomes the counterpoint to 'preventative partnerships' as the means of reducing crime rates (Garland, 1999). The two strategies are not so much opposed or contradictory, as complementary. By 1996, risk of re-offending had become as important a theme as risk of serious physical harm: prevention of primary victimisation becomes the responsibility of the individual citizen as potential victim; prevention of repeat victimisation emerges as the main responsibility of state crime control apparatus.

Although not clearly stated in legislation or policy documents, the distinction between violent and non-violent offences has been a key to much thinking on criminal justice in England and Wales. Penal reformers in the 1980s consistently referred to the numbers and proportions of property offenders in prison; policy and legislation innovation throughout the decade bifurcated parole and remission, restricting early release for violent offenders and extending it and making it automatic for property offenders; strengthened community penalties were aimed largely at burglars and other property offenders. By 1996, this distinction was either blurred, or less important.

Although the CJA 1991 left definitions of seriousness largely to the courts, the spirit of the Act was clearly to separate violent and sexual offences, which were assigned to the risk track, from property offences, assigned to the proportionality track, a separation accomplished by the concept of serious harm. The inclusion of 'psychological injury' in the definition of serious harm in the 1991 Act had left the way open for non-violent offences to be on the risk track, but it was generally understood that this mainly applied where property offenders targeted unusually vulnerable victims, such as the elderly, who might be specially traumatised by the offence. The coupling of 'dangerous' and 'persistent' in the later legislation makes the distinction between violent and non-violent offences far less significant.[1]

Burglary provides an interesting example of this tendency. This was the offence most innovatively and rigorously targeted for the more robust 'alternatives to custody' in the 1980s. If the expectation is that custody is for violent offences, then most burglaries would not lead to imprisonment. The framing of the CJA 1991 seems almost tailor-made to allow for burglary to be generally below the 'so serious that only a prison sentence will suffice' threshold, with exceptional above-commensurate sentences for cases with especially vulnerable victims. Burglary is a high-recidivism offence, so the battles between justice-model advocates and politicians and others over the significance to be accorded to previous convictions are particularly meaningful for burglary. If risk of re-offending is the primary criminal justice theme, then most burglaries can be expected to lead to imprisonment. Sentencing trends (as usual, somewhat in advance of the legislation) reflect this thematic shift: there was a significant rise in the proportionate use of imprisonment for burglary after the implementation and almost immediate demise of the CJA 1991, and the implementation of the Crime (Sentences) Act 1997.

---

1   Ralph Henham (1998) points out that robbery using a knife, which would come under the definition of a violent offence for the purposes of s 2(2)b of the Criminal Justice Act 1991 would not qualify as a 'serious' offence under the Crime (Sentences) Act 1997 which legislated the 1996 White Paper.

Table 1: Percentage use of imprisonment for burglary, 1988–97

	Crown Court		Magistrates' court	
	Under 21	21+	Under 21	21+
1992	48	55	11	14
1993	55	60	16	18
1994	61	66	17	22
1995	66	70	18	27
1996	72	78	19	28
1997	67	78	18	31

Source: Home Office Statistical Bulletins 30/92; 18/98

The C(S)A 1997 put burglary firmly on the risk management rather than proportionality track, by including it in mandatory sentencing provisions. By USA standards, a mandatory sentence of three years' imprisonment for a third offence might not seem particularly draconian; the significant point of principle, however, is that it is unusual for England and Wales to have mandatory minimum sentences rather than mandatory maximums, and this provision put burglary on the same track as violent and sexual offences, rather than with other routine property offences. The Bill was going through Parliament at the time of the change of government from Conservative to Labour; when it completed its legislative passage, although the new government left the burglary provision on the statute, the provision was not implemented alongside the others. It has, however, since been implemented.

What is happening to the idea of 'danger' (as opposed to 'risk') is that it is shifting from acts to people. As many commentators have noted, commission of an act is no longer required as evidence of being dangerous or risk-posing. Dangerousness, risk-posing, is a property of a data self which is constructed out of the possession of designated 'risk factors'. Conviction for an offence occasioning or threatening serious physical harm as the criteria for adverse risk assessment has been replaced by 'categorical suspicion' (Marx, 1988). People are assessed as risk-posing on the basis that they display 'whatever characteristics the specialists responsible for the definition of preventive policy have constituted as risk factors' (Castel, 1991, p 285).

There are many ways in which we can see that sense of a necessary connection of punishment/exclusion to an actual act, is being lost. Like the USA, there has been much concern about sex offending, particularly paedophilia, and schemes for compulsory supervision and community notification have been introduced. Debates around these issues reveal little grasp of how firm the connection should be between actual crimes and penalisation, with no professional consensus about how long periods of supervision and notification of change of address should be. The prevailing sense of the mood in England is that once convicted, or even suspected, a sex offender is to be criminalised virtually for life. Recent proposals concerning disclosure of offences to potential employers covered people who have been arrested or accused of sex offending, not just those who have been convicted; a television programme and subsequent reaction to it made no distinction between paedophiles who had been recently convicted or recently released, and others who had been without arrest or conviction for periods of up to thirty years.

New DSPD proposals from the present Home Secretary provide that persons declared 'dangerous' by psychiatrists should be subject to detention – possibly for life – even without a criminal conviction (discussed in more detail in the chapters by Eastman and Fennell). This proposal responds to a moral panic fed by two notorious cases. A few years ago a young music teacher, John Zito, was murdered by a schizophrenic man. His wife, Jane, has led a campaign for the enforcement of compulsory treatment of mentally ill persons resident in the community. This campaign and the official response might have remained at the level of enforcement of treatment in the community, but for the more recent case in which Michael Stone was convicted of the murders of Lin and Megan Russell, the wife and daughter of a university lecturer, and the attempted murder of the other daughter. The conviction was widely regarded as shaky. It was overturned on appeal, but Stone was reconvicted in a retrial, even though there was no substantial new evidence. Evidence based on testimony of convicted offenders, hoping for extra remission as reward for co-operation, that he had 'confessed' to the crime in prison conversation, was the basis of the prosecution case. This testimony was supported by some circumstantial, but no forensic or eye-witness evidence. Michael Stone, however, is diagnosed as having a severe personality disorder, but because of negative assessment under the 'treatability' criterion, could not be detained in the absence of a criminal conviction, under present legislation. What seems to be apparent to those who have dealt with him is apparently that even if the evidence in the case is weak, he is *the sort of person* who would have committed such a crime, and is extremely dangerous. The details of the proposed legislation have been published in a White Paper and there is considerable public and political support for the idea.

It is clear that ministers sponsoring the legislation are aware that it breaches due process safeguards concerning no detention without conviction, but that they do not regard this as sufficient reason not to proceed:

> Ministers have admitted that their plan to detain psychopaths deemed to be dangerous could mean unconvicted people being locked up until they die. Paul Boateng, home office minister, told MPs that the overriding interest of public protection meant some people should be held until a time, 'if ever', that the risk they posed was minimised [*The Guardian*, 26 June 2000].

These examples of sex offenders and personality disordered persons demonstrate that adoption of the principle of risk control as the dominant goal of criminal justice not only blurs the distinction between violent and non-violent offending, but also blurs the crucial due process distinction between offender and suspect.[2]

6.3 SOME PERSPECTIVES ON RISK

> It is now possible to contend that we live in a 'risk society' ... in which the demand for knowledge useful in risk definition, assessment, management and distribution is refiguring social organisation ... Discourses of risk penetrate a range of institutions and have bearing upon how the criminal law institution and its operatives think and act ... There is a drift in the public agenda away from economic inequality to the distribution and control of risks. The values of the unsafe society displace those of the unequal society [Ericson and Carriere, 1994, pp 102–03].

Given the obvious importance of risk to criminal justice, it is hardly surprising that many commentators are complementing their use of the 'governmentality' perspective by drawing upon the 'risk society' analysis of Beck (1992) and Giddens (1990). These analyses centre on the way in which risk has become a generalised preoccupation of modern life: the reflexivity of modernism induces critical attention to the problems caused by modernity itself; the expectation of mastery of the social and natural environment encouraged by modernism demands that risks be countered. 'Risk society theory' also emphasises the individualisation of modern life, and the progressive loss of tradition and social bonds as parameters for structuring identity and life courses.

This theory is clearly consistent with many of the developments in crime prevention and risk management penality noted by commentators on 'new' and 'post-social' penology such as Feeley and Simon, and O'Malley. Whilst it

---

2   A further, alarming incident of this tendency was reported in *The Guardian* in 1998. A person accused of offences against young people was stoned and beaten to death. Commenting on the conviction of those responsible, the judge pointed out that there was no way of knowing whether the victim had committed the acts or not.

accounts for the emergence of community and individual strategies to avoid victimisation, the centrality of risk assessment in prison and probation administration, and other such developments, it cannot throw much light on the apparent turn from justice to vengeance, from due process to gloves-off crime control. Mary Douglas' cultural-anthropological perspective on risk is helpful here. Where Beck and Giddens discuss sociocultural phenomena in terms of risk, Douglas discusses risk in terms of sociocultural phenomena (Crook, 1999). In other words, Douglas takes risk as her constant, and investigates different sociocultural traditions of explaining and dealing with risk, and argues that social institutions such as law and criminal justice are shaped to a large extent by societies ideas of the source of, and responsibility for, various kinds of risks (Douglas, 1992; Douglas and Wildavsky, 1982).

Douglas' more recent writings on risk and culture share the contemporary interest in the constitution of the Other as dangerous, alien outsider. She emphasises the role of the concept of risk in maintaining cultural boundaries of member and non-member, insider and outsider. Risk, on this account, acts primarily as a locus of blame, whereby individuals and groups are singled out as dangerous, posing a physical or cultural threat to individuals and communities. Developing a theme from her earlier work on *Purity and Danger*, or stigma and taboos (1966), risk becomes a predominant 'forensic resource', attractive to contemporary Western societies because of its scientific, neutral, impersonal stance, but nonetheless analogous to ideas of 'sin' or 'taboo' in more primitive societies (Lupton, 1999). Douglas' work is important for understanding the implications of risk for justice, because it shows how 'risk' is blame-laden, and therein provides a counter to earlier analyses of the shift to risk as the new 'master pattern' of social control which predicted a decline of concern with individual morality and responsibility (Cohen, 1985; Simon, 1988). If risk-posers are perceived as a threat to the culture of society, indeed to its very existence, then they are thereby constructed as subversive of institutions of culture, such as justice, and not as equal claimants upon them.

While some commentators have tried to distinguish dominant trends in penality (Feeley and Simon, 1994; Pratt, 1995) for good or ill, and others, notably Garland, have identified major but competing or coexisting trends (Garland, 1996, 1999), in a recent article O'Malley (1999) has commented on the volatile, contradictory and incoherent state of penal affairs, with a plethora of initiatives appearing at more or less the same time, often espoused by the same people, initiatives which are based on different and often incompatible principles. Restorative justice and zero tolerance, both pursued in relation to youth crime, are two obvious current examples. O'Malley explains this in terms of the contradictions within 'new right' political ideology. At another level of analysis, Crook brings together the three dominant theoretical approaches to risk to elucidate the coexistence of apparently contradictory regimes of risk management. Drawing on the governmentality, risk society, and cultural-anthropological perspectives mentioned above, he argues that there are three different kinds of ordering of risk management operative in contemporary late-modern societies:

- *modern ordering* which operates at the level of national societies through differentiated, rationalised and organised institutions and through technologies of mass communication. The exemplary modern institutions are those of the state and the market;

- *hyper-reflexive ordering* which is global in scope and which operates through networks of highly reflexive individuals rather than stable institutions. It is dependent on computerised communications, and engages individuals in selected, shifting coalitions of interest;

- *neo-traditional ordering* operates as intense group solidarity, such as that associated with ethnic, religious or lifestyle groups. The intensity of solidarity with the group is matched by intensity of antagonism towards outsiders. (Crook, 1999, p 164.)

The prefix 'neo' indicates that this traditionalism is not a residue of an earlier form of ordering, which is giving rise to a new regime. This new traditionalism is self-chosen rather than ascribed, and it is variously celebrated as a revival of community, or regretted as a contemporary 'tribalism' (Maffesoli, 1996). Whilst we associate this new tribalism most clearly with inter-communal conflicts such as in the former Yugoslavia, there are parallels in the response of 'respectable' communities and individuals to crime and risk of crime associated with certain groups (eastern and central European Romani, as well as sex offenders and young offenders, at the time of writing) and with certain locations.

Drawing these perspectives together, we see that what emerges as the key change in late-modernity is not the emergence of risk as a crucial concern, but the individualisation of blaming risk and of defending against it. Discussing blaming systems found in different types of society, she comments that our present society is one in which risk-posing is attributed to individuals – not just risk of crime, but risk of all kinds:

> Of the different types of blaming system we can find in tribal society, the one we are in now is almost ready to treat every death as chargeable to someone's account, every accident as caused by someone's criminal negligence, every sickness a threatened prosecution. Whose fault?, is the first question [Douglas, 1992, pp 15-16].

We are a society which no longer attributes risk to providence, or the gods, or the unfathomable laws of nature, but to an individual, Plane, train or coach crashes result in search for a culprit – the pilot, the driver, the maintenance engineer, the traffic controller. There is nothing new about fearful consciousness of risk; societies have always sought to protect themselves against risk. The foundations of any social contract is that of giving up some rights in return for protection against risks. The defining difference between the ancients sacrificing children to appease the gods and preventive incarceration today is surely that the former ceremonies, cruel though they may seem to modern sensibilities, were not blaming ceremonies. Today's risk ceremonies are not rituals of appeasement, but of censure (Von Hirsch, 1993).

Corresponding to the individualisation of blame is the individualisation of risk protection. What links the various recent accounts of risk and criminal justice (risk society, post-modernity, neo-liberalism, governmentality) is the conception of retreat from the social. There has been a retreat from approaching risk as something to be shared between the members of a society. This is evident in relation to the kinds of risks which welfare systems were constructed to deal with, and is also evident in relation to the risk of crime. Social insurance systems are in decline, and 'private prudentialism' (O'Malley, 1996) is the normal response to risk.

The retreat from the social and the embrace of individualism means that the social elements of crime causation are underplayed, and of course resonates well with the new right crime ideology which apportions blame to offenders and refuses to recognise social reasons for high crime rates. This individualism means that although crime control strategies are targeted at aggregates – burglary, car crime rates; the underclass, aggressive beggars – the individuals within those groups are blamed, and punished.

If the social is in decline, two kinds of relationship are enhanced: that between individuals, and that between individuals and the state. Whilst contemporary society may have less collective action, more private action, there is also more repressive, centrally funded and centrally controlled, action in relation to crime. There is a decrease in social action, but an increase in state action. What individuals cannot do for themselves, they call for the state to do. Whilst the ideal of the modern state is that it should derive from and represent society, it is not surprising that a diminishing sense of the social should lead to a strengthening of the repressive aspects of state – as a defence against each other, and against those defined as outsiders. What we are seeing is a narrowing of the bounds of sociality to those must obviously 'like us' – through kinship or lifestyle.

At various times in this chapter, I have used the term 'risk control', rather than 'risk management'. Clear (2000) has argued persuasively that what has happened is not the emergence of risk as the dominant idea of criminal justice, risk is the very core of the penal idea. What has happened, he says, is a move from risk management to risk control. Risk management is an acceptance of the inevitability of risk, with pooling of risk among people who see themselves as a group of some sort; risk control is a refusal of risk, an attempt to eliminate risk, and is the response to risks posed by people whom we do not recognise as consociates. In criminal justice, risk management is the basis of due process: rights are distributed as equitably as possible between probable risk bearers and probable risk-posers. This distribution of rights and risks is what is at stake in the changing balance between crime control and due process. It is this distribution, in the context of changed relationships between individuals, society and the state, that must be addressed in any new thinking about justice.

6.4 TOWARDS A RENEWAL OF JUSTICE

Foucault and others using his or similar analytic frameworks have shown us the technological possibilities of modernity for repression, and demonstrated that the logic of governance in the age of regulation by norm involves utilising techniques and disciplines which constitute dichotomies of normality and deviance, dichotomies which tend to become fissures of inclusion and exclusion. Bauman (1989, 1993) among others has vividly warned us of the dangers of defining groups as 'dangerous other' and excluding them from the community of those entitled to justice. Contemporary events show us that the potential for ultimate policies of exclusion remain latent, never far from realisation in action. We cannot reassure ourselves by regarding events such as the Nazi German extermination of the Jews as one-off aberrations. There may be differences in scale and technological sophistication, but the instinct to describe the stranger (including the cultural stranger, who may simultaneously be one's neighbour) as dangerous alien other is strong and ever-present. As well as events in Rwanda, Burundi, Sierre Leone, and closer to home in former Yugoslavia, in our own countries racial violence, the suspicious categorisation of most refugees as probable 'bogus asylum seekers', should alert us to the need to keep alive a vigorous commitment to justice, and to address the intellectual task of reformulating our theories and institutions of justice to meet the challenges of the politics of safety.

Any possible renewal of justice as ideal and as institutional practice involves, I would argue, bringing together the ideas of *rights* and *difference*. This section of the chapter therefore focuses on two developments: first, the incorporation into domestic jurisdiction of the European Convention on Human Rights; and, second, the growth of a literature of recognition of difference.

6.4.1 The European Convention on Human Rights

Interest in Packer's *due process* and *crime control* models (Duff, 1998; Packer, 1969) has been much more marked recently, because of the way they allow for succinct description of recent shifts in criminal justice strategies. Most commentators would say that in many Western criminal justice systems there was a movement in the due process direction in the 1980s, and that there has been an equally marked shift towards crime control in the 1990s and into the new century. During the so called rehabilitation era of the 1960s and early 70s, penal strategies were principally targeted at offenders as individuals, whilst in the 'just deserts' era of the late 1970s and 1980s, attention was focused on the acts the offenders had committed, with proportionality and consistency the primary values expressed in policy and legislation. In the 1990s, control of crime rates rather than fair and consistent sanctioning is the principal penal objective.

Although some commentators have objected to the presentation of the two models as dichotomous, arguing that crime control is the overall aim of criminal law and criminal justice, whilst due process is concerned with procedure (Ashworth, 1979), others maintain that Packer's formulation points up some useful distinctions, and that the models represent the two polarities of a basic and enduring tension within criminal justice. The current debate sees the two models not so much as expressing competing aims, but as representing different sets of values; the question then becomes the extent to which the values of due process may be allowed to restrict the aim of crime control (McConville, Sanders and Leng, 1997; Sanders and Young, 1994). In previous works I have followed Braithwaite and Pettit (1990) in seeing the two clusters of values as *goals* and *constraints*, which like the current legal version of the debate, prompts the question of the right balance between them (Hudson, 1993, 1995). The tension between goals of crime control and values of due process can be seen in the disagreements between politicians and senior lawyers about mandatory sentencing and other issues.

Crime control displacement of due process values is also apparent in changes in procedures in recent years. It has been thought (by police and politicians) that too many professional criminals are escaping justice because of their manipulation of proceedings, and there has come to be a widespread view that rules of evidence and rules of disclosure have tipped the balance too far in favour of defendants. Some changes in procedure have redressed the balance, the most important being altering the implications of remaining silent under police questioning. The right to remain silent still exists, but its exercise can now be taken as inference of guilt. There was almost no popular or political opposition to this change: in terms of my present theme, it does seem that in general, British society now places crime control above due process.

While the old adage that it is better for ten guilty persons to go free than for one innocent person to be convicted seems to have very few adherents now, there also seems to be disturbingly little concern for upholding the principle that the prosecution should have to prove guilt, rather than the defendant having to prove innocence. It is interesting that the civil suit in the

OJ Simpson case prompted a newspaper article from one of Britain's leading lawyers, Sir Louis Blom-Cooper, who had formerly been thought of very much as a liberal, to the effect that greater use of civil procedures should be considered here (cf Dershowitz, 1997). There is a danger that we could be moving towards combining civil law standards of proof with criminal law penalties – some of the provisions of the Crime and Disorder Act 1998, as well as the proposals about people with dangerous personality disorders mentioned above, and proposals which seek to put people who have been suspected of, or cautioned for, sex offences on the same footing as those who have been convicted with regard to their civil rights, are worrying steps in this direction.

Andrew Ashworth (1995) has argued that human rights should become the anchor of criminal justice, superseding any idea of 'balance' between crime control and due process. He states that human rights should be an absolute constraint on criminal justice pursuit of crime control goals. Ashworth seeks to establish a firm normative foundation for criminal justice processes in the European Convention on Human Rights. The Human Rights Act 1998, which came into force in October 2000, provides for the incorporation of this convention into British domestic legislation, something which has been campaigned for vigorously by human rights groups. Ashworth's is a substantial contribution to the defence of justice, and its significance for substantive justice is that it incorporates recognition that 'due process' might not of itself embody human rights.

Ashworth and other human rights legal theorists seem to have in mind rights to do with process rather than sentence. Important though these are, they leave unresolved key questions about rights not to be punished excessively, and not to be punished for possible future offences. This latter right – the right not to be punished for acts which one has not (yet) done but may (or may not) do if at liberty, is the principle of 'just deserts' penal theory which is threatened by the shift to risk control as the dominant penal principle, and this right which needs robust defence in the interests of 'justice'. The requirement that a conviction by a court must precede punishment (Art 5(1)(a) of the European Convention) at first sight looks promising here, but there is considerable doubt about its likely efficacy, since most provisions for more than offence-proportionate detention are defined as 'protective detention' rather than 'punishment'.

Similarly, interpretation by the European Court of the requirement that there be 'sufficient connection' between sentence and subsequent detention has made it clear that the self-declared objectives of the relevant legislature constitute such connection (Henham, 1998 p 599). Henham considered the likely impact of this legislation on the non-commensurate detention of mentally disordered offenders and those defined as dangerous, and points out that Article 5 allows for the detention of persons with infectious disease, those of 'unsound mind', alcoholics, drug addicts or vagrants. There is no precision given to standards of proof or diagnosis of being of unsound mind. His somewhat pessimistic conclusion is that:

> ... the Convention adopts a minimalist approach to questions concerning the legitimacy of state sentencing policy and the protection of individual rights and, since no protection exists in domestic law against the potential injustices described, the maintenance of fundamental rights against procedural unfairness in this context has no foundation [Henham, 1998, p 600].

Challenges to the European Court on the basis of breaches of human rights have been procedural rather than substantive: in the James Bulger case, for example, the main challenge was that the use of standard criminal proceedings rather than welfare/juvenile procedures was oppressive, and unfair because the boys were not likely to be able to understand and instruct their legal representatives in the way that adults would be. There has also been a successful challenge to the Home Secretary's altering the tariff period of the boys' detention; again a procedural issue rather than on the basis that the detention might simply be too long.

My reason for taking the Human Rights Act 1998 as important for the renewal of justice is that it could make a difference beyond its technical provisions, if it encourages the growth of a rights culture among the judiciary, penal practitioners, and above all, policy-makers. Penal progressives in eastern Europe are placing considerable emphasis on the Convention to support the need for reform; successive UK governments having copied so much that is reprehensible in US penal innovation, penal reformers could well learn from their US counterparts who have used constitutional rights to challenge excessive, inhumane and discriminatory punishments.[3]

6.4.2 Justice and difference

Western theories of justice are based on a philosophy of identity. Philosophers construct their subject of justice by abstracting from actual personalities, social groups, contexts and situations, qualities which all people share. That which is shown to be universal is the ability to exercise rational will. This universal rational subjectivity is notably represented in Kant's theory of the transcendental subject, and Rawls' reasonable person. Such a subject is presumed able to act on general principles rather than subjective impulses, to speak as 'the voice from nowhere', representing the

---

3   On a visit to Hungary, I witnessed the vitality of commitment to European human rights standards among academics, officials, lawyers and prison governors; the use of rights-based legal challenges is beginning to happen more frequently in England. For example, The Howard League for Penal Reform has mounted to challenges to the imprisonment of under-18s under anti-discrimination and child protection provisions.

common good over sectional interests. Questions of justice are then cast as what principles and what social institutions would be acceptable to all such rational beings, *qua* rational beings rather than as representatives of communities of interest (Rawls, 1971). Impartiality and objectivity are primary virtues for this 'justice as fairness'.

Philosophical expulsion of difference is reflected in law's model of the abstract subject of law, with all legal subjects constructed as equal in their possession of agency and free will. This assumption of sameness has been the focus of critique by post-modernists, for whom the abstract universal turns out to be the characteristics associated with the white, Western citizen of the Enlightenment, and feminists, who point out that the so called universal norm is in fact predicated on the middle-aged, middle-class male. Philosophical critiques (Bauman, 1993; Cornell, 1990; Young, 1990) of theories of justice predicated upon a logic of identity have thus paralleled the arguments of feminist and Marxist critics of law in action (Kerruish, 1991; MacKinnon, 1989; Smart, 1995). Law based on this logic of identity is castigated for its lack of appreciation of alternative standpoints, and for its failure to recognise that what it presumes to be universal is in fact very partial.

The move to risk control has brought difference very much to the fore in penal policy. Current penal strategies recall the old 'social defence' strategies, aiming to separate high risk from low risk offenders, the dangerous from the normal; their logic is thus the opposite of proportionality's precept of treating like offences similarly. One very significant implication of this is that if the aim is no longer to punish fairly, to treat like offences the same, then 'discrimination' loses any meaning. Discrimination is a term whose meaning is entirely dependent on a norm of equality. Under a risk control rationale, however, someone assessed as higher risk should be punished more – kept away from the public for longer – than someone assessed as low risk. This has obvious implications in relation to race: since so many of the risk indicators, such as employment record, previous imprisonment, are racially correlated, risk rationales would be expected to lead to greater imprisonment of black offenders compared to white (Morris, 1994; Hudson, 1998).

We have seen the mass incarceration of black Americans accelerate as penal strategies have shifted from the desert ideal of 'doing justice' to a risk-control oriented 'new penology' concerned with preventing the risk of re-offending, and with managing a 'dangerous' underclass of people who are assumed to be likely to become more rather than less criminal as they grow from youth to adulthood. Morris was envisaging risk as an occasional departure from a predominantly proportionate system; his allowance of departures from equal, proportionate distribution of punishment because of considerations of dangerousness takes on a new import if the due process ideal of justice-as-fairness is abandoned. The CJA 1991 approximates Morris' formulation; the post-1993 developments with their movement towards risk as the dominant principle part company with the principle of equal penal treatment. These developments thus expel 'discrimination' whilst they re-centre 'difference'.[4]

Feminist criminologists and legal theorists have for a long time been arguing that treating people the same is not necessarily treating them all equally in the sense of giving them equal consideration (Carlen, 1990; Hudson, 1998b). 'Woman-wise penology' was proposed as an alternative to the equality of just deserts which in practice meant fitting women into a penal system designed for men. Arguments for reducing or even abolishing imprisonment for women have been predicated on the low numbers of women committing violent offences.[5] Any decrease in the significance of the violence/non-violence divide, therefore, has implications for the punishment of women. Kelly-Moffat (1999) describes the development of new risk assessment guidelines in Canada, which, she says, recast what were formerly 'needs' as risk factors. I understand that the women's policy section of the Prison Department in the UK is working on a similar development now.

Considerations of race and gender, and also varying social and economic conditions of offenders, pose what Martha Minow describes as 'the dilemma of difference':

> ... when does treating people differently emphasise their differences and stigmatise or hinder them on that basis? and when does treating people the same become insensitive to their difference and likely to stigmatise them on *that* basis? [Minow, 1990, p 20.]

Minow explains that law's usual categories distinguish the normal from the abnormal, the capable from the incapable, and the autonomous from the dependent. In terms of the present discussion, those who are defined as normal, capable, autonomous, are dealt with in juridical mode, with their deeds responded to (more or less) consistently and fairly, without their whole selves being investigated and placed under continuing control. The abnormal (the dangerous), the incompetent (the mentally disordered) and the dependent (those whose legal identity is a function of their relationships – children and, to an extent which varies with time and place, women) will

---

4   In the UK we have not seen the same rise in proportion of black prisoners as in the USA. This is because many of the so called 'underclass' in Britain's degenerated cities are white. The over-penalisation and criminalisation of black youth continues, but the custodial response has been extended to white, workless young men. In the UK risk penality has led to harsh treatment of all youth, with the penal treatment of young black men becoming the temperate for the penal response to all impoverished, marginalised youth.

5   'Abolition', in this context, means treating imprisonment as an exceptional measure for exceptional cases, rather than the penal norm, rather than in the more fundamental sense of abolition of categories such as 'crime' and 'punishment' associated with some, mainly European, theorists.

be dealt with by disciplinary mechanisms (surveillance, institutional care, preventive detention, psychotropic medication, and maybe even expulsion or elimination). The problem is that present institutions presume similarity, and see difference as a difficulty which will be encountered from time to time, and for which special arrangements need to be made. These special arrangements (preventive incarceration, for example) will generally be worse than the normal arrangements, because difference – however statistically normal, given for example that half the population is female, that the factors associated with persistent offending are shared by a large proportion of the male, economically marginalised population – is treated as an aberration or deviation.

There are plenty of examples which show the deficiencies of the unitary standpoint. We can think of the struggle to gain recognition for a feminist account of domestic violence: the male question is always, 'why didn't she leave'; feminist understanding shows that women in a situation of serious and long-lasting abuse cease to think of themselves as active agents with the capacity to make things happen to improve their situation. Another example is the distinction between regulation of alcohol and cannabis: consumption of alcohol, the recreational drug-of-choice for most middle-aged white persons is not of itself illegal, whereas consumption of cannabis, the recreational drug-of-choice for many Afro-Caribbean communities and for many young people, remains illegal, even though new guidance discourages formal prosecution.

Difference is denied in those who come within the definition of normal, capable and autonomous, and is repressed in those who are defined as abnormal, incapable or dependent. The boundaries of inclusion as 'the same' change from time to time, but the cost of successful challenges to designations of difference is false identification with an unacknowledged norm. Thus the price for women of challenging the paternalism, infantilism and lack of acknowledgment as persons rather than possessions of men, has been to be treated the same as men; the price for minority ethnic groups challenging prejudice and lack of legal equality is denial of their cultural specificity and insensitivity towards their needs and sensibilities.

Attempts by feminists or others to question law's male-centredness, to acknowledge female or black standpoints, may widen categories and definitions, but they do not disturb the univocity of ideas and institutions of justice. They merely add more types of people to those who can be included in the identity of reasonable person. Such advances may broaden the definition of sameness, but they do nothing to solve the problem of difference. For every dimension of difference that is encompassed within the circle of similarity, new definitions of difference will be discovered. Genetics, psychology and new versions of positivist criminology are prolific in giving us new categories of difference: the attention deficient child, the sexual predator, the bad parent, the persistent offender, the bogus asylum-seeker, are new labels which put those to whom they are ascribed outside the constituency of justice as fairness.

A difference which is crucial to current penal strategies is that of victim/offender. Ashworth's concern to secure a rights-based approach to justice is prompted in part by the growth of victim concerns as influences on sentencing as well as mandating better provision of victim services (Ashworth, 1996). The rights-based approach advocated by Ashworth, Henham and others still has in mind the rights in standard cases to be secured to standard offenders and standard victims. Even where they have in mind 'different' groups such as mentally disordered offenders, these writers are envisaging procedural rights which will obtain in these sorts of cases. But as Lacey makes clear, emphasis on procedural rights and fairness does not guarantee substantive justice, a just outcome in the individual case (Lacey, 1987, p 225). Consideration of the balancing of victim and offender interests shows that this standard case/difference as exception to be coped with, cannot provide satisfaction to all parties. If an offender is dealt with more harshly than someone convicted of a similar offence, because of some greater-than-standard impact on the victim, then that offender will believe him/herself to have been unjustly treated; if some special circumstance means that an offender receives less than the 'going rate', then the victim will feel that s/he has been denied justice.

What needs to happen to promote substantive justice is the development of a rights-based approach which is predicated on difference, on conflicts of rights that will be generated by individual cases. For this to emerge, criminal proceedings would have to become more like the discursive procedures of restorative justice, underpinned by the process model of Habermas' discursive rationality (1984, 1987). The problem with many formulations of restorative justice, however (and indeed the weak point of Habermas' formulation, according to some critics) is that it still presumes that the outcome of discourse will be a consensus (Benhabib, 1986; Hudson, 1998c). Contemporary recognition of so many claims on justice – the offender, the victim, the community – and so many standpoints – black/white, male/female, young/middle-aged, religious/secular – forces acknowledgment that such consensus is not generally possible. Once the subject of justice is given back her social context and flesh-and-blood reality, it is clear that difference is the standard case, and that differences are routinely irreducible: criminal justice needs to find ways of balancing legitimate but competing or conflicting rights and of accommodating irreconcilable standpoints. As Lyotard puts it in his critique of Habermas, whilst justice remains as important as it has ever been, the idea of consensus has lost plausibility; there needs to be a new ideal of justice which does not depend on consensus:

> Consensus has become an outmoded and suspect value. But justice as a value is neither outmoded nor suspect. We must thus arrive at an idea and practice of justice that is not linked to that of consensus [Lyotard, 1984, p 66].

Minow and others provide an important first step towards thinking what a discursive jurisprudence attuned to difference would be like, and towards bringing discourses of rights together with discourses of difference, by advocating a relational approach to rights. Rights dilemmas are relational difficulties – the respective rights of victims and offenders; the balance of rights of the individual offender to limited punishment and the rights of communities to concern for their safety; the rights of a female offender to have the difference of her circumstances from the male penal norm recognised; the right to recognition of male and female perspectives on what constitutes 'provocation'; the right to recognition of affluent and poor perspectives on what constitutes economic 'coercion'; the recognition of black as well as white perspectives on what constitutes racial motivation.

The developing perspective of *legal guaranteeism* (Van Swaaningen, 1997; Hudson, 1998c) seeks a role for formal law in guaranteeing the rights of the different parties in individual cases. A starting point for writers in this perspective is recognition that at present, criminal law due process offers better protection of the rights and liberties of those defined as dangerous, as criminal, than other processes of social control. This certainly seems to be true at the moment in the response to sexual offending and to youth crime. Those classified as different or dangerous need protection by a criminal justice system that is respectful of their rights, against a potentially vengeful community. In the past, proponents of ideas such as restorative justice or abolitionism have had to deal with the argument that communities would probably not provide adequate controls on offenders, or censure sufficiently strongly; now, perhaps, the argument is that they would not be sufficiently temperate.

Legal guaranteeism is as yet little developed, and not so far sufficiently detailed nor clearly enough differentiated from the standard due process model. As I envisage, the role of the legal adjudicator would be to identify what rights are endangered in particular cases or (in the terminology of discursive justice process) in particular deliberations, and need to be safeguarded. This would mean that the task of law would be to make sure that rights which we hold in general, are protected in individual cases, as well as being operative in the framing of penal and protective legislation. It might mean, for example, the right of an offender not to have a 'cruel and unusual punishment', or to punishment without conviction. This would extend beyond sentencing to the administration of penalties: the length and extensiveness of community surveillance of sex offenders; the degree of interventiveness of probation supervision, as well as issues such as parole decision-making are in need of active rights-thinking.

Such a justice would follow a model of 'reflective' rather than 'determinant' judgment. As Ferrara (1999) argues, new philosophies of justice such as those developed by Habermas (1996), and the various formulations of restorative or alternative justice, move towards a reflective judgment but do not complete the transition. With determinant justice, the particular case must be fitted to the universal rule: the role of the proceedings is to determine what type of case this is an example of, and then must apply the prescribed rule. Determinant judgment is thus 'top-down' justice, and only those aspects of a case which are relevant to the general type can be admitted. There is a deductive relationship between principle and its application. With reflective judgment, the particular takes precedence. The case must be discussed – in whatever terms they choose – by all those concerned, to generate questions such as what type of conflict is this; whose interests and well-being are at stake here; what are the differences between the parties. Instead of the deductive process from principle to application, there is a generative process from instance to principle.

Discursive modes of justice fail to complete the move from determinant to reflective judgment insofar as they aim for consensus, or for the agreement of one participant to the point of view of others, or to the adoption of the viewpoint of one party as the view of all parties. Forms of 'restorative justice' where cases can only be taken if the accused admits guilt, or where the aim is to make the offender assume responsibility for his/her actions without any reciprocity of responsibility-bearing by the other parties or the community, are examples of this incomplete turn towards reflective judgment. Developments from within both restorative and retributive orientations are taking theories of justice further in the direction of reflective judgment as they formulate the opening of conceptual and procedural discursive space (Braithwaite, 1998, 1999; Duff, 1996, 1999). They still, however, leave too much of the discursive content pre-constituted to shift fully from determinant to reflective judgment.

In discursive processes based on a reflective model of judgment, the aim will not be to reach consensus or to induce one participant to adopt another's viewpoint, but to identify any areas of overlap between different viewpoints. Examining what is valued by different parties within these areas of overlap will generate the principles that are to be upheld or encouraged in the process. The only constraints on discussion and outcome will be those conventions of modernist theories of justice which survive the tests of justice as the guarantor of freedom from oppression and which are to be found in most areas of overlap: equal respect, and equal freedom to pursue one's chosen life course. Universal statements of human rights such as the United Nations Declaration of Human Rights, and attempts to interpret them as a practical guide to governance, such as the European Convention, provide guidelines for these sorts of procedure, and should lead to the development of a jurisprudence of rights geared to deciding conflicts and upholding rights in specific cases.

Although human-rights based legal guaranteeism needs substantial theoretical elaboration and also needs the accumulation of a substantial body of case law, its aim is clear. The objective is to establish a system such that human rights can 'function as a moral standard which sets limits to purely instrumentalist law enforcement, while leaving enough space for normative pluralism in a democratic society' (Van Swaaningen, 1997, p 239). Much work remains to be done to develop a jurisprudence of rights, and to bring this together with the growing politico-legal theorisation of difference. Such work is vital, however, if 'justice' is to survive, even as an aspiration, in the risk society. For risk society to be a society where justice sets limits to power, a vibrant culture of rights, and a non-repressive respect for difference, are pre-requisites.

CHAPTER 7

RISKY MONEY: REGULATING FINANCIAL CRIME

Michael Levi

7.1 INTRODUCTION

It may be helpful to begin by addressing the question 'risk to whom of what?'. Financial crime takes many forms, and has very different sets of victims – if, indeed, any specific victims at all: these forms may have as a common core only the legal presumption that by virtue of their having been criminalised, they offend against the State or public weal.[1] In addition to the laundering of the proceeds of diverse crimes from drugs trafficking to tax evasion, committed within or outside the jurisdiction of the financial institution's territory, it includes:

- crimes by elite against consumers, clients or other, lower status businesspeople;

- crimes by small businesspeople against consumers and employees;

- crimes by professional criminals against elite/large corporations;

- crimes by blue-collar persistent offenders/opportunists against financial institutions;

- crimes by individuals of various status against government (tax evasion/social security fraud);

- computer hacking by insiders/outsiders for the purpose of financial gain.

I take the phrase 'financial crime' to mean something more than fraud and to include money-laundering, but to exclude the arena often described as 'corporate crime' – violations of health and safety at work, pollution – on the grounds that though the latter may arise from the desire to benefit the corporation by saving money, and they are indeed crimes,[2] they (a) raise too

---

1   In this sense, the concept of a victimless crime is nonsensical.

2   This may not be universal in technical terms, for it does not apply to the many countries that will not countenance corporate criminal liability on conceptual grounds. One plainly must distinguish here between 'convictability', ie, whether the behaviour was likely to have been defined as criminal had it been competently investigated and prosecuted, and some doctrine of functional equivalence of criminality, such as recommended by the OECD in its 1998 Convention prohibiting the bribery of overseas public officials by trans-national corporations.

many other issues to be conveniently discussed here, and (b) are broadly dealt with in the vast socio-legal literature on regulation that has somehow largely avoided fraud.[3] This exclusion criterion is pragmatic rather than principled, however, since much money-laundering may be done 'by the firm, for the firm' rather than being motivated solely by the pecuniary interests of the human actors. (There is, however, something slightly spurious about this contradistinction, which sometimes arises in the sentencing of 'white-collar criminals': especially in the age of performance bonuses, acts that benefit the corporation also usually benefit the individuals who 'do the business', directly and/or in terms of promotion/retention prospects.) The simpler contrast of financial crime 'for the firm' and 'against the firm' might be a better way of making the distinction of 'altruistic' and 'selfish' white-collar crime, though one might also want to differentiate between acts intended or expected at the time to benefit the firm and those that actually do so over 'the long run' (whenever that is): thus, the market 'manipulations' by some of those involved in the Guinness takeover of Distillers during the 1980s were intended to benefit Guinness as well as the covert participants directly, even though Chief Executive/Chairman Ernest Saunders and three others convicted considerably understated the downside risks and consequences of detection (see Levi, 1991 for a discussion of the sentencing issues). Although – whether or not convicted – those prosecuted in Guinness all sustained net financial (opportunity cost) and reputational losses, this particular case satisfied both the 'intended at the time' and 'achieved in the long run' benefit tests, but sources state that the reputational damage to the business caused was one factor behind the later change in corporate name from Guinness to Diageo,[4] though the broad spread of corporate activities was also vital.

One of the key difficulties of disentanglement is between the risks of financial loss and the risks of financial crime. Commercial risk management has been a preoccupation of firms, banks and regulators for the past two centuries, though the level of attention given to the risk of fraud – 'moral hazard' – compared with other sources of economic loss has varied substantially. Insolvency and insolvency fraud is one the most difficult areas to determine fraud since the notions of wrongful and reckless trading, and of fraudulent trading, are even more clearly issues of social and cultural construction than some other terminological overlaps.

---

3 A limited exception may be made for the work of McBarnet (1991) and McBarnet and Whelan (1999) on tax, though this is more an exploration of how the law is used to insulate potential and actual taxpayers and 'tax planners' from incrimination than it is an examination of risk.

4 Firms may suffer reputational loss not only from crimes carried out 'for the firm': even if the crime was neither intended to benefit them nor actually did, they may suffer damage from perceived incompetence and laxity of controls.

Even where, as in the case of the UK Financial Services Authority, there is an official core objective of 'contributing to reducing financial crime' – a phrase of wonderful subtlety – what forms of financial crime against what sorts/classes of victim are unspecified. Sometimes, criminal justice agencies such as the FBI have explicit priorities – currently health care fraud, previously Savings and Loans frauds – these are seldom absolute and reflect political priorities in those systems in which there is some political lead given to the police. Even in devolved systems such as the UK, there is some guidance for priorities, but fraud has never remotely approached a Home Office Key Performance Indicator and intra-fraud priorities are not specified even by the small City of London police, one of the very few ever to mention fraud in the force objectives. The position of regulators is more likely to be politicised. As for the reduction of systemic versus (presumably) non-systemic risk, one knows that a risk (like the ineptly named Long-Term Capital Management or even BCCI) is systemic only after one has decided not to intervene or has failed to intervene and the economy has collapsed. In this sense, financial risk regulation in a not-for-profit context is rather like secret intelligence and conflict/war prevention: what constitutes evidence for the purpose of measuring success?

A further dimension of this is caused primarily by economic but secondarily by political risk. Certain sorts of victim can do more harm to the party in power (though such commitments can be cross-party) than others, and thereby may ascend the ranking of those deserving protection. Whereas in most Western countries, the political and populist policing priority may be protection of large numbers of small investors, in Russia, for example, the protection of a very small number of large investors may be the crucial motivator. What is the moral or intellectual basis for such prioritisation of classes of investor and can it ever be 'rational', for example, based on some Rawlsian conception of distributive justice? To what extent do any equity principles of prioritisation apply also to resources devoted to addressing 'fear of financial crime', a subject that – with the exception of telemarketing against the elderly – has been wholly absent from government agendas, though 'fear of crime' is, as we are often told, often a bigger issue than crime itself. (This may be a little unfair, insofar as investor protection is the business of the regulators: so what portion of UK fraud reduction and fear of fraud reduction properly belongs to the Home Office as opposed to the Treasury or the Financial Services Authority?) That there are such effects of fraud on insecurity is known only to a modest extent. The Goode Report (1993, p 188) into the reform of UK pension law noted that 'Security [of pensions] is not usually a substantive worry – no one would probably have raised it pre-Maxwell. But nearly everyone did bring up Maxwell unprompted – though they have only a very limited understanding of what it is all about'; and (p 431) that the number of OPAS (Occupational Pension Advisory Scheme) enquiries 'rose from 7,240 in 1991 to 20,034 in 1992', reflecting post-Maxwell concerns. (These are not proper longitudinal data, but there seems no other plausible explanation for these rises in anxiety.) The US Savings and Loans frauds and bankruptcies affected swathes of depositors of varied social status in many parts of the country (Zimring and Hawkins, 1993), as did the collapse in Australia of the Pyramid Building Society in Victoria, the South Australian State Bank (which arguably resulted at least in part from fraud), and Christopher Skase's Quintex Corporation in Queensland. More restricted groups are also affected by frauds, such as members of professional bodies by the compensation payments to victims of frauds by their colleagues: English solicitors often express disturbance at their professional payments, as did the Australian New South Wales and the Victorian Legal Practice Board following revelations in 1999 of embezzlement by murdered lawyer Max Green. There is a growing geographical spread of cases, and though there are clusters of fraud in some locations (for example Florida, London, Vancouver), the notion of 'where fraud happens' is analytically confused, since one should take into account not just the spread of where victims are or offenders live but also the sub-components of financial crime:

- financing;

- staff recruitment;

- places (including media) where deceptions are made;

- places where deceptions are received;

- places where deceptions are acted upon by victims and their financial institutions;

- places through which funds are spent or laundered;

- places where funds come to final rest if stored and/or where laundered funds are reconstructed.

As share ownership widens – as it has done throughout the advanced world[5] – the social spread of the population at risk increases, and the somewhat patronising bifurcation at the time of the Financial Services Act 1986 by the former UK Securities and Investments Board of the population into professional investors (who can look after themselves on *caveat emptor* principles) and 'Aunt Agathas' – a forename that itself is redolent of a particular class – who 'need' protection becomes excessively crude. Nevertheless, the problem of outreach in communicating both specific and general risks of both fraud and loss remains central to the risk management

---

5   The concentration of share ownership may not have altered dramatically in some countries, but the crucial thing is the proportion of the population who own shares directly or indirectly and see securities fraud as relevant to them.

enterprise. Far more can be done for the investor who takes steps to verify the credentials of the agency with which s/he deals than for the trusting/gullible/greedy or other adjective for the person who assumes that if it is advertised somewhere it must be true.

As Financial Services Authority Chair Howard Davies observed in March 2000:

> Much more demanding is the challenge of educating a consumer to equip himself with the technology to obtain basic warnings and information, before he starts buying products or services. Again, the technology is available to give warnings and information if the request is made [italics not in original]. We have examined solutions based on PICS (Platform for Internet Content Selection) and have also looked at the possibility of a specific financial URL for regulated entities.

(A PICS-type solution could mean a consumer, equipped with regulator-provided or approved software, would be automatically provided with warnings and information whenever he logged on to a financial services site. The warning or information might do no more than say 'company X is regulated by the FSA' but equally it could say 'don't touch this with a ten foot pole, we've just arrested the CEO'. And there is great potential for then creating intelligent hyperlinks to sources giving specific information about the firm, the individuals it employs, its regulatory track record, or generic information about the products or services, or indeed the questions that the consumer should be asking.)

Under the Financial Services and Markets Act 2000, the Financial Services Authority has four statutory objectives:

- to maintain confidence in the UK financial system;

- to promote public understanding of the financial system;

- to secure an appropriate degree of protection for consumers; and

- to contribute to reducing financial crime.

In pursuing these objectives, the FSA will be required to have regard to:

- the need to be efficient and economic in its use of resources;

- the responsibilities of regulated firms' own management;

- the need to balance the burdens and restrictions placed on firms with the benefits of regulation for consumers and the industry;

- the desirability of facilitating innovation in the financial sector;

- the international character of financial services and markets and the desirability of maintaining the competitive position of the UK; and

- the value of competition between financial firms.

Note the absence of any specific reference here to the relative deserts of different sorts of depositor and investor: in this sense, there can be a tension between the more abstract economic conception of 'risk' (which does not distinguish between classes of person) and notions of desert that prioritise individuals. It is less than clear how those objectives – especially, perhaps, the reduction of financial crime – will be achieved or demonstrated, given the problematic nature of the evidence on the extent and distribution of financial crime. It is to that that I will now turn.

7.2 FRAUD: COSTS AND RISKS

Crime data:

- are always the product of organisational processes for the defining of events, and that this is true *a fortiori* for activities such as fraud where there is more uncertainty in making attributions of intent or recklessness than is present in most other areas of crime for financial gain; and

- are sometimes used for entrepreneurial purposes by public and private sector groups interested in creating a particular perception of their 'product'. Thus, internet fraud risks are inflated by those selling security and computer crime insurance, while they are understated by financial services and telesales firms selling confidence to depositors or traders.

The range of analytical 'entrepreneurs' – both moral and economic – is enormous. There are radical criminologists who wish to reframe perceptions of the nature and extent of 'fraud' by including a variety of rip-offs, irrespective of whether or not they are illegal.[6] There are people who have lost money from investments, who want to be treated as victims of fraud rather than simply as losers. Finally, and probably most important as 'primary definers' of 'the fraud problem', there are (a) the public anti-fraud agencies demanding extra powers and staff (for example, to deal with the 'growth of organised crime involvement in business'), and (b) the array of corporate security consultants, including those seeking to increase sales of computer security software/consultancy by emphasising the risks firms face, for example of computer fraud and damage. In other words, impact as well as risk probability 'data' play a key role in the bureaucratic political (with a small or even a large 'p') process: the more independently generated

---

6   Zimring and Hawkins (1993) point up the ways in which white-collar crime also leads criminologists and politicians to reverse their normal processes of causal and blame attribution. As an individual, I take the view that some lawful acts are far more harmful than are many unlawful ones, including some classified as frauds. But transcending legal categories in the interests of some broader morality will always induce counterallegations that one is redefining crime according to personal likes or dislikes, as in the famous dictum 'one person's terrorist is another person's freedom fighter'.

and 'objective' the data, the more weight they may carry – though major public figures may be able to get away with ludicrous estimates about the extent of white-collar crime and money-laundering before a credulous media happy to swallow any alarmist data[7] – but by mere dint of repetition, some opinions become 'evidence'. If agencies can show that the problem is large enough, they can get greater powers and more resources from politicians and the public, who become more alarmed as the figures soar. Likewise, fraud prevention – like other sectors of the private security industry – is a source of profit for those selling services and hardware, and 'awareness' needs to be created by fear enhancement, whether this is based on any reasonably valid methodology or not. In this process, the unclear and unbounded nature of the laws relating to fraud are paradoxically an advantage, for this gives space for intentional and unintentional fudging of 'the nature of the problem'. Some of this fudging is entirely legitimate: some studies might include 'consumer fraud', others not; and some (when aggregated, major and certainly numerous) frauds such as credit card and counterfeiting conspiracies dealt with by some non-police or local police would not be included in data supplied by national squads. Nor should we assume that fraud data are always overstated: the fact that low numbers are prosecuted can be used to show that there is only a small problem when, in reality, that may itself be a reflection of the 'problem' of lack of police or prosecution motivation, or even political interference. Finally, and importantly, to point to the interests that are served by high or low fraud estimates is not to tell us anything about how accurate or inaccurate those data are: it is merely to alert readers to the forces that shape the popularity/unpopularity of impact data.

By contrast with the daily diet of politicians' condemnation of the impact of street and household crime, 'social welfare scroungers' and telemarketers excepted, political condemnation of fraud tends to be noteworthy by its absence. Some law enforcement bodies provide data on the breakdown of types of fraud they deal with – the US ones offer the most helpful data here – but the little corporate victimisation data that exists tends to focus on fraud against retail and manufacturing industry, ignoring both financial services and the 'new economy', perhaps because e-tailers are harder to 'mug'. Those data that are available show that in purely financial terms, when one factors in attempts, losses from fraud dwarf all other types of property crime.

Such bald statements of cost data are misleading, however, for they do not illuminate the interaction between the stocks and flows of fraud cases. Particularly where businesses do not keep or destroy their records, the

---

7 The difference is that in other areas of crime, there are victim surveys, self-reports and other data to act as a reality check. Transparency International's 'Corruption Perception Index' is often 'read' as if it were an index of actual corruption levels, rather than an index of the respondents' perceptions of which countries are the most corrupt.

length of time that elapses before reporting and, after reporting, for all creditors to be contacted by the police and/or to realise (or accept) that they have been defrauded, means that it is less meaningful to produce annual fraud cost or case figures than is the case for other types of crime which take little time to happen and to define as 'crimes'. For instance, many of the frauds prosecuted in the UK and North America actually were committed many years earlier: the time lapse occurs partly because it sometimes takes time for a financial empire based on false valuations and on 'robbing Peter to pay Paul' to unravel, and partly because of the time taken to investigate and prosecute (including delays occasioned by defence lawyers). Furthermore, not only are current prosecutions a very poor reflection of contemporary risks – private or public sector preventative measures may have been taken in the meantime – but also these data do not by themselves tell us anything much about the relative riskiness of different investments, not least because they are not expressed as ratios of the amount of funds invested, loaned, etceteras in different regions of financial activity and of the country or globe: in this respect, they are similar to other crime data which do not tell us how much theft there is as a proportion of property in circulation, or violent crimes as a proportion of interactions in public or private space. Such data obviously do not tell us what fraud patterns would be like if we, or sub-sets of us, took different decisions that ignored our perceptions of moral hazard. In that sense, as in other areas of fear of crime, social and personal constructions of 'riskiness' affect the incidence and prevalence rates. Finally, unlike most other forms of crime, the whole concept of using the police force area or even the Nation State as a unit of analysis is deeply problematic. In some frauds, the victims and offenders live in the same area, but in others – both personal and institutional victims – the geography from initial plan to final resting places of the proceeds of crime may be truly global (Blum *et al*, 1998): unless one allows double-counting, there is no obvious method for allocating crime properly, even if one uses the places of residence of the victims as the criterion for 'place of fraud'.

We cannot readily accept victim claims about their volume of fraud losses as reflections of amounts taken fraudulently – for how can victims and criminal investigators validly 'know' whether or not suspects had the requisite criminal intent or recklessness, and for what proportion of the overall business losses any such intent or recklessness applied? – but they are clearly a 'significant' amount of money, both in absolute terms and relative to the cost of other crimes. Taking fraud in its broader sense, to include victims of consumer fraud, the data are impenetrable and/or unrecorded. However, it is instructive to compare even the fraud data set out above with losses from other types of recorded property crime. In doing so, we should note that some householders and commercial victims of burglary inflate their losses in order to defraud and/or to 'compensate' in advance for the expected reduction of their claims by the insurance company: industry sources 'estimate' (or guess) that at least one in ten claims is fraudulent, at least in part. The total UK loss from insurance fraud was estimated (albeit on the basis of poor survey responses) at £650 million in 1998 (ABI, 1999), but this excludes 'frauds' that are dealt with by Lloyd's of London and by other regulators. These may not be reported as crimes or, if reported, no prosecutions may ensue. (Even where, as in Australia and the US, there are federal securities regulators, there are still non-governmental ones that undertake a great deal of monitoring and compliance work.)

To give one illustration of the potential scale of such disputed cases, in 1996, Lloyd's of London negotiated – not without further litigation from American 'victims' – a global settlement with its members (or 'Names') of £3.1 billion to cover all the claims for misrepresentation and underwriting agent recklessness (including fraud) made against it to date. But resistance continued to legal rulings that 'Names' had to pay contributions to this fund first and sue later, and the United Names Organisation questioned how their debts to Lloyd's were calculated, one representative observing: 'People's lives have been destroyed: 30 people have committed suicide and many have spent their last years in misery as a result of Lloyd's' (*The Observer*, 11 January 1998).[8] The lawsuit ended in victory for Lloyd's in November 2000, but Sir William Jaffray, the lead plaintiff, estimated the average losses suffered by the 230 names stood at £5 million and hinted they would be seeking compensation in excess of £1 billion on appeal. Though none of these cases involved behaviour successfully prosecuted as crime, very large fines and expulsion from membership have been imposed and will continue to be imposed. (For discussion of insurance 'fraud' at Lloyd's, see Mantle, 1995, and – on behalf of US Names – the vitriolic www.truthaboutlloyds.com. See also Clarke, 1990.) My point here is that there is no doubt that the insurers properly lost huge sums of money from underestimating the risks of payments sanctioned by the courts or settled in favour of victims of industrial diseases such as asbestosis: in that sense, the risk was higher than expected, both for insurers and for the unfortunate workers, residents and smokers exposed to these substances. The key question reviewed by the courts was whether or not these were crime risks, which could be addressed by reviewing whether companies and/or their agents had unlawfully hidden impact data, and whether the Lloyd's underwriters and/or those acting on their behalf as agents had concealed their own knowledge about the scale of damages in prospect when actively recruiting new Lloyd's Members who in effect became their victims by spreading the risks to existing underwriting syndicate members and

---

8   One does not recall similar amounts of humanitarian concern being expressed by the Lloyd's Names for the victims of corporate crime and ill health in places such as Bhopal, where insurers did not pay out sufficient to keep the victims alive or healthy.

therefore reducing the financial losses to the latter. Thus, gains are privatised and losses are socialised (though in this case, socialised to other fairly wealthy people rather than to the taxpayers, as happened in the Savings and Loans bailouts).

Finally, there are 'frauds' that are dealt with by other departments such as tax and local government. We may know a considerable amount about the risks of personal and corporate insolvency, and credit bureaux have developed extremely sophisticated mathematical models to predict the risks of inability to pay debts, but the probability of intentional fraud is much harder to model.

Using passenger data, HM Customs & Excise estimated the revenue lost from excise fraud. For 1998–99 (Customs and Excise, 1999), the target for prevention of civil and criminal VAT and excise fraud was £920 million (against an emerging actual total of £954 million, £154 million of which was 'saved' in one case); and £373 million was 'saved' as the revenue value of detected alcohol and tobacco fraud and smuggling (in which one case led to £92 million 'savings'). Fines and penalties (excluding drugs trafficking proceeds confiscation) were expected to total £120 million in 1998–99.

Measuring the 'risk' of income tax evasion is even more difficult than indirect taxation. Moreover – except for the smuggling of illegal drugs and the entry of former drug traffickers into excise fraud – 'crime' is not a core conceptual category for this form of policing the risk society. Rather, with some exceptions, non-payment of what the Revenue perceive to be the correct amount due is seen as non-compliance, with some people and companies being more averse than others to persuasive tactics.

7.3 THE TYPES OF FRAUD DEALT WITH BY THE UK SERIOUS FRAUD OFFICE

The Serious Fraud Office (SFO) deals with 'serious or complex' fraud totalling normally at least £1 million but this can be made up of many small sums. The SFO itself classifies the cases with which it deals as follows:

Table 1: Serious Fraud Office cases, 1993–2000

Types of victims	93–94	94–95	95–96	96–97	97–98	98–99	99–2000
Central/local government	4	5	8	10	9	7	6
Company creditors	25	21	18	17	15	12	10
Financial institutions	20	21	16	17	15	9	9
Investors	11	14	29	42	41	42	37
Market manipulation	9	4	3	3	5	5	5
Others	12	7	18	14	17	19	22
Total	**81**	**72**	**92**	**103**	**102**	**94**	**89**

Many of the cases result from (and at least contribute to) huge corporate insolvencies and one should not take the above table too literally: in most cases, financial institutions are involved as losers (even if they are not primary losers or offences against them are not charged), and in many cases, insurers holding professional indemnity and/or other forms of liability insurance are at risk of substantial losses. Cases dealt with by UK police forces and the SFO – which has a remit of investigating on behalf of overseas agencies – may involve victims overseas, and in this respect they overstate official fraud cases against British victims: the cost statistics are organisational activity data rather than victimisation data. These data, like crime data generally, are not expressed in risk terms. Some construct of harm and seriousness enters the loose criteria for case adoption, but the work of the SFO and fraud squads generally is not based around risk management.

The European Commission (1998) states that in 1997, reported fraud and irregularities on its 'own resources' (from import tax, VAT and Member State contributions) rose to ECU 1 billion (plus about ECU 3 billion lost by national budgets from excise and VAT fraud in the same cases); fraud on the Common Agricultural Policy fell to ECU 317 million; and fraud on structural funds fell to ECU 77 million in 1997. The proportion of this that was fraud rather than mistake is speculative, but some clue may be gleaned from the fact that only 35% of money lost before 1994 had been in any degree found by 1998. On the other hand, during 1998, there was widespread criticism of the Commission itself for failing to act against frauds suspected of containing an element of collusion with its own staff, so the 'true' total may be higher still.

7.3.1 The 'dark figure' of unrecorded fraud

With the possible exception of car theft, no crimes are fully reported and recorded. However, fraud does present some special problems, because it offers the possibility for the 'offender' of inducing into the victim an erroneous interpretation of what has happened. The victim may believe that he or she has been unfortunate or has made a commercial misjudgment: capitalism, after all, is about taking risks and profiting or losing by one's risk-taking. Victims may even remain unaware that they have lost money at all. How does a shareholder, or even a company director, know that the purchasing officer has a corrupt deal with a supplier in exchange for kickbacks, or even beneficially owns through a nominee the supplier with whom the business is done? Similarly with 'insider dealing', which may be unnoticed by anyone except the conspirators, though modern technology in stock market surveillance can pick out any material fluctuations in share prices prior to the announcement of price-sensitive information, generating an investigation which, in most countries, is extremely unlikely to lead to any criminal prosecution or even regulatory action. How do the victims of what the person carrying it out knows to be an insolvency fraud know that they have not lost money to just another legitimate failed business (see Levi, 1981)? The point about fraud is that the offenders can manipulate the victims' perceptions of 'what happened' so that it may never even occur to them that they have been victimised improperly or criminally. There are no other crimes of financial gain in which victims never become aware that they are losers (though some victims of pickpockets may believe that they merely lost their wallet, and some mere losers may believe that their property was stolen).

The interpretative process may also work the other way: out of outrage and the desire to find someone other than themselves to blame, or from the desire to claim compensation or fidelity insurance, people who have exercised poor judgment, have simply been unlucky or have had their investments poorly managed may believe that they have been swindled. This is in essence what Lloyd's argued had happened to the plaintiffs.

Not only shifts in recording practices so that each (reporting and recorded) victim counts as a separate crime but also technological factors may have accounted for a small part of the rise in fraud statistics in the UK, as better data matching techniques connect up individual frauds (on, for example, credit card applications) as part of a series of behaviour. It may also not be convenient organisationally to define behaviour formally as a fraud: in Asian countries where much shame attaches to being cheated, losses may not be formally crystallised for that reason, hoping that either retirement or a change of job may happen before formal recognition has to take place; while in the West as well as the East, less personal questioning of the manager may take place if the loss was just another bad debt.

From a theoretical viewpoint, the 'at risk' estimates are even worse. In some cases, the sums are readily justifiable, where sums of money are actually about to be collected by deception, but in other cases – especially advance fee frauds in which the dupe plans to launder, say, $25 billion of diverted Nigeria oil revenue in exchange for a percentage, but the target is actually an upfront set of 'good faith' payments to the Nigerians from the dupe that seldom exceed £500,000 – the notional attempts are inappropriate. Sources state – probably guesswork – that one in 100 such letters received lead to loss averaging £18,000, so the scale of risk is plainly considerable even if one is sceptical about the 'hit rate'.

The number of cases in which overestimates occur probably is not large, for the corporations who are the primary clients (by amounts lost and by volume of cases reported) of the fraud squads usually have well-defined losses. But the resolution of these issues makes a critical difference to the fraud figures, because multi-million pound sums discussed in advance fee frauds make a sizeable difference to the total fraud costs dealt with by the police: one advance fee fraud alone, in 1985, was estimated at $242.5 million in police records, having a substantial effect on the fraud squad data (and being seven times more than the largest ever British robbery, Brinks' Mat, which had occurred not long before).

The analytical framework within which one chooses to review data makes a huge difference. One could pick:

- a company framework – apportioning losses within a multi-national corporation would not fit at all neatly into national data, and, unless local problems (for example, corruption) become so great that locating the company in a particular country becomes non-viable, this calls into question how meaningful some national fraud statistics are;

- a country-based framework, as in the consumer fraud and corruption questions that are now part of the International Crime Surveys (which, for some fraud types, would bring difficulties in deciding whether or not a fraud resulted in loss within the country); or

- a regional base such as the European Union or NAFTA.

But criminal law has often experienced problems in defining the locus of the offence as being where the deceit operated on the mind of the victim. Given the ability of modern technology to patch forward telephone calls so that a London telephone number dialled (by British or overseas victims) can in fact be received in Lagos, the practical venue of where the deception was made or the property was obtained may be hard to define. These difficulties would apply even to definition as crime, let alone the reactions of the police or other enforcement agencies. Despite ignoring the problematic area impact of some international frauds and the omission of tax fraud from their brief, a study for the EU by Deloitte and Touche (1997, para 1.14) concludes:

> We have tentatively suggested that fraud within the European Union may lie in the range ECU 12 to ECU 120 billion, of which between ECU 6 and ECU 60 billion may be international. We emphasise, however, that notwithstanding the width of this range, we have no means of verifying this assumption.

Though their research instruments remain inaccessible, an acknowledged margin for error of ECU 108 billion demonstrates the caution with which aggregate regional and national estimates must be approached. These end points appear to be derived solely from taking guesstimates of the proportion of GNP accounted for by fraud and dividing aggregate GNP for EU countries by these percentages (1997, p 35). One might applaud the refusal to give a spuriously confident single figure but in practice, this conclusion is worthless.

7.3.2 Some survey findings about the cost and distribution of fraud against large companies

The estimation of the extent of unreported fraud against companies remains in its infancy. Organisational victimisation surveys have begun to look at conventional property crimes against business such as burglary robbery, and arson – see for example, the thoughtful reports on retail crime (most recently, British Retail Consortium, 2000; Burrows et al, 1999), which covered firms accounting for half the retail sales (and which sector employs some 10% of the UK workforce), and the 1994 Commercial Victimisation Survey (Mirrlees-Black and Ross, 1995) – but they have not tapped fraud (other than junior employee fraud) to any significant extent, and have not extended to the financial (or any other) services sector, which has been the growth area in major post-industrial societies.

Some insight may be gleaned from the findings of some modest exploratory surveys conducted by this author in collaboration with the international accountancy firm Ernst & Young, though these remain subject not only to the usual survey response problems (discussed further in Levi and Pithouse, in press) but also to the endemic problem of the 'correct' identification by victims of the frauds they have suffered: this requires more intensive case study examination than has proved possible to date. I have resisted the temptation to gross up the survey responses to present an estimate for the total of 'real fraud', because variability in company size and type of business would make this an analytically misleading exercise: even had the response rate been higher, it would make no sense to generalise from *Times 1000* companies we surveyed to the medium and small business sectors, which we did not. (For some comments on fraud against small business, see Barlow, 1993, and for findings on fraud against manufacturing and retail firms, see Mirrlees-Black and Ross, 1995, and Gill, 1998.) This is an important methodological point in international as well as national surveys, because the mix within 'the business sector' varies enormously between countries, especially where there is a large 'grey' or 'black' economy in which many businesses remain unregistered to avoid taxation. Consequently, it may be misleading to write about 'the problem' of fraud within business. In Eastern Europe, for example, multi-national companies may bring their own security apparatus with them, which may mean that their vulnerability to extortion (though not necessarily to fraud) may be far less than the vulnerability of the emerging business sector. In a different way, very small firms who may find it hard to get credit may be vulnerable to tempting offers from 'advance fee fraudsters' or apparently prosperous long-firm fraudsters (Levi, 1981), but not so much as large corporations to internal employee fraud, because there is less distance between employer and employee and therefore greater guardianship.

7.4 INTERNATIONAL CORPORATE FRAUD SURVEYS

Data about levels of white-collar crime internationally are extremely patchy. Corporate crime surveys have been conducted internationally by some accountancy firms. For exemplé, in the 2000 International Fraud Survey (Ernst & Young, 2000), it was found that 45% of respondents suffered between one and five frauds, 15% have suffered between six and 50 frauds, and 8% have suffered more than 50. Notably, 11 Australian and 12 UK respondents have suffered more than 50 frauds in the last 12 months. The largest single fraud suffered in the last year was US $28 million and was within Continental Europe. The total losses from the single worst frauds suffered by each respondent during the last 12 months added up to US $172 million, of which only 29% was recovered. Those companies that are relying on insurance or third party liability to compensate them may be disappointed: only 7% of this loss was covered by insurance and 2% by third party liability. The main source of recovery was fraud perpetrators themselves. Surprisingly, the value of losses recovered from perpetrators was higher than the value recovered through insurance channels. One of the largest losses suffered in the last year was approximately US $25 million and was not insured, but half of the loss was recovered from the perpetrator. By business sector, 18 of the 43 respondents who have suffered more than 50 frauds, of any size, in the last year were from the banking and financial services sector, and three of these frauds were greater than US $25 million. It should be noted, though, that high value frauds are not restricted to a particular sector or country: organisations in 19 sectors suffered losses of more than US $1 million. France was the only country where all respondents reported experiencing at least one fraud in the last year, although it was one of only two countries, the other being Ireland, where the value of each respondent's worst fraud experienced during the last 12 months was less than US $500,000.

7.4.1 'Computer crime'

There is no space here to discuss risks for many crimes in a great detail, but it may be illuminating to turn to a separate dimension of fraud costs – computer fraud – which does not fall against any particular set of victims, though unlawful (and lawful) major transfers of funds almost invariably involve a financial institution as intermediary, if not as a victim, of fraud.

Grabosky and Smith (1998, p 8) approach this 'harm measurement' issue with some delicacy:

> Quantification can also be deceptive ... Often these [financial losses] amount to billions of dollars ... Some estimates need to be treated with caution, however, since they are based on figures extrapolated from relatively small surveys to represent losses suffered by industries which have an enormous customer case and daily deal in turnovers amounting to vast sums of money ... However ... there are abundant examples of substantial and quantifiable sums being stolen throughout the world.

They add that qualitative dimensions are also important, not least because hackers may inflate their achievements. These statements are true as far as they go, but this does not address the deeper problem that official sources may deliberately or paranoiacally inflate the threat and may conflate experience of with theoretical risk from computer crime. This is not simply the attempt to gain more resources acknowledged (p 8) by the authors: it is part of the intelligence threat-assessment mental set, encouraged also by the 'concerns' (also known as self-serving PR) of security consultants whose income depends on shocking (or as they put it, 'creating awareness among') senior executives and government agencies who complacently fail to spend 'enough' money on security.

It is important to think through whether what we are concerned with is corporate (and national security) loss or corporate/individual/governmental fraud. The latter speaks to traditional criminal law notions of blameworthiness and the precise allocation of blame to individuals; the former speaks to harm reduction and prevention, irrespective of whether anyone is blameworthy in a way that fits into the curious categories of the criminal law. Actual and potential damage to data can be catastrophic for the operation of computer-dependent businesses and can provide the basis for corporate blackmail in exchange for unravelling the damage (*Sunday Times*, 2

June 1996), but this 'cyber-warfare' is different from fraud risks. The same difficulties apply to American studies of computer crime (Computer Security, 1998, 2001). A recent British corporate survey by Barnes and Sharp (1998) found that technology was identified very seldom by insurance (6.3%) or retail (13.6%) sector respondents as a cause of the rise in fraud, largely because those sectors were exposed more to thefts and false claims outside the cyber-sphere. By contrast, 42.9% of services and of oil and gas sectors attributed the rise in fraud to technology. Whether correct or incorrect, this at least focuses us to more finely tuned analysis of risk by the nature of the activities.

Hitherto, I have focussed on cyber-crime against the corporate and governmental sectors – which is also the core of political concern, especially in the defence and 'National Security' industries (as stressed in President Clinton's State of the Nation address in 1999) – but this is far from the exclusive preserve of organisational real or potential victims. The Financial Services Authority has not yet taken legal action against online fraudsters, although one case is thought to be pending. Most online breaches of the rules were believed to be accidental, and were dealt with by warnings. The UK watchdog will continue regular sweeps of the web to identify illegal and unregulated advisers, but a 'surf day', carried out in November 2000, identified fewer suspicious UK-based websites than the first, undertaken in the spring. This identified 58 suspicious sites, nine of which remain under investigation. The Washington-based Internet Fraud Watch (IFW) noted an alarming rise in the number and proportion of internet frauds arising from online auctions – where goods are generally paid for by cheque or money order – which rose from 26% of frauds reported in 1997 to 68% in 1998 and 87% in 1999, while the total fraud complaints rose tenfold over the same period. Other top frauds for 1999, in order, are non-auction sales of general merchandise, internet access services, computer equipment and software, and homeworking plans. In 1999, the IFW reported that consumers lost over $3.2 million to internet fraud. This figure might look insubstantial compared with other crime costs, but according to the IFW, 'a 38 percent increase in internet fraud complaints in 1999 coupled with an average consumer loss of as much as $580 indicate an urgent need for consumer education about shopping online'. Hence, a National Consumers League special warning on 'Shopping Safely from Home'. Telemarketing frauds, stock price manipulation via internet 'chat group' demand stimulation of interest in lawfully quoted securities, and advertising of offshore investments to tempt the needy and greedy are all methods by which remote persons can commit frauds with even less human contact and risk of arrest than in normal frauds: they also alter the 'capable guardianship' component of fraud prevention. The US Securities and Exchange Commission detected 10–15 violations per day in 1997, rising to 200–300 a day in 1999. In August 2000, an American was put on five years' probation and ordered to pay restitution for planting a false takeover rumour simulating Bloomberg's Business News, generating massive activity in the stock. On 1 April 1999, the Australian Securities Commission put an advert on the Net offering shares in a phoney firm that would offer millennium bug insurance: it got 10,200 visits in a few days, and 233 people offered £1.7 million as investments. In short, gullibility is, if not enhanced, at least not reduced, by the offerings of the Net. The latter also generates a set of low-investment crime opportunities.

In short, I am not suggesting that concern about computer crime is irrational: on the contrary, I agree with Grabosky and Smith (1998) and with Mann and Sutton (1998) that computer security is going to be a major issue in the 21st century. However, the term must be unpacked into sub-types of crime and we believe that concern about computer fraud should normally be less than concern about (a) many other types of fraud, especially those by senior insiders, and (b) other types of computer crime. For example, it may be that 30 British banks detected fraud on their systems in 1998–99, but the amount of money defrauded was modest, and – despite headlines of 'Hackers hold City banks to ransom' (*Sunday Times*, 19 September 1999) – even the amount extorted was modest compared with product contamination threats. (For a more developed empirical treatment of electronic theft, see Grabosky *et al*, 2001.)

Risk also has a component of 'who the offenders are' and implicitly or explicitly contains a construction of social dangerousness, entailing repeat serious offending. One form of 'social cost' – the 'threat to society' – is often attributed to 'organised crime' as if, merely by being organised by a syndicate rather than one or a small group of professional criminals or anarchic 'pranksters', that made the impact much worse. Such a concept is implicit in the criminalisation of money-laundering, for the assumption is that the integration of 'organised criminals' into 'society' and business will be only superficial, and that they will continue to cause harm.[9] This is an arguable point, though under some circumstances, people outside traditional crime groups may be regarded as a less manageable risk and therefore more dangerous even than gangsters. Battles over social definitions of social harm are not restricted to computer crime, but they are particularly salient to whether those hackings that do not involve pecuniary gain for the perpetrator but may involve substantial pecuniary loss for the victims (and those using allied systems, should they hear about the penetration) should be defined as serious crimes or as what – in the delinquency literature – might be termed 'play vandalism' (Sterling, 1993).

---

9   There is an arguable line that the prevention of laundering reduces the level of crime, in the same sort of way that the availability of competence 'fences' increases burglary and theft rates.

In making these remarks, I am not debunking the cost to firms of protecting their systems against unlawful use by outsiders of insiders: actual and potential damage to data, for example, can be catastrophic for the operation of computer-dependent businesses (for example, the Melissa and 'I love you' email viruses) and can provide the basis for corporate blackmail in exchange for unravelling the damage (*Sunday Times*, 2 June 1996; 19 September 1999), but this 'cyber-warfare' or 'play vandalism' – depending on one's ideological and material perspective – is different from fraud risks.

7.5 THE EXTENT OF PERSONAL FINANCIAL CRIME: SOME INTERNATIONAL COMPARISONS

Somewhat paradoxically (and perhaps reflecting colonialist élitism that corruption is not a problem in the First World), it was in the Third World that, initially, a greater attempt was made – through the 1991 International Crime Survey (del Frate *et al*, 1993, especially Zvekic and del Frate, 1993) – to measure the extent of corruption and consumer fraud. However, in 1991, the industrialised countries were asked about consumer fraud and in the 1995 survey, they were asked also about corruption (though national sample sizes are small and participating countries vary – see Mayhew and van Dijk, 1997).

Within Europe and North America, in 1996, the proportion of the surveyed population who stated that they had been victims of consumer fraud that year ranged from 4% (Northern Ireland) and 5% (England & Wales) through 7% in Canada and 10% in the US – though the US response rate was only 40% – to 15% (Finland) (Table 2.4 and Mayhew and van Dijk, 1997, Appendix 4 Table 5). The UK countries had separately and collectively the highest rates of reporting such frauds to the police and non-police agencies, though the US topped the reporting to the police, with 13% (International Crime Survey 1996 data, unreported). But in every Third World country surveyed, consumer fraud was the form of criminal victimisation experienced by the highest proportion of the population, with corruption typically being the second most common (except in Jakarta, Indonesia, where it was by far the most common, being experienced by over a third of the sample).

In a US national telephone survey of 1,246 American respondents in 1991 associated with the National Crime Victimisation Survey, Titus *et al* (1995) report their experience of 21 different types of fraud, including investment and consumer fraud. 58% had experienced one or more lifetime victimisation's (including attempts); 31% within the previous 12 months, of which just under half (48%) were successful. Thus, fraud is a very common experience for US citizens: more so than for most other crimes. As for the demographic data associated with victimisation, those aged 25–44 were most likely to be victims, while those aged 65 or over were least likely to be victims, though they reported disproportionately often. (This follows the pattern of general crime victimisation.) The likelihood of actually losing money through fraud has no significant association with any demographic variables such as age, education, ethnicity, area of residence, gender, and income. Frauds that occur most often and are most likely to be successful included appliances / car repairs, fraudulent prices for goods on sale, fraudulent subscriptions, and fake charities.

Finally, in 1999, the US National White-Collar Crime Centre (Rebovich and Layne, 2000) conducted a representative (if modest in size) telephone survey of 1,169 Americans about their experiences within the previous year of frauds by financial planners / stockbrokers, car repair firms, and other merchants, as well as internet transactions, unauthorised use of credit cards and ancillary phenomena. 36% stated that they had been victims in the previous 12 months, of which 41% were actually reported externally (compared with 95% who said in the abstract that they would report such offences). The highest proportions victimised were for (minor) product pricing fraud, frauds that offered people 'free prizes' that turned out not to be free, and car repair frauds (13–15%). After that, there is a sharp drop in proportions victimised to 3% for unauthorised credit card use, unauthorised Personal Identification Number (PIN) use (often by family members and friends), telephone and internet frauds and finally, to financial planning fraud (2%).

7.6 GENERAL COMMENTS ON FRAUD SURVEYS AND RISKS

I have explored a variety of data sources in order to build up what, of necessity, has been a dense and not always compatible portrait of unreported and recorded fraud (and, in a more modest way, internationally). (See further Levi and Pithouse, in press.) These kinds of estimation problems are universal in the white-collar and corporate crime arenas.

There are many areas that I have not touched upon here. There seems little reason to suspect that medical fraud in the UK is anything approaching the magnitude in the US. My scepticism is not based solely on cultural factors, but arises because most UK operations and prescriptions do not involve any significant cash payments and there is still relatively little scope for manipulation (outside matters such as exchange of cash for the improperly rapid advancement of private patients' places in queues for publicly funded operations). Nor, given modest awards for personal injury in the UK, are insurance frauds likely to reach American levels, with accusations of widespread conspiracies between doctors, lawyers and gangs arranging artificial crashes costing millions of dollars. On the other hand, privatisation of health care can generate the risk of over-billing and other massive scams.

On one view, criminal statistics should be read as indices of conduct that 'somebody wants something done about' (Wilkins, 1964). Looked at in this way, it is quite irrelevant that much conduct potentially recordable as fraud goes unreported: researchers are simply creating an artificial crime panic by opening up new phenomena via crime surveys. However, not only are people's estimates of the risk of fraud based on estimates even more uninformed than their perceptions of the risks of other crimes, but also people might want things done about crime under conditions – for example conditions of anonymity or the absence of sensational publicity, or without paying for a costly private investigation before the report will be recorded as crime – that do not currently exist, and therefore their 'wants' are artificially deflated.

Furthermore, rather than simply set out the costs of crime, risk-based data are more illuminating (and not just for fraud). In payment card fraud, for example, losses as a proportion of turnover have dropped in 2000 to almost a third of their 1992 peak figure in the UK, though the absolute amount of fraud on UK-issued cards is now higher in money terms (over £290 million compared with £165 million): these figures are reliable except for some bad debt that could be fraud. For large corporations (and, in many respects, for individuals also) the impact of fraud depends not so much on the absolute loss but on what it would take to replenish their profits. In other words, losses from fraud (and from bad debt/'non-performing loans', which can actually be unrecognised fraud) logically should be set against profits, not just sales volume. One might take this 'replenishability' approach also with other forms of property crime, and in relation to individuals as well as business and government. There is thus a social justice as well as efficiency component in determining which classes of victim should receive priority not just in proceeds of crime restraint orders and criminal justice responses but also in prevention strategies.

It is entirely appropriate to transcend conventional definitions of crime and to supplant them with indicators of 'social harm', provided that those harms are defined sufficiently tightly and the transcendence is made explicit: (see also Shapiro, 1980; Pearce and Tombs, 1992 for two contradictory positions). The social and criminal definition of interpersonal and commercial behaviour as 'fraud' does and quite properly should remain a contested site, in law as well as in practice. The way in which during 1999 and thereafter, long-term violations of the International Olympic Committee code on accepting presents suddenly became defined publicly as 'corruption' is an illustration that moral and even legal categories are flexible. However, while sharing the classic view that we can call 'crimes' things that have not been adjudicated as such in the courts – otherwise, there could be no meaningful crime surveys at all – I do not regard it as appropriate to resolve this by criminological fiat: not all conflicts or social harms are 'crime'. Crime control partly entails a struggle for definitional legitimacy, and it is better to keep that struggle going and render it explicit than to wish away the conflicts or to treat them as if they were merely technical rather than ideological decisions about what sort of social phenomena we ought to be counting.

Risks and opportunities are closely intertwined. When law enforcement agencies discuss the 'risks' of money-laundering, they are implying that this causes harm to the societies and the institutions which launder the money. This may be quite misleading. If taking crooks as bank customers leads to financial instability – the money may be 'hot' in the conventional economic sense and may therefore flow rapidly out of the system, undermining the capital base if lending has taken place on the assumption that the accounts are stable – then this is harmful in a readily understood way. Indeed, it was fear of global money flow instability that led the Swiss Banking Commission to prohibit the active solicitation of capital flight funds in 1977 and to the Statement of Principles by the Basle Committee in 1988. Similarly, if crooks are allowed to own banks and if they run the bank as an opportunity to fleece depositors or simply incompetently, because they have no idea how to run a legitimate business, then these clearly are risks and harms. However, what the probability is that these events will follow from criminals depositing the proceeds of crime either simply in accounts or in bank ownership and management, no one currently knows. In 'policing the perimeter', regulators aim to keep out the 'riskiest' sector of the population from conducting banking and investment business: those who are deemed either unfit or improper. I would deem it risky to deposit funds in a bank run by Colombian or Mexican narco-trafficantes, or in any country that has inadequate deposit protection. However, if Citibank handles Raul Salinas' Mexican money, if Barclays handles General Noriega's Panamanian money, or if Credit Suisse does so for General Abacha, is that truly harming the bank? Is it really bad for Bulgaria or Switzerland if they launder the proceeds from crimes committed elsewhere? There is a 'one world' argument – paralleling the analysis of stolen property markets by Sutton (1998) – that institutions and countries that facilitate the laundering of proceeds stimulate the criminal market, and that they thereby increase risks and harms to others. But whatever the harm caused by the primary crimes – from drugs and people trafficking to tax evasion – the launderers themselves are at risk principally because international and perhaps (variably) national regulators are determined to clamp down on them and may impose massive fines and personal incapacitation through the criminal process or through banning them from operating in the business. That is a risk from the regulators rather than directly from the crimes. Whether financial institutions anthropomorphically 'know' that they are taking a risk depends partly on how vigilant their bonus-inspired sales staff are and how skilful the criminals are in presenting a plausible rationale for the funds. (They can, alternatively, simple bribe or threaten the bankers.) Here, too, the scope for ambiguity in determining whether 'what happened' was a crime or not offers a substantial difference from most other crimes in which harm can readily be determined by the observation of loss.

SECTION THREE

RISK IN SOCIAL CONTEXTS

CHAPTER 8

THE LANGUAGE AND TECHNOLOGIES OF RISK

Tom Horlick-Jones

8.1 INTRODUCTION

In recent years there has been a significant growth in the use of risk-related ideas and techniques within various domains of activity concerned with the management of people variously described as 'dangerous'. In fact the very notion of 'dangerousness' (Hinton, 1983) has largely given way to 'risk' as both a basis for evaluation and as a category for the articulation of policy and practice. Practitioners in fields as diverse as probation (Kemshall, 1998), clinical psychiatry (Duggan, 1997) and social work (Parton, 1998) have all found the decision-making processes in which they are involved framed in terms of the assessment and management of risk. For some commentators (Castel, 1991; Feeley and Simon, 1992) these changes amount to no less than a shift away from clinical considerations towards actuarial calculation: from a focus on the individual to one on aggregates of statistical entities.

These developments have taken place in the context of an increasingly powerful political discourse of risk within Western industrialised nations (Beck, 1992; Giddens, 1991; Horlick-Jones, 2001). We are living through times of rapid change, economic restructuring and globalisation, featuring a huge expansion of media and electronic communication. For many citizens, everyday experience has increasingly become one of feeling assailed by threats from crime and unemployment, and by the disappearance of familiar ways of life (Giddens, 1990). Risks to our food, our health and our environment have become daily features of media news reports. Significantly, the risks of failure faced by professionals charged with responsibility for the management of risk – one of the 'risks of risk' as it were – have themselves become grave; in terms of blame, public humiliation and job insecurity (Horlick-Jones, 1996).

Public sector bodies responsible for the management of the criminally inclined – the mentally disordered, the paedophile and others regarded as posing a threat to society – are not alone in adopting a risk-based approach to their operations. During the last decade there has been an enormous growth in the application of risk ideas and techniques like risk assessment in government departments and agencies, across the policy portfolio, and throughout the various sectors of the corporate sphere (Mandel, 1996; Ericson and Haggerty, 1997; Rose, 1999a; Horlick-Jones, 2000). It seems that the language of risk has acquired a generic appeal for all manner of organisations, including those with preoccupations rather different in nature from the high-hazard industries and insurance bodies where risk analysis and risk management have their intellectual roots.

This growth in risk awareness, and in the use of risk ideas as interpretive categories and analytical frameworks, has been accompanied by something of an explosion in scholarly work concerned with risk. Lupton (1999) points to the exponential rise in risk-related academic journal papers over the last few decades, and Rose (1998) notes a similar rise within the psychiatric literature. In this chapter I draw upon some of this literature to explore the significance of the transition 'from dangerousness to risk' in areas of practice related to criminal justice. In this sense, I seek to situate the discussions of risk-related practices to be found elsewhere in this book within a wider context of organisational and political change.

In the following pages I first consider some of the merits and shortcomings of certain influential theoretical approaches to understanding the 'growth of risk'; looking in particular at the circumstances in which those developments have taken place within British institutions. This leads to an examination of how the 'risk object' is constructed, and to the roles played by formal expert knowledge and of informal, experiential and practical knowledge in allowing people to make sense of risk issues. Throughout my discussion I stress the need to understand how people in specific settings use risk and risk-related ideas, and the resulting situated practices and associated micropolitics. I illustrate this situated view of risk with some findings from research into the management of crowds at a major public festival.

I then turn to some specific applications of risk ideas in the management of 'dangerous people'. Here I draw on recent empirical work to illustrate some of the contrasting patterns in which risk ideas are used within these spheres of practice. Again, I suggest a micropolitical view of risk most satisfactorily accounts for observed patterns of situated risk-related behaviours. Significantly, as the papers by Vivian Leacock and Richard Sparks, and by Hazel Kemshall and Mike Maguire, also, in their own ways, argue, the 'pure logic of risk' is not alone capable of accounting for this diversity of risk-related practices at different locations within the criminal justice system.

Finally, I question the extent to which framing issues in terms of the language of risk is value-free, and I then go on to suggest that, on the contrary, the language of risk seems to embody a tacit utilitarianism and, often, an impoverished conception of human nature and action. In this way, the transition to a 'risk management society' poses important ethical and political questions which need to be addressed by policy-makers and practitioners.

8.2 THE RISE OF RISK

During the 1990s, a significant growth in the use of risk ideas, especially risk assessment, took place within United Kingdom Government departments and agencies (McQuaid, 1995). A new cross-departmental body, the Interdepartmental Liaison Group on Risk Assessment (ILGRA), which included participation by the Home Office and the Department of Health, came into being and made a significant contribution to co-ordinating this process. Around this time, several important factors contributed to building an awareness in UK government circles of the need to improve risk handling practices: a number of high profile controversies, including the one concerning the Brent Spar oil platform, and the crisis over BSE and British beef, concentrated the minds of those in government, as well as ringing alarm bells throughout the corporate world.

Similarly, during the last decade, numerous high profile cases within the criminal justice sphere have occurred. These included the alleged 'ritual abuse' of children; the controversy about the release of convicted paedophiles into the community, which led to vigilante attacks and a 'naming and shaming' campaign by a national newspaper; and two particularly well publicised murders: that of Jonathan Zito by the schizophrenic Christopher Clunis, and of Lin Russell and her daughter Megan by Michael Stone (see, for example, Cleaver, Wattam and Cawson, 1998; Reed, 1997; and other chapters in this book: especially those by Barbara Hudson, Anthony Maden, and Hazel Kemshall and Mike Maguire). Although these controversies prompted many calls for 'something to be done', I suggest that the form of policy developments like the recent Home Office proposals for indefinitely detaining individuals suffering from certain personality disorders (Home Office/Department of Health, 1999), which are rooted in ideas concerning 'managing risk in the community', need to be understood in terms of a wider agenda within government agencies.

A new Government came into office in 1997 with a programme of 'modernising' the Whitehall administrative machine. During the election campaign, Tony Blair had a great deal to say about the trustworthy character of 'New Labour', and a preoccupation with trust and with the management of risk seems to have taken root within the heart of the British government; interestingly reflecting some central motifs in the theorisations of the 'Risk Society' articulated by Ulrich Beck and Anthony Giddens. These changes are, however, more profound than the contents of a racy 'sound bite' or paragraph in an election manifesto. The *Modernising Government* White Paper (1999) is clear about the central role of risk management and risk communication in the 'modernisation' process; and the recent Government response to the Phillips Inquiry into BSE (2001) indicates the extent of this influence.

A number of contextual factors appear to have pre-disposed British state institutions towards embracing risk-based thinking and management. The adoption of the language of risk necessitated the formation of an alliance of interests, and it is therefore important to understand how risk came to satisfy a variety of needs that were possibly not related to its ostensible purpose in any simple way. It is possible to identify four key underlying factors (Horlick-Jones, 2000).

First, global developments in the nature of capitalism led to the corporate sphere embracing risk in new, 'risky' ways, in what was seen as an essential pre-condition for growth and success (Mandel, 1996). These changes also served to encourage the adoption of risk thinking by states, and shifts in the management of Western political economies towards deregulation, cost-cutting and performance-driven resource allocation (Osborne and Gaebler, 1992; Power, 1994) prompted the adoption of risk assessment as the basis for 'rational' decision-making. In the UK during the early 1990s the then Conservative Government's Deregulation Initiative invoked the authority of risk assessment in order to legitimate measures to combat the 'tide of red tape' and what was seen as 'unnecessary and harmful' European Union legislation. The associated rhetoric argued that this approach would 'ensure we get the balance of regulation right to everyone's benefit' (DTI, 1993, p i).

Secondly, there exists circumstantial evidence that the idea of introducing risk assessment into the politics and practice of deregulation, was 'imported' via policy networks from North America (Marsh, 1998). The American political and legal systems place great importance on openness, negotiation and on appeals to objective forms of knowledge (Porter, 1995). US Federal Government under the (first) Clinton Administration introduced risk analysis in the broader context of regulatory priority setting and decision-making (Cantor, 1996). In this way, what is seen as the objectivity of a scientific process is introduced as a basis for political decisions. A cynical observer might note that this development amounts to 'taking the politics out of policy' (cf Horlick-Jones, 1998, p 86).

Thirdly, within the British State, risk provided a shared language between different groups and individuals, thus addressing fragmentation that had resulted from radical changes during the Thatcher years. In this way the language of risk seemed to provide a means to facilitate a more cohesive, 'joined up government' administrative approach.

Finally, as noted above, certain theoretical accounts of society, in particular those associated with Ulrich Beck and Anthony Giddens, have been influential in policy development. These perspectives seemed to chime with perceived political difficulties associated with the management of risks and an apparent erosion of trust in science and expertise, in the manner that has become common in the United States. Recent risk controversies seem to have convinced those in some quarters that similar changes were indeed taking place in the UK. A corresponding preoccupation with risk assessment and concerns about public trust has been manifest throughout UK government departments and agencies, and loomed large, for example, during the establishment in 1996 of the Environment Agency (Löfstedt and Horlick-Jones, 1999).

8.3 LIVING IN A RISK SOCIETY?

Risk, as we are constantly reminded, has become a central concern of contemporary life in Western industrialised nations. As Giddens (1991, p 28) puts it: 'to live in the 'world' produced by high modernity has the feeling of riding a juggernaut'. Giddens and Ulrich Beck both point to an epochal shift in societal dynamics towards the production and distribution of 'bads' rather than goods and services, and the generation of reflexive social agents, whose lives are increasingly preoccupied with a bewildering multiplicity of choices. These theorisations, whilst having many similarities, differ in important ways; with Beck seeing the 'motor' of these changes as being located in the growth of pathological by-products of technological development, and Giddens suggesting that enhanced sensitivity to risk has arisen from shifts in the nature of subjectivity.

These conceptual developments have provided important insights into certain arenas of contemporary risk politics; in particular those associated with environmental controversies and certain consumer issues. However these theories have also been subject to severe criticism, especially with regard to the shortcomings of their analysis of class and power (Lash, 1994; O'Brien, Penna and Hay, 1999), the suggested lack of universality of the Risk Society thesis beyond a specifically German context (Dingwall, 1999), and their alleged implicit 'rational choice' conception of human agency (Wynne, 1996).

Perhaps the most significant criticism from the point of view of this chapter has been made by Rose (1998; 1999a; see also Horlick-Jones, 2000) who argues that, rather than the homogeneity implied by the Risk Society theory, one can in fact observe a diverse range of practices which are now articulated in terms of the language of risk or make use of the techniques of risk. Risk assessment, for example, may be regarded as a 'technology' in the sense that, ostensibly, it is a tool designed to achieve some end. However a recognition that such 'technologies of management' are not necessarily (politically) neutral in their impact forms the basis of a literature which has considerable significance for attempts to understand the 'growth of risk' within the British State. This work is concerned with 'governmentality', a concept introduced by the French thinker Michel Foucault, and which recognises the way in which state power can be exercised in complex and shifting ways through the application of such technologies. The important characteristic of the approach adopted by Nikolas Rose and others working within a broadly Foucauldian perspective (for example, Ewald, 1991; Ericson and Haggerty, 1997) is that they regard risk as being a particular style of thinking that has 'brought the future into the present and made it calculable' (Rose, 1999a, p 247).

The political impact of this discourse of risk, and the practical effects produced by its penetration of societal institutions has been recognised by a number of areas in the literature, in particular criminology (Feeley and Simon, 1992; Ericson and Haggerty, 1997; Stanko, 1997). Here, it is argued that a shift from a traditional concern with the responsibility of individuals for their actions is being replaced by an 'actuarial' approach which is managerial in nature: seeking to regulate levels of risk. Rejecting grand theories such as *Risk Society*, Rose (1999, p 41) draws on Foucauldian notions of discourse and genealogy (Foucault, 1977, 1979; Dreyfus and Rabinow, 1982) to situate risk within a fine-grained process of shifting patterns of governance and subjectivity:

> ... a little, variegated, multiple history of the objectifications of human beings within the discourses that would govern them, and their subjectification in diverse practices and techniques.

Whether this 'governmentality' view of risk can indeed account for the diversity of risk-related practices is a matter necessitating empirical investigation. Elsewhere I have argued that further explanatory resources need to be invoked in order to provide such an account (Horlick-Jones, 2000). However in methodological terms, I suggest that Foucault's (1972, 1979) 'archaeological' approach to the evolution of knowledge – an examination of the situational specificity of the trajectory of ideas – is precisely what is needed to understand what is going on. This approach is nicely captured (in slightly more transparent form) in another of Rose's books (1999b, p x):

> This involves an attempt to trace, in very concrete and material forms, the actual history of those forms of rationality that compose our present, the ways of thinking and activity in which they have been caught up, the practices and assemblages which they have animated, and the consequences for our understanding of our present, and of ourselves in that present.

This discussion has taken us far from conventional interpretations of the nature of risks associated with aspects of criminal justice, and, not unreasonably, the reader may wonder how this is related to the practicalities of evaluating and managing risk. What I am trying to do is to not only situate such practices within wider organisational and political processes, but also to disentangle those underlying interactions which together constitute the ostensibly objective activity of risk assessment.

The shift from traditional notions of dangerousness to a discussion in terms of risk entails a process of abstraction which gives birth to what has been termed the 'risk object' (Hilgartner, 1992). Elsewhere (Horlick-Jones, 1998) I have attempted to dissect the overlapping social and material processes entailed in the coming into being of these entities by utilising a rather similar approach to the one termed 'archaeological' above. In that case, I was concerned largely with risks associated with dangerous substances and failures of material infrastructures. In the section below, I begin to explore the relevance of this approach for risks associated with 'dangerous people'.

8.4 THE CONSTRUCTION OF RISK

The analytical approach termed 'constructionism' is a perspective that recognises that the categories we use to understand and describe the world to each other are socially negotiated (see for example, Velody and Williams, 1998, and the excellent critical analysis by Hacking, 1999). One might respond to this observation by saying that it is clearly a truism, and to some extent this is indeed the case. The interesting questions arise however, when one starts to consider the relationship between some entity's ontological nature and the categories we use to describe it. To what extent does some entity's 'innate nature' (if it makes any sense to speak of such things) demand its description takes a certain form; and, conversely, to what extent do ideological and value 'spin' impose what one might call our 'ways of seeing'? The dynamic may be seen, therefore, as a tension between materiality and sociality.

In the case of risks associated with dangerous people, we are faced with potential hazards arising directly from human behaviour. It could be argued that such risks are rather different in nature from those associated with, for example, a cloud of toxic fumes, or perhaps a railway accident. In the latter cases, risk analysts perform calculations that draw heavily on engineering and physical scientific knowledge. In evaluating risks associated with dangerous people, professionals tend to strike a balance between clinical assessments, drawing perhaps on psychological, physiological or medical knowledge, with actuarial calculations which rely on statistical indicators which typically embody both clinical and social factors such as employment status and socio-economic factors, and patterns of previous behaviour (Snowden, 1997; Cleaver, Wattam and Cawson, 1998; Copas, 1998; Kemshall, 1998; Rose, 1998). However, I will suggest that perhaps the differences are not as categorical as one might expect.

Constructionist views of risk recognise that, above all, the identification and assessment of risk is both a human and a social activity and, as such, is concerned with the production of meaning and a shared understanding of reality (Renn, 1992; Lupton, 1999). The role of the social in the construction of meaning needs to be invoked in order to appreciate how different societies, and indeed subcultures, have sometimes radically different beliefs and sense of what is real and true. This multiplicity of meaning lies at the heart of why a given risk is sometimes perceived by different social groups as posing a very different degree of threat. Of particular importance here, of course, are the contrasting perceptions corresponding to a scientific assessment and that of 'non-expert' audiences. Contrasting meanings associated with risks also contribute in pivotal ways to complicating the processes involved in their management.

Constructionism is most often associated with Berger and Luckman's (1967) well-known book, and their reading of Schutzian phenomenology. However it also has distinct intellectual roots within the sociology of knowledge, and especially the sociology of scientific knowledge (for example, Collins, 1985; Woolgar, 1988), and the North American 'social problems' literature (Spector and Kitsuse, 1987). It is very important to draw a clear distinction between constructionism as an approach to investigating the social and material processes entailed in understanding and describing the world, and the long philosophical tradition of idealism: an outlook that suggests the world is a thing of the mind, and that there exists no reality independent of socially-organised representations. This idealist view is certainly not a necessary component of constructionism theory.

The inherent nature of risk necessitates value judgments, but the social is also incorporated from the human, and judgmental, activity of assessment, the organisational and social context in which it is embedded, and the fundamental ambiguity of meaning inherent in human understanding and action. None of these observations is intended to attack or discredit scientific knowledge, or to question its utility; rather, it argues that risk assessment should be seen for what it is an essentially human activity.

8.5 AN ARCHAEOLOGY OF RISK

One might usefully begin a process of examining the social and material construction of risk by observing that our understanding of the world is fundamentally ambiguous by virtue of the existence of symbolism, resulting in any given entity assuming a multitude of different meanings, according to context (for example, Sperber, 1975). However even within a purely positivist perspective that views risk as being a measure of objective facts about the world, the social inevitably intrudes. Any assessment of risk involves, by necessity, a summation over a variety of potential harms posed by a given hazard, in this case arising from a criminal act. Such a summation involves a weighting process that either implicitly or explicitly introduces valuations of the relative importance of each harm, and hence generates a politics of the process of risk management (Fischhoff, Watson and Hope, 1984; Horlick-Jones and Peters, 1991).

Similarly the process of risk assessment itself, as conducted by scientific or technical experts, introduces valuations and potential biases. These emerge by virtue of the need to use imperfect and uncertain knowledge, and to make professional judgments that call upon experience, assessments of the quality of data and other subjective elements (Freudenberg, 1988).

It is important to appreciate, however, that even in those cases where scientific knowledge – perhaps of a psychological or medical nature – plays an important role in the assessment process, ambiguities arising from human subjectivity cannot be avoided. There is now a considerable body of evidence, largely from research into the sociology of scientific knowledge, which seem to demonstrate that scientific 'facts' are underdetermined by data. The conclusion of these findings has been that commitments and pre-conceptions held by scientists, and processes of negotiation involved in scientific activity, play central roles in the construction of the form of scientific facts (for example, Collins, 1985; Latour and Woolgar, 1986; Jasanoff, Markle *et al*, 1995).

For some, especially practitioners of applied science, this suggestion of the contingent nature of scientific knowledge may be particularly unsettling. An implied relativism, in which there is no special epistemological status for scientific knowledge, set against other forms of knowledge, appears absurd or dangerous to many. Resulting disagreements have sometimes become quite acrimonious, with the sociology of science recently coming under sustained polemical attack by some of its critics (for example, Wolpert, 1992; Gross and Levitt, 1994). Despite the details of these sometimes-arcane debates, it is difficult to disagree with Collins' (1985, p 167) view that:

Neither anarchy nor nihilism follows from the recognition of the human basis of expertise; instead comes the recognition that there is no magical escape from the pangs of uncertainty that underlie our decisions.

Turning now to a third mechanism by which the social is incorporated into the risk object, one needs to consider the organisational and social setting in which a risk assessment takes place. This perspective has been shown to be important in order to appreciate the nature of failures associated with many disasters; for example, Diane Vaughan's (1996, p 394) analysis of the explosion of the Challenger space shuttle in 1986, where she demonstrates that the disaster was rooted in the apparent normality of day-to-day operations:

... its origins were in routine and taken for granted aspects of organizational life that created a way of seeing that was simultaneously a way of not seeing.

Finally, I return to the question of symbolism, and the sometimes-contrasting ways in which people make sense of risk issues. One influential body of work that has addressed this issue is associated with the anthropologist Mary Douglas (for example, Douglas and Wildavsky, 1982;

Douglas, 1990, 1992). Douglas argues that cultural formations determine both the selection of certain risks for special concern, and the adoption of risk handling styles, with people displaying different, or 'plural', rationalities, in such a way as to reinforce and not contradict their chosen ways of life. Despite its apparent relativism, Douglas does not seek to deny the reality of risks; as she puts it:

> Note that the reality of the dangers is not at issue. The dangers are only too horribly real ... this argument is not about the reality of the dangers, but about how they are politicized. This point cannot be emphasized too much [Douglas, 1990, p 8].

Meaning lies at the heart of this human-centred perspective on risk. When Brian Wynne (1982a, p 127) stated that:

> The risk assessment fraternity is well aware by now of the limited role played by various 'technical', 'rational', or 'analytical' approaches to risks in real decision making contexts

he was, of course, identifying a phenomenon widely recognised by anyone with experience of these matters. Technical risk assessments tend to fail in identifying the multiple social meanings associated with a given 'risk object'. These may include perceived threats to community, home, jobs, ways of life and so on. A given risk issue may come to play a symbolic, or proxy, role according to an apparently unrelated agenda (Wynne, 1982b; Manning, 1992; Bloor, 1995; Horlick-Jones, 1996; Horlick-Jones, 2000; Horlick-Jones, Rosenhead *et al*, in press). These considerations may apply in organisational or public arenas, and they are every bit as real as scientific assessments, even if they are more obviously judgmental.

8.6 CONTEXTUALISATION

Risk practitioners, like other professionals, need to employ a significant amount of skill and judgment in their work in order to operate effectively (Schön, 1983; Dietz and Rycroft, 1987). Such craft skills require experience and the ability to improvise and adapt that can only be learned by practice. They are distinct in nature from formal disciplinary-based knowledge. Evidence presented in the 1980s to the Sizewell B nuclear power station public inquiry in the UK was clear in recording the views of the plant's design engineers:

> [They] do not believe that risks can be accumulated into single numbers or that any given safety investment necessarily reduces collective risk. They look at design parameters and their implications for operator error and accident sequences ... Risk regulation cannot be achieved by regulation alone, nor can risk-cost-benefit analysis provide an answer [O'Riordan, Kemp and Purdue, 1987, p 368].

The craft skills involved in this work draw on formal procedures like mathematical modelling not so much as 'gateways to truth', but as what Polanyi (1958) termed 'heuristics'; namely as devices to assist intuition. According to this human-centred view of scientific activity, the tacit knowledge and skill of the scientist forms a key ingredient in the production of scientific knowledge.

It follows that in the practice of risk assessment, experts need to recognise the limits of narrow instrumental knowledge, and develop an appreciation of the complexity of the problem context. Risk professionals are therefore involved, to some extent, in contextualising technical scientific knowledge for application in specific problem situations.

Wynne (1989, 1996) has provided a number of useful case studies where official scientific assessments of risk have proved wildly wrong because the characteristics of the context in question had not been properly taken into account. The practical circumstances in which the herbicide 2,4,5-T was applied was one of these, and perhaps the best known example concerns the movement of radioisotopes from the Chernobyl nuclear accident fallout through the Cumbrian hill top environment. In this latter case, official estimates of the necessary length of bans on the sale of sheep meat proved inaccurate as knowledge of the local geology and of hill farming practices proved inadequate.

A number of recent strands of risk research have recognised the need to contextualise expert scientific knowledge and to extend the range of knowledge that is seen to constitute 'expertise' (Wynne, 1991; Funtowicz and Ravetz, 1992; Horlick-Jones and De Marchi, 1995; Horlick-Jones, 1998; Horlick-Jones, Rosenhead et al, in press). Taking into account a wider range of both expert and tacit knowledge, it is argued, allows both contested values and sources of uncertainty, as well as possible impacts on related policy areas, to be incorporated into the decision-making process.

Funtowicz and Ravetz's (1992) theoretical rationale of this perspective is the most highly elaborated, recognising at it does the emergence of a range of practical problems where typically facts are uncertain, values in dispute, stakes high and decisions urgent. In these circumstances, scientific 'truth' is, as they put it, a 'chimera', so necessitating the development of new forms of scientific practice ('Postnormal Science'). Central to their concept is a concern for the quality of scientific knowledge in decision-making, and a commitment to the democratisation of such knowledge by the establishment of 'extended peer communities': including members of lay publics 'who are prepared to commit themselves to the quality assurance of scientific inputs' (p 96). This approach seems to offer the possibility of addressing the interconnectedness of facts and values in risk issues which emerges from the constructionist analysis above. There are now a number of arenas of risk practice where such interactive approaches to risk management are beginning to be used, or discussed in policy development (for example, Rip,

Misa and Schot, 1995; UKOOA, 1999; Horlick-Jones, Rosenhead *et al*, in press).

This matter has been taken up in the context of probation practice by Hazel Kemshall (2000), who identifies a number of pathologies of professional practice arising from epistemological barriers between policy makers and practitioners, and between professionals and their clients. She points to the challenge of finding ways of integrating differing, and sometimes competing, knowledges of risk to produce negotiated and effective systems of risk management, and indeed, she and Mike Maguire take up this theme in their chapter in this book. There is clearly a need for more empirically-based work in criminal justice-related areas to investigate both the situated practices of professionals engaged in evaluating risks, and in the ways in which multi-disciplinary teams collectively accomplish such tasks.

8.7 RISK AND INTERACTION: THE CASE OF THE NOTTING HILL CARNIVAL

Here I consider some organisational and inter-organisational risk management processes in order to illustrate some of the diversity of risk-related practices that may be observed in specific, concrete, situations. This example is concerned with the Notting Hill Carnival, an annual celebration of Afro-Caribbean culture, which is, in essence, a huge street party, combining loud music, dancing, a procession and street trading, and which attracts up to one million revellers to a relatively small area of West London each year. The Carnival involves a complex web of relationships between culturally diverse parties with sometimes competing interests. This tension and diversity provides the context for a number of linked risk management processes. Such risks present a number of potential hazards to Carnival-goers and local residents, and include threats to public order, public safety, environmental health, and from crime. A recent two-year (1996–98) ethnographic study of planning and operational aspects of the Carnival yielded a number of interesting findings concerning interactional aspects of risk management practices (Horlick-Jones, Rosenhead *et al*, in press).

Risk management at the Carnival is achieved by a combination of careful planning and real-time activities. The latter is dominated by a huge police operation. Policing the Carnival requires sensitivity to the needs and perceptions of the various interests involved, including ethnic, local community and commercial groups. It also requires efficient and co-operative relations with other organisations and emergency service agencies. The policing operation is co-ordinated by a special operations room based at New Scotland Yard, which acts as a communications centre, collates information and provides a liaison point with the emergency services.

An important finding is the perhaps surprising extent to which Carnival decision-making (or at least the framework for decision-making) is pre-programmed, certainly at the strategic level or involving inter-organisational relations. The Carnival has become a mature, well-practised operation in which a multitude of tactical decisions, predominantly made 'close to the ground', serve to steer the huge, complex process.

Despite this level of control, it is important to recognise that all organisations involved in the Carnival's planning and operation run risks by virtue of their participation. These are the risks associated with legal liability and financial loss, and the risk of damage to an organisation's public image and credibility. All the organisations involved in the Carnival seemed to have similar underlying agendas associated with the avoidance of blame and liability, and each needed to be seen to be taking all possible reasonable measures to protect public safety, so generating a tendency to account for actions in 'safety audit'-like terms. Transferring blame to other agencies was another potential escape mechanism; a factor which manifestly tended to undermine inter-organisation trust. In a fundamental way, these considerations shaped each organisation's approach to taking part in the Carnival process, and so contributed to the fashioning of its culture of engagement.

During field work we were struck by the observation that all agencies involved in planning for the Carnival tended to talk a great deal about safety; this factor constituting the event's key criterion of success or failure. It became clear, however, that there was a certain formality to the use of the concept; and by virtue of the fact that no one could be seen to be arguing against safety, arguments advanced on safety grounds could be potent rhetorical devices, and therefore powerful resources in pursuing various other organisational agendas. As a consequence, power relations formed and re-formed in shifting patterns with the skilful and tactical deployment of risk-related arguments in a range of specific settings.

During the process of the management of the Carnival by the Metropolitan Police, we noted yet another risk-related rhetoric, this time concerned with a trade-off associated with public order. Its logic seemed to work like this: 'this is a legitimate safety concern, but we cannot act because it might cause public disorder, and that itself would be a public safety problem.' This amounts to the adoption of a semi-technical risk trade-off explanation as a rationale for inaction. Importantly, it also provides an audit-type cover in the context of possible liability or blame. Ambiguity over the legal position of the police fuelled this logic: what seems to amount to clear grounds for action in public safety terms may not constitute the stronger 'imminent threat' criterion, which is necessary to provide immunity should anything 'go wrong'. We heard this 'risk trade-off' rhetoric used on a number of occasions as the basis for police officers rationalising their reluctance to act in what seemed to us manifestly 'risky' situations.

In this way the existence of informal 'rules' which provide local rationales of action were identified. These seem to emerge naturally from the 'force of circumstances' rather than being operational orders, imposed from above. Risk issues (including liability) played a key role in the construction of such rationales. These findings are reminiscent of Bittner's (1967) work on police decision-making, and point to the importance of studying the detail of situated actions as a means of understanding the relationship between the tacit skills of policing, the exercise of discretion and the difficulties inherent in specifying sufficiently rich operational instructions to cope with the variety of policing situations.

8.8 RISK AND PRACTICE IN THE MANAGEMENT OF DANGEROUS PEOPLE

Having first developed a framework for understanding the context within which the rise of risk thinking and the application of risk techniques has taken place, and then considered some interactional aspects of corresponding practices, I now wish to examine in a little more detail some aspects of risk-related practices associated with the management of 'dangerous people'. I have, of course, already drawn attention to examples from an emerging literature which has started to chart the contours of such practices (Ericson and Haggerty, 1997; Rose, 1998, 1999; Kemshall, 1998, 2000; plus the chapter by Hazel Kemshall and Mike Maguire in this book).

I have argued that any attempt to appreciate the nature of risk-related practices needs to take into account both the context and the specific circumstances in question. It is therefore useful to recall that risk thinking came to be adopted within criminal justice-related areas during a time when a pervasive political discourse of risk ensured that organisations took their own risk management practices very seriously. Of all the risk controversies, perhaps those associated with 'dangerous people' had been most significant in capturing the imagination of lay publics, grabbing newspaper headlines and prompting politicians and officials to be seen to be 'doing something'.

Street-level mobilisation and direct action against sex offenders and others has focused attention on the strength of feeling within communities, and the widely perceived shortcomings of a range of public sector workers, seen in some circles as hate figures: probation officers, social workers, physicians and so on. In many of these cases, the sociological concept of a 'moral panic' (Cohen, 1972; Goode and Ben-Yehuda, 1994) has been relevant, combining as it does notions of deviance and media 'amplification'. Indeed, we have been living through times where what is arguably an 'overreaction' has occurred in response to a range of scare stories and to events like the death of Princess Diana (Anderson and Mullen, 1998).[1]

Against this backdrop, professionals charged with the management of 'dangerous people' have been hamstrung for many years by the unreliability of clinical assessments of 'dangerousness' (Hinton, 1983; Hamilton and Bullard, 1990), and have therefore been vulnerable to high profile failures. This has led to a situation in which attempts have been made to strike an acceptable balance between 'false negatives' – failing to identify future offenders – and 'false positives' – in which people are perhaps unnecessarily incarcerated. As Kemshall (1998, p 51) observes, even with the advent of actuarial devices like statistical risk assessments, striking such a balance is 'often a matter of social and political acceptability rather than a matter of methodology'. In such circumstances there is a real threat to the civil liberties of people for whom political support may be regarded as something of a liability.

Interestingly, the shortcomings of clinical assessments of dangerousness by psychiatrists prompted a very significant critique of existing practices by Stephen Pfohl (1978) which formed part of a wider critical evaluation of positivist psychiatry during the late 1970s (for example, Ingleby, 1981). Pfohl's empirical investigations indicated that, in practice, expert diagnoses of dangerousness were inherently 'political' in nature, in the sense that their accomplishment reflected pre-existing categories, and so reflected the interests of dominant processes of social control. In such cases, expertise became the basis for rationalising a decision that, in effect, had already been taken. In response to his findings, Pfohl went on to advocate a very similar broadening of the basis for decision-making to that identified in the section on contextualisation of risk knowledge that we considered above.

We have already seen that risk-based regulation offers the promise of decision-making processes being seen to be independent, scientific, apolitical, auditable, transparent, and, above all, defensible. Therefore in times of enhanced risk awareness, a propensity to blame, and a tendency for all failures to be regarded as unacceptable, the adoption of a risk-based approach to practice among vulnerable professions was perhaps almost inevitable. However it is important to ask how, in practice, the adoption of a risk-based approach has influenced the way that professionals act. They may now account for their actions in terms of risk categories, but does this correspond to what they may be observed to be doing?

---

1 An interesting analogy exists between the perceived threat to communities posed by 'dangerous' individuals and from, for example, contamination or explosion hazards. In this sense, studies designed to investigate 'Not In My Back Yard' (NIMBY) reactions to proposals for the siting of, say, hostels for the mentally ill (for example, Dear and Taylor, 1982), take a rather similar form to those which examine reactions to the siting of some industrial complexes (for example, Zonabend, 1993). The complex way in which certain risks are 'amplified' by media attention has recently been subjected to a critical empirically-based investigation (Petts, Horlick-Jones and Murdock, 2001).

The possible contrasts between accounting behaviour and situated practices in risk-related fields has formed one of the foci of recent research in which I have been involved. During this work I have been able to investigate the ways in which risk ideas and techniques are being used in practice in a wide range of government institutions and corporate bodies (for example, Horlick-Jones, 2000). These investigations have included the opportunity to interview officials from agencies responsible for the management of 'dangerous people', to speak with a number of individuals possessing inside knowledge of these bodies, and to gather documentary materials which related to their working practices. I hasten to add that my work which relates to these areas of professional practice is preliminary in nature, and I would claim nothing of the competence and level of knowledge of researchers who have specialised in these areas, some of whom I have cited above. The following observations therefore take the form of a few remarks which may be suggestive of the need for further detailed investigation.

The first point I would like to make concerns the ambiguity of the word 'risk' in these professional settings. The language of risk conveys a sense of systematic organisation, and without doubt provides authority in statements and arguments. Yet I found quite dramatic differences in the precise meaning that officials were associating with the word. In one area, policy shifts had resulted in risk changing its meaning from the 'risk of an adverse incident re-occurring' to the 'risk of potential harm' of an incident, should it occur. There are clearly significant practical differences here. This confusion between potential harm (or 'hazard') and 'risk' is an important source of potential inconsistency and difficulty. In some areas, I found that risk, in an engineering sense, appeared to be selectively used for what one might term 'low harm' hazards, but slippage occurred when a potentially 'high harm' hazard was considered, no matter how unlikely was the potentially damaging event.

My second point is concerned with attempts to introduce the use of formal risk assessment procedures, which utilise actuarial devices drawing upon indicators and statistical patterns. In one area I found that these developments were being greeted with concern among 'front line' practitioners. Sometimes such resistance was rooted in worries about de-skilling, and linkages with other agendas; for others, there were ethical worries that relatively crude assessments of risk could result in people 'thought dangerous' being incarcerated in error. In contrast to the worries which I heard at an operational level, senior management often seemed to adopt a rather different view on these matters which chimed with the notion of the 'decontextualised' perspective, discussed above, which has been found by other researchers.

Among the people with whom I spoke, some had real concerns about the impact of actuarial approaches to risk assessment. One official observed:

> ... who is going to argue that we should be fairer to potential offenders? ... pressure from the public, the media and politicians means that the release of a dangerous person in error is just not acceptable at the expense of locking someone up by mistake ...

Others, however took a more positive view; for example one academic noted:

> ... they forget the liberal ballast of British society ... we'll end up with a compromise combining actuarial screening and clinical judgement ...

In other words, this person argued that a conflation of multiple agendas would ensure that the logical consequences of risk thinking, with its perhaps worrying implications, would not be pursued in practice.

My final point is concerned with the use of multi-agency fora in managing risks associated with dangerous people. This matter is examined in detail, for one specific area of professional practice, in the chapter by Hazel Kemshall and Mike Maguire. Interestingly, I found that this type of practice has emerged in a number of areas where different professionals with overlapping responsibilities are working together (discussed in Ericson and Haggerty, 1997; Cleaver, Wattam and Cawson, 1998; Rose, 1998). Perhaps significantly, this development has a number of similarities with interactive processes which are increasingly emerging as part of corporate sector risk management (UKOOA, 1999; Horlick-Jones, 2000). In both spheres of practice, risk seems to provide a shared language and a structured framework for negotiation, so facilitating a mutual auditability of actions (Power, 1994).

8.9 CONCLUSIONS

A risk-based approach has been adopted by a number of professional groups charged with the responsibility of managing the behaviour of individuals who are regarded as potentially dangerous. I have suggested that the range of risk-related practices, which one can observe in different locations, cannot be understood in terms of the 'pure logic' of risk alone. Rather, people in specific settings have the capacity to use risk and risk-related ideas, perhaps by making linkages with other agendas. A micropolitical view of risk, rooted in an appreciation of the central roles of practical reasoning and situated practices (cf Bittner, 1967; Garfinkel, 1967; Anderson, Hughes and Sharrock, 1989), seems to possess greater explanatory potential than either an instrumental interpretation or one based on some readings of a Foucauldian 'governmentality' model, which appear to leave little room for agency and situational specificity (see for example, Ericson and Haggerty, 1997, p 33).

Returning for a moment to Pfohl's (1978) critique of clinical assessments of dangerousness, my conclusions seem to provide an ironic twist to the story, as the replacement of the category of dangerousness by a risk-based approach, rather than providing an objective, scientific framework, has simply shifted the nature and range of possibilities for micropolitical practices.

My conclusions do not, however, deny the importance of recognising that articulating issues in terms of the language of risk brings with it a framing which is not neutral, and which may bring a range of undesirable unintended consequences. It seems to me that this capacity is not widely appreciated, so I will explore this observation in a little more detail. In her excellent study of the role of risk in probation practice, Hazel Kemshall (1998, p 294) has pointed to the dangers of:

> ... an inexorable widening of the risk net as those held accountable for risk attempt to reduce its inherent uncertainty through the use of precautionary techniques and invasive systems of information collection,

and she goes on the conclude that:

> In our attempt to 'colonise the future' through risk ... we may make that future very bleak indeed.

Is there evidence to support this warning? Well, consider the bizarre case of a Prison Service spokesman citing 'risk assessment' as justification for chaining a woman prisoner with multiple sclerosis to a hospital bed after she had suffered a stroke (*The Guardian*, 10 July 1998, p 7). This, I suggest, is an example of how things might start to go wrong. Whether this was an anomaly or an indicator of a sinister trend is clearly the key question.

Risk thinking and techniques, one might argue, have certain similarities with cost-benefit analysis which has been criticised on the grounds that it is ideological in nature, and facilitates the exercise of power (Rosenhead and Thunhurst, 1979). In North America concern about the civil liberty implications of the growth of the use of risk assessment in US Federal government have been voiced by some pressure groups (cited in Cantor, 1996). In Britain, worries in connection with the growth of risk ideas have been expressed in connection with violence against women and the safety of children. Stanko (1997) has pointed out that the threat of violence from strangers inherent in contemporary discourse about safety effectively polices women to behave in public in certain constrained ways by embodying the expectation that 'the ordinary is risky'. Similarly, talk about the threat of strangers arguably directs parents to adopt over-protective practices towards their children which, as a recent report suggested, may itself be harmful ('Lack of risk in play is damaging children', *The Guardian*, 24 June 1999, p 7).

Risk may be viewed as both a language and a set of techniques, however it is not neutral in its framing of the world, or in its associated accounts and practices. Pushing the analogy still further, it is possible to observe that, in the same way as with language, where a speaker's talk is oriented towards, but not determined by, the structures of that language, and purposeful articulation of meaning is possible by using the structures of the language as a resource (Sacks, 1992), so the discourse of risk offers resources for the pursuit of diverse agendas.

Two main conclusions finally emerge from this discussion. First, a plea for scholars not to get too carried away with theoretical accounts of risk; rather, there is a need for a much greater emphasis on empirical investigations of patterns of risk-related practical reasoning and situated practices in all areas of professional practice. Secondly, there is an urgent need for practitioners in the criminal justice sphere, and elsewhere, to develop a reflexive risk practice, which permits critical reflection on the possible unintended consequences of utilising risk techniques, and an awareness of the dangers as well as the benefits of adopting a risk-based description and analysis of the world.

Acknowledgments

This chapter draws on research supported by a number of sources, in particular, the award of a fellowship during 1998–2000 by the Economic and Social Research Council in association with the *Risk and Human Behaviour Programme* (award L211272006), and support provided by the Leverhulme Trust via the *Understanding Risk* programme. I would like to thank Nikolas Rose, Hazel Kemshall, John Copas, Tony Colombo, Richard Sparks and Mick Bloor for a number of useful conversations which helped to shape my thoughts on these matters, and the editors of this book, for their patience and helpful encouragement. My access to various arenas of risk practice would not have been possible without the co-operation of numerous professionals who have been generous with their time, and to whom I am most grateful.

PUBLIC PROTECTION, PARTNERSHIP AND RISK PENALITY: THE MULTI-AGENCY RISK MANAGEMENT OF SEXUAL AND VIOLENT OFFENDERS

Hazel Kemshall and Mike Maguire[1]

9.1 INTRODUCTION

This paper focuses on a relatively new set of measures for dealing with both sexual offenders and the much wider category of 'potentially dangerous' offenders, which is already firmly established throughout England and Wales, but which – despite the serious questions it raises about the rights of individuals, and despite its obvious relevance to broad theoretical debates about new modes of crime control and penality – has so far received surprisingly little attention from criminologists. Its key features are the setting up of formal 'public protection' or 'risk management' partnerships at a local level between police forces, probation services, social services and other agencies; the drawing up of protocols to allow the exchange of confidential information about people thought to pose a risk of harm to others; the creation of multi-agency 'public protection panels' (or similarly named bodies) to consider individual cases; the maintenance of special databases of offenders; routine classification of offenders into specific risk groups; and the development, implementation and monitoring of individual 'risk management plans'. The latter may include home visits, police surveillance or, on occasion, the controlled disclosure of information about offenders to potential victims or to interested parties such as local head teachers (as yet, despite media pressure, demands for full community notification have been resisted). In the case of sexual offenders, application may also be made to the courts for a 'Sex Offender Order' to place legal restrictions on an individual's movements (though this avenue, again, has been used only rarely to date).

These risk assessment and management procedures are directed, in the main, at people who have been convicted of serious violent or sexual offences, although they are sometimes used in relation to other types of offender and even suspected offenders who have not been convicted. At

---

1   This paper is partly based on research conducted by the authors jointly with Lesley Noaks, Karen Sharpe and Emma Wincup (with additional assistance from Rob Jago and Professor Tim Newburn) and funded by the Home Office. The authors gratefully acknowledge the contribution of all the above to the research project and to the development of ideas arising from it. However, this paper is solely the responsibility of Professors Kemshall and Maguire, and should not be assumed to represent the views of any other individual or organisation.

present the majority of cases dealt with involve sex offenders.[2] This is because, while similar procedures to deal with 'potentially dangerous offenders' (PDOs) of any kind had existed in some areas for over a decade previously, the catalyst for their countrywide expansion was the implementation of the Sex Offenders Act 1997, which imposes a requirement on most convicted sex offenders to register their address with the local police. This has been interpreted by the government to place a corresponding obligation on the police, in consultation with the probation service, to assess, and where necessary to 'manage', the risk that each registered offender poses (Power 1999; Plotnikoff and Wolfson 2000).

The empirical data used in the paper derive from a Home Office funded study of such systems, carried out in 1998–99 by the authors and others in six police force areas in England and Wales. Detailed findings of this study, which focused mainly on issues of policy and practice, can be found in the published report (Maguire *et al*, 2001).

The current paper has much broader aims. The above developments – which are broadly in tune with policy changes in several other countries – will be discussed within the framework of the growing number of claims that we are witnessing a process of fundamental change in the field of crime control. This is portrayed by some as a series of adaptations by governments and criminal justice agencies to a 'crisis of penal modernism' (Garland, 1996), brought about by the destruction of old certainties (such as faith in 'experts' and in the capacity of penal-welfare techniques to change offenders and reduce crime) which characterises the late modern period. Others detect the beginnings of a totally new 'risk penology' (Feeley and Simon, 1992; Simon and Feeley, 1995) or a fully-fledged 'post-modern penal world' (Pratt, 2000), fuelled by the insecurity inherent in the globalisation of national economies and the fragmentation of social relations, and driven inexorably by the 'logic of risk' (Ericson and Haggerty, 1997) – a world in which an all-consuming desire to eliminate threats to safety produces ever more sophisticated technologies of information-gathering, classification, surveillance, control and exclusion; in which attention shifts from the individual to the aggregate 'risk group'; and in which concepts such as individual justice, rights and accountability lose their meaning.

Clearly, the development of multi-agency public protection panels is of central relevance to these debates, as their 'core business' is risk assessment and risk management, and many of the cases they deal with involve types of behaviour which play a prominent part in contemporary fear of crime and the stoking of such fear by the media – behaviour like paedophilia, stalking and 'irrational violence'. The specific issues to which we shall direct our attention are:

---

2   The proportion varied between the areas studied, but was generally in the region of 80–90%.

(a) the extent to which the evidence from our research is consistent with the above kinds of accounts of current trends in crime control practice;

(b) the role and importance of 'partnership'; and

(c) the implications of these developments for the accountability and regulation of a system which contains potentially major threats to individual rights.

The remainder of the paper is divided into three main sections. The first provides a brief recent history of policy developments in England and Wales relating to 'dangerous offenders', including the 'dangerousness debate' of the 1970s and key legislation in the 1990s. It also fleshes out the argument of some social theorists, that the most recent changes can be understood as part of a broader shift in modes of crime control, and lists some specific features which have been identified as indicative of a new ('post-modern') penality. The second section looks for evidence of such features in the findings from our empirical research, concluding that, while some are present to some degree, the overall picture is mixed and contradictory. The third section focuses on what is perhaps the strongest evidence of the emergence of 'post-modern' social forms in this field – the relationship between the development of new ('risk driven') kinds of partnership and the dispersal of accountability. This is followed by a brief concluding section.

9.2 HISTORICAL BACKGROUND: FROM THE 'DANGEROUSNESS DEBATE' TO 'RISK PENALITY'

The issue of how to protect the public from 'dangerous' offenders is clearly not a new one, and recent developments bring to mind many echoes of the so called 'dangerousness debate' which continued among criminologists and policy-makers in Britain, as elsewhere, for much of the 1970s and early 1980s. At the same time, however, they flag up quite starkly some of the major differences between then and now in the general 'climate' of criminal justice and in the kinds of discourse which receive a serious hearing from decision-makers.

The 1970s debate in the UK was sparked off in earnest by a highly publicised homicide case involving a diagnosed psychopath, Graham Young, who had been committed to a Special Hospital after poisoning members of his family but was later released without any effective monitoring or supervision and committed further murders by a similar method. The eventual outcome was a variety of proposals for sentencing reforms, including indeterminate prison sentences (Butler Committee, 1975) and exceptionally long fixed term sentences (Floud and Young, 1981), to 'incapacitate' offenders judged to pose a risk of serious harm to the public.

However, although their architects were anxious to insist that they would be used very sparingly (for example, the Butler Committee saw its proposed 'reviewable sentence' as applying to only about 40 offenders per year, while others used names such as 'special' or 'exceptional' sentences), such proposals were resisted strongly and effectively by opponents, including civil liberties groups and leading criminologists, who saw this type of legislation as a constituting a threat to society almost as great as that of the offenders it was aimed at (see, for example, Radzinowicz and Hood, 1981). It was pointed out that the concept of 'dangerousness' is vague and subject to shifts of meaning, so that the numbers of people it is applied to can easily expand, and that laws allowing preventive detention on such grounds are potentially open to serious abuse. Some also argued that it was wrong in principle to punish people on the basis of what they might do in the future, and even those who were prepared to do so to achieve a 'greater good' were generally anxious to balance the rights of the individual and the community and to set strict limits to such punishment (Floud and Young, 1981; Bottoms and Brownsword, 1983). Others saw the unreliability of the science of prediction as a major stumbling block, regarding it as morally unacceptable to incarcerate at least two people who would not have committed another offence for every one who would have done so (the problem of the 'false positives': see Bottoms, 1977; Monahan, 1981, 1997).

However, since the early 1980s objections on the grounds of ethics and principle have had decreasing impact on legislators and policy-makers, and the number and severity of preventive measures against 'dangerous' offenders have grown rapidly. In 1983, the Home Secretary restricted parole for serious violent and sexual offenders (see Maguire, 1992) and in 1991 the Criminal Justice Act – despite its general advocacy of 'just deserts' in sentencing – allowed longer sentences for such offenders on the grounds of public protection. A highly significant step was taken in 1997 with the introduction, under the Crime (Sentences) Act, of a mandatory life sentence on a second conviction for a serious violent or sexual crime. What was remarkable about the passage of this draconian law was not so much the absence of political opposition ('toughness' on law and order being a key stance of both major parties in the imminent election campaign), but the relatively small amount of argument it engendered in other influential circles, including among academics. The contrast with the 1970s 'dangerousness debate', in which philosophers and criminologists played a prominent part in protracted discussions of principle which eventually persuaded the government not to introduce new legislation, is striking. It remains to be seen whether there will be a similarly muted response to new legislation which is currently under consideration to allow the possibility of long-term incarceration of potentially dangerous 'psychopaths', even if they have not been found guilty of a criminal offence (Home Office, 1999).

In parallel with these moves towards longer or indeterminate prison terms for dangerous offenders, increasing attention has been paid to ways of monitoring and controlling their behaviour in the community – most commonly, to extend the incapacitative effect of imprisonment by lengthy (and, if considered necessary, indefinite) periods of surveillance after release. Two key elements in this have been the development of multi-agency co-operation and the rise to centre stage of the practice of 'risk assessment'. Inter-agency co-operation in this field dates back in some areas for over ten years. Much of the early impetus came from the probation service, to some extent in response to sustained government attacks during the 1980s on its 'social work' ideology and its alleged lack of effectiveness in reducing re-offending. In their search for new ways of demonstrating the value and effectiveness of the service, local probation managers began to seek improvements in methods of identifying and supervising offenders who might pose a serious threat of harm. Formal risk assessment began to become standard practice, both in the preparation of pre-sentence reports and in advance of the supervision of prisoners released on licence. Probation services also began to engage in much closer liaison and information-sharing, initially with prisons, but increasingly with the police and social services.

A small number of probation services then moved to place this co-operation on a firmer footing by brokering the establishment of formally constituted public protection panels, which met at intervals to exchange information, assess the level of risk and formulate plans in relation to offenders identified as potentially dangerous ('PDOs'). The number of such panels grew during the mid-1990s as other areas followed their lead. They also expanded in size and scope, most coming to include representatives at fairly senior level from probation, police, social services, housing departments and health authorities, and some including a variety of other agencies, including voluntary groups. While initially the main focus was upon offenders leaving prison under statutory probation licence, many panels also began to consider cases – which might be brought forward by any of the partner agencies – of individuals who were considered dangerous but were under no statutory control. Again, although convicted violent and sexual offenders have always remained the most frequent object of their attentions, the panels have also come to discuss potentially dangerous offenders of many kinds, including on occasion, suspected offenders who have never been convicted.

However, while these kinds of arrangements would probably have continued to expand gradually as probation services copied each other and the Home Office offered encouragement, the catalyst for their sudden growth in the late 1990s was the rapid increase in attention – on a worldwide scale – to the problem of sexual abuse of children. This has included concerns about intra-familial abuse and abuse in children's homes, as well as claims of organised abuse by networks or 'rings' of 'paedophiles'. Responses have been strongly influenced by the image of paedophiles – to some extent supported by research – as recidivist offenders who are stubbornly resistant to attempts to reform them, and who in some cases move around the country seeking new opportunities to 'groom' children for sexual abuse (Hughes *et al*, 1996; Hebenton and Thomas, 1997, p 22; Grubin, 1998). This has led to much less emphasis being placed upon 'treatment' than upon a search for effective ways of monitoring and controlling their movements. For example, 'tracking' systems, entailing requirements for sex offenders to register with the local police, spread rapidly in the USA in the mid-1990s (Hebenton and Thomas, 1996, 1997). Another important consequence has been the growth of official disclosure of information about sex offenders (and particularly offenders against children) to local schools, neighbours and even the whole community. Indeed, community notification is now mandatory in the USA under the federal 'Megan's Law' (1996) in cases where it is adjudged 'necessary and relevant for public protection' (Hebenton and Thomas, 1997, pp 7, 24–32) and at least 16 states routinely list sex offenders' details on the internet.

In Britain, in the wake of considerable media attention to the risk posed by 'predatory paedophiles' (focused around the release from prison of some major offenders), the government partly followed the American lead by introducing the Sex Offenders Act 1997. Under Part 1 of this Act, people convicted of most forms of sexual offence are obliged to register their address with the local police within 14 days of caution or conviction and within 14 days of moving into a new home. This obligation continues for a period ranging from five years to life, depending on the offence and sentence length (Cobley, 1999; Power, 1999; Plotnikoff and Wolfson, 2000). While this is clear enough, the Act gives no firm guidance to police forces on what they can or should do with the information collected, nor does it deal with the difficult and controversial issue of disclosure. The general understanding, based mainly on subsequent communications from the Home Office (especially Circular 39/97), has been that:

> ... in consultation with the local probation service, police forces should undertake a formal risk assessment of every offender who registers;
>
> where the level of risk is considered high enough to warrant it, a plan should be drawn up to 'manage' the risk, where appropriate sharing information and tasks with other agencies; and
>
> decisions on whether to notify other organisations, private individuals, or the whole community, should be made by the police on a case-by-case basis, taking into account their common law duty to prevent crime, as well as data protection law and relevant Articles of the European Convention on Human Rights.

These procedures apply only to sex offenders (rather than to 'potentially dangerous' offenders as a whole) and primary responsibility for their implementation falls upon the police (rather than the probation service), but the basic approach is clearly very similar to that developed earlier through the public protection panels. For this reason, most areas responded to the Sex Offenders Act by either wholly or partially integrating the two sets of procedures into a general multi-agency system of risk assessment and management. The fact that one set was based on legislation and one not, does not seem to have hindered this process of integration. Many areas systematically 'risk assess' any people who come to their notice as potentially dangerous offenders, and maintain shared databases of 'PDOs', akin to those held on officially registered sex offenders. In fact, the government has recently (September 2000) announced plans to place statutory obligations on both police and probation services to undertake risk assessments of violent as well as sex offenders – a move which will greatly extend and accelerate the integration process.

The specific issue of community notification was thrown into sharp relief by a series of events in the summer of 2000. A Sunday newspaper obtained and published the names and addresses of large numbers of known and suspected 'paedophiles'. With public feelings inflamed after the murder of a young child, Sarah Payne, this triggered a spate of vigilante attacks and a campaign for full public access to the sex offender register: a 'Sarah's Law' to match the American 'Megan's Law'. The government resisted these calls, arguing (in accordance with the views of most practitioners) that such a course of action would lead to offenders being 'driven underground', thus increasing rather than decreasing the risk to the public. Instead, it announced that general information would be made available about the numbers of sex offenders in a particular area and about the measures in place to protect the community. At the same time, the risk management of registered offenders would be tightened by creating new legislative powers for the police to enter their homes without a warrant, as well as through stricter rules on notifying their movements (*The Times*, 3 September 2000). Whether this will be sufficient to curb the intensity of the campaign for full notification remains to be seen.

9.3 A POST-MODERN PENALITY?

Before looking more closely at particular features of the new public protection systems, it is necessary to say a little more about the kinds of contemporary social theory which seem most obviously relevant to an understanding of why they have developed – namely, those postulating the centrality of risk as an organising principle of social life, as the developed world undergoes a transition from 'modernity' to 'late modernity' or, according to some writers, 'post-modernity'. We are neither competent nor inclined to venture into current debates about the precise nature of the post-modern condition or about what properly constitutes post-modern theory, which Kellner (1999, p 639) aptly describes as an intense 'firestorm of controversy'. For our purposes, it is sufficient to draw attention to some of the basic and generally agreed elements of this way of interpreting social change, and then to focus on the ideas which have been most prominent in criminologists' applications of such theories to the realm of crime control and penality.

In broad terms, many sociologists argue that the developed world has entered a period of late capitalism, characterised by processes of both globalisation and localisation, in which the stability and continuity of traditional cultural and social forms (including Nation States, families and secure forms of employment) are undermined, and the universal claims to knowledge, reason and progress produced in earlier phases of modernity are no longer uncritically accepted (Leonard, 1997). At its most extreme, this is characterised as a radical transformation of society and culture, representing a 'fundamental rupture with the modern era' (Kellner, 1999, p 641). Others see it as a much more gradual, complex and unclear process, viewing the present period – which they often describe as 'late modern' rather than post-modern – as essentially transitional. Either way, a common theme is the peculiarly uncertain and reflexive nature of the current social condition, with many inquiries directed at 'life under conditions of uncertainty' (Parton, 1994) or at the centrality of risk and insecurity to many forms of discourse. This is most famously encapsulated in Ulrich Beck's (1992) coined phrase, 'the risk society', but has also been prominent in the work of writers such as Giddens (1990) and Douglas (1992). Another major theme is the emergence of new forms of governance and control. For example, Rose (1996, 2000), who uses the term 'advanced liberal' to describe the nature of late modern societies, argues that one of their central features is a shift from direct state power to a more subtle and dispersed 'government at-a-distance'. This means that disciplinary social forms give way to a high degree of individual freedom, and hence that the 'responsibilisation' of individual citizens (getting them to take full responsibility for their own actions and to engage constantly in self-regulation) becomes a core project. This involves processes of both inclusion and exclusion: a continual patrolling of social boundaries to determine which kinds of people are deemed competent to participate in this kind of society and which are not.

For criminologists, the above perspectives raise important questions about the social construction of 'crime' and 'criminality', and in particular the understanding and explanation of current developments in crime control and penal policy. Over the past few years, a growing number of writers have drawn attention to features which appear consistent with sociologists' accounts of transformations in other fields, and a debate has developed around the core question of whether we are really witnessing, or about to witness, a 'fundamental rupture' between modern and a new post-modern penality. We end this section by briefly outlining some of the specific developments which have been identified as harbingers of this 'new penality' – or, to use Pratt's (2000, p 127) phrase, 'pointers to the emergence of a postmodern penal world'.

Two linked claims, in particular, tend to dominate the literature. The first is that there has been what Garland (1995, p 193) refers to as a 'collapse of the grand narrative of penal reform and penal progress': in more concrete terms, widespread acknowledgement of a fundamental failure of the modernist criminal justice and penal (or 'penal-welfare') system to deliver its implicit promises – repeated over a period of nearly 200 years – of transforming offenders and reducing crime. This, it is claimed, has entailed a major loss of faith in penal experts (in particular, their capacity to 'change' offenders) and has opened the door to an essentially pessimistic new mode of penality.

The second claim is that this new penality (usually referred to as 'late modern' or 'post-modern', though the distinction is by no means always made clear) is characterised by a major shift from a disciplinary focus upon individual behaviour and the possibility of change, towards the management of risk distribution – what Reichman (1986, p 153) has called 'an insurance concept of crime control' (see also Simon, 1988). A particular manifestation of this is the spread of 'actuarialism' (the mathematical calculation of levels of risk) and a consequent focus upon aggregate risk groups rather than individuals – a trend accorded major significance by several commentators, most notably Feeley and Simon (1992, 1994). Systematic risk management strategies are evident in various guises in many currently popular crime control approaches in the UK, including profiling, targeted policing and incapacitative sentencing. As documented by Kemshall (1998), the concept of risk has also assumed a growing centrality in probation practice, traditionally an area with a strong individual 'welfare' focus. Maguire (2000, p 316) has likewise identified several examples of a shift in policing practice from the 'reactive investigation of individual crimes' to a 'strategic, future-oriented and targeted approach to crime control'. A basic aim of all these approaches is the management of crime opportunities. They are partly driven by new technologies and the possibilities these provide, but more importantly, it has been argued, they reflect wider changes in patterns of social regulation. As Pratt (1995) expresses it, there is a marked shift away from traditional disciplinary practices to an 'informative' system, in which the production and exchange of risk knowledge becomes the key mechanism by which some groups control others. This position has since been reinforced by Ericson and Haggerty's (1997) powerful thesis on the role of the police as 'communicators of risk knowledge' – servants to a mushrooming public and private security network, driven by the 'logic of risk', in which their main task has become a constant process of reappraisal, refinement and exchange of information for the use of other agencies.

Within this general framework, a variety of trends have been identified as indicative features or manifestations of this 'new penality'. Many of these can be directly linked to the claimed pervasiveness of the 'risk climate' (Giddens, 1990) and of the sense of insecurity which underpins it. The following list is by no means exhaustive, but gives a fair flavour of the range:

1   The foregrounding of dangerousness and public protection, and the prominence of these concepts in social regulation and social exclusion at many levels.

2   Increased willingness to contemplate lengthy preventive detention or stringent 'control in the community' for people who have not yet committed serious offences but are nevertheless defined as a risk.

3   The replacement of professional clinical diagnosis and assessment by formalised, actuarial risk tools, encouraging more 'automatic' decision-making (rather than individualised judgment) about the disposal of those subject to assessment.

4   A shift away from reliance on the formal criminal justice and penal systems towards more use of informal and regulatory mechanisms (though, as several writers have pointed out, this has not meant a decrease in the use of imprisonment – on the contrary, the use of both penal and regulatory modes of control has expanded greatly: see, for example, Christie, 1994; Garland, 1995).

5   The extension of criminal powers into previously non-criminalised areas on the grounds of public safety and protection, and a blurring of previously clear distinctions between 'criminal' and 'anti-social' behaviour (as, for example, in the introduction of Anti-Social Behaviour Orders – see Ashworth *et al*, 1998; Maguire, 1998).

6   A relative lack of priority and importance attached to the rights of individuals.

7   Ever-increasing importance placed on the development and use of technology (and surveillance technology in particular) as a tool of control.

8   Despite the apparent rise of 'cold' and 'rational' actuarial methods of determining risk and hence of actions against those assessed, a parallel rise in the value attached to the expressive function of penality and an increased role for the public and media in determining both individual

punishments and penal policy. This has been dubbed by Bottoms (1995) a growth in 'populist punitiveness', a trend accompanied by a corresponding decline in the importance and respect accorded to the role of the penal expert.

9 A general focus on 'signs and symbols' (Garland, 1995) rather than on substance. This is manifested in superficiality, 'short-termism' and sudden swings in penal policy, often without serious consideration of principle or of longer term implications; a taste for fashion and 'flavour of the month' approaches; and 'knee jerk' reactions to individual events and media campaigns.

10 Increasing involvement of non-state agencies and institutions – both private and voluntary – in key areas of crime control and criminal justice.

11 A rise in 'managerialism', with ever-increasing attachment to organisational targets, audits, performance indicators, and so on. This is sometimes associated with the notions of 'reflexivity' and of 'autopoetic' (or 'self-referential') crime control systems: the irony that, as 'modern' organisations improve their knowledge, they become more aware of their own failings (in this case, to control crime effectively), and hence tend to retreat into a narrow focus on process outputs and systems management, rather than examine their effectiveness in the broader terms of 'final outcomes' (Simon, 1993). It is also associated with new, dispersed forms of accountability (Kemshall, 1998).

Recognisable as many of these trends are to anyone who has recently studied or worked in the crime control 'business', the question remains whether they really are indicators of some radically new form of penality, or whether they represent simply a new shift of emphasis, albeit a significant one, within the long-existing 'modernist project'. Garland (1995) argues, for example, that the focus on actuarial risk represents a continuance of, rather than a break from, existing penal forms. Certainly, the use of mathematical calculations of risk has been with us for some time, with its roots in the marine insurance and slave trade of the 17th century, fuelled by the explosion of statistical technologies to assess and predict risk at the close of the 19th. The 'taming of chance' (Hacking, 1991) continued throughout the 20th century with probability accorded an important place in key disciplines of control such as psychology, psychiatry, social work and criminology (Rose 1996) – although, as Pratt (1995) has pointed out, policy desires to predict risk accurately have often outstripped the technologies available to deliver them.

Developments such as 'managerialism', targeting and strategic approaches can also be discerned in other arenas, not least in the organisation and delivery of state welfare during the 'Thatcher years' and as such have at least some of their roots in neo-conservatism (Clarke and Langan, 1993). Knowledge production and exchange was also a significant site of power and control for much of the 20th century, not least in the 'psy' disciplines of the benevolent welfare state (Foucault, 1971; Rose, 1996). Again, the rise of 'populist punitiveness', including the apparent re-emergence in some developed countries of 'pre-modern' forms of punishment (involving physical harshness, public involvement, and so on), is by no means necessarily a sign of a new form of penality. While Pratt (2000) sees it in this way, Garland (1995) argues that such punitiveness is simply an 'archaic symbol of sovereignty' which has raised its head many times during the modernist period in opposition to the dominant penal narratives. 'All that has changed,' he writes, 'is the balance of power in the struggle to define what punishment should mean.'

Finally, the general question has to be asked – though we say no more about it here – whether this very diverse set of developments can convincingly be portrayed as part of one definite movement in a particular direction, or whether current developments are better seen as forming an unclear and 'messy' picture, exhibiting a number of trends in different directions. To be fair, Pratt is careful to state that the shift to a 'post-modern penality' he discerns may be evolutionary rather than radical in nature, and that 'its exact contours are still somewhat vague and ill defined': evidence of discontinuity and defining characteristics will therefore be restricted during this period of transition. As he puts it, 'We have not yet seen a completed historical change' (Pratt, 2000, p 140). However, he does maintain that:

> New initiatives appearing on the scene are likely to have the penality of postmodernity as their referent ... and it is likely that we shall see more and more initiatives being introduced and tested as it were, as the boundaries of penal possibilities come to be redrawn [p 141].

Most of the debates that have so far taken place within criminology on this important topic have been pitched at a high level of generality. Rather less attention has been paid to the quality of the evidence used to support the various claims, and relatively little empirical research has been utilised systematically to query them. Most writers have discussed the main features of penal discourse and practice which one would expect to see emerging as part of a major shift in penality, drawing on brief accounts of selected developments from around the world as illustrative examples or counter-examples. Thus, for example, Pratt (2000) gives diverse examples of offenders being publicly shamed which he sees as indicative of a general revival of pre-modern modes of penality. He characterises this as 'the return of the wheelbarrow men' – a reference to an 18th century practice in Philadelphia in which convicts were made to wear distinctive uniforms and undertake humiliating street cleaning tasks. However, while we agree that exploration of major questions about the nature of penality ultimately requires a broad brush approach, and that imaginative insights of the above kind are of great value, we would argue that a useful light can also be thrown upon them through empirical research on particular areas of penal practice. As Garland (1995, p 30) notes, such transformations should be visible in the 'material forms' of penality as well as in its 'objectives and orientation'. Valuable contributions have recently been made in this direction by Mona Lynch (1998, 2000) in her detailed analyses of changes in parole practice in California, and it is hoped that our own research may also provide some insights in a similar way.

Drawing upon our detailed study of local practice, then, let us now consider to what extent recent developments in the multi-agency risk assessment and management of sexual and dangerous offenders in England and Wales can be said to take postmodern penality as a 'referent', whether in terms of expressed 'objectives and orientations' or in terms of 'material forms'. In particular, we shall ask whether any of the key features we have listed above can be discerned in the day-to-day functioning of public protection panels and their members.

9.4 MULTI-AGENCY RISK MANAGEMENT: PERTINENT FINDINGS

The fieldwork for our study was carried out in six police force areas, varying widely in size and character. Altogether, 117 interviews were carried out with police and probation officers, and a further 30 with a variety of staff from other agencies, including social workers, prison officers, psychiatrists, health officials and housing officers, and ranging from very senior managers to 'front line' staff. The interviews covered their views and experiences in respect of risk assessment, the operation of the sex offender register, the operation and effectiveness of panels, and the nature and effectiveness of multi-agency working. The research team also observed panel meetings and training, analysed agency records and collected a large amount of documentary material, both local and national.

The research took place in an environment which was changing very rapidly. Virtually every area visited was in the process either of introducing new policies and practices or of reviewing its procedures. This included changes in the structures of multi-agency bodies, in joint protocols, in training, and in the use of risk assessment instruments. For this reason, we set out not so much to compare or evaluate the work of individual areas, as to look at the range of practices to be found. We also took note of the directions in which changes in policy and practice were generally moving, and practitioners were questioned about changes they wished or expected to see.

The findings we focus upon in this paper are those which bear most directly on debates about the advent of new forms of penality, as outlined in the previous section. They will be couched in summary form, rather than presented in detail (for more detail and findings on other aspects of the procedures, see Maguire *et al*, 2001).[3]

The first general comment to be made is that many features of the basic edifice of multi-agency public protection arrangements which we observed – the use of risk assessment instruments, the classification into risk groups, the formulation of risk management plans, the availability of technical surveillance, and so on – would be immediately familiar to any casual reader of the 'new penology' literature, suggesting that we are dealing with a prime example of 'risk penality' in action. The stated aims of the system, the language used in official documents and meetings, and the names of the panels themselves, all reflected an overriding concern with issues of risk, control and exclusion, while references to transformative aims such as 'rehabilitation' or 'resettlement' were rarely heard, even among probation officers.

However, on closer inspection, by no means every aspect of the system as operated in practice fitted so neatly into the 'new penality' mould. We organise our remaining comments under six headings.

1 Actuarialism or professional judgment?

As discussed earlier, a frequently mentioned element of the apparent shift to risk penality is the increasing replacement of professional judgment by reliance on actuarial instruments for assessing levels of risk. Certainly, we found a general trend in this direction, as well as a desire for more

---

3 The main policy-related findings other than those discussed in this paper were:

(i) The risk assessment and management systems in operation were highly diverse in structure and variable in quality. Some were largely police-led, others probation-led, and the involvement of other agencies (especially health) was patchy. The fora for inter-agency discussions ranged from regular panels to ad hoc meetings, covered offenders of different levels of risk, and involved staff of varying seniority.

(ii) While the work in some areas was actively overseen by management committees with senior representatives from several agencies, in others there was little overall direction and policies were left in the hands of a few individuals. The quality of chairing, minute-taking and case monitoring and review also varied widely.

(iii) All areas suffered from resourcing problems (not least managers' time), which were increasing as the numbers of registered sex offenders rose. While high risk offenders generally received close attention, difficulties were sometimes experienced in sustaining effective risk management of low and medium risk offenders. Panels in some areas were also 'swamped' on occasion with too many cases, allowing insufficient time for proper consideration of all of them. The main recommendations put forward were for the promotion of more standardisation and consistency; better resourcing (including pooling of agency resources to provide dedicated panel coordinators); and more attention to the managerial oversight, monitoring and accountability of public protection systems.

standardisation of practice between areas and agencies. In particular, there was growing use of a shortened version of the Structured Anchored Clinical Judgement (SACJ), a prediction tool which assesses the level of risk that a sex offender will commit another sexual offence (see Kemshall, 2000; Hanson and Thornton, 2000).[4] This is a simple instrument, quick to administer, and requires only data which is readily available in most cases – features which were found, unsurprisingly, to be very attractive to busy police officers. The scores obtained are used to place each offender into one of three risk categories – 'low', 'medium' or 'high' risk.

However, it is important to note that use of the SACJ did not imply slavish acceptance of the outcomes. On the contrary, we found that the eventual categorisation depended on a great deal more than a mechanical scoring process.

First of all, most panels used the results of instruments such as the SACJ only as a screening tool or as a starting-point for discussion, seeing it as a core part of the panel's task to arrive at its own 'expert' classification of risk, based on consideration of all the information available. There were often long debates about individual cases, and in many cases offenders were personally known to probation officers or others on the panel. Indeed, it was quite common practice to invite to panel meetings, on a one-off basis, probation officers or others responsible for particular cases, specifically in order to gain a 'better picture' of the person being considered.

The character of the risk assessment debates, too, was often anything but 'scientific' or 'technology-driven'. On the contrary, researchers noted that many discussions were unstructured, even rambling, and that close attention was paid to the views and 'instincts' of members who knew the offender in question, even if unsupported by hard evidence. It was not unusual for panels to revise instrument-derived risk classifications, in essence backing their ability – through a combination of 'gut feelings' and professional experience – to make a better prediction than one based purely upon actuarial risk.

The above observations do not fit well with the picture (associated particularly with the work of Feeley and Simon) of a form of penality in which expert judgment is replaced by actuarial decision-making, and attention is directed at risk factors and aggregate groups rather than at

---

4   This instrument was developed by David Thornton of the Home Office. In its full form, it takes account of both static factors (a current or past conviction for a sexual or violent offence, and four or more previous convictions of any kind) and a variety of dynamic factors (including substance abuse, psychopathy and deviant sexual arousal), in order to allow for changes in risk status over time. The shortened version, officially named SACJ-MIN, omits most of the dynamic factors, as information on these is often unavailable or unreliable. Most forces employed a further recommended modification of the SACJ, producing an assessment of the degree of harm which an offender was likely to cause, should he or she reoffend, in addition to an assessment of the likelihood of reconviction *per se*.

knowledge of the individual. Clearly, human judgment and a degree of interest in individual motivation (albeit to inform control strategies rather than 'disciplinary' or 'transformative' interventions) remain alive and well.

Even so, it should be emphasised that actuarial risk assessment instruments do play an important (and expanding) role as an initial filtering mechanism. Although some areas continued to consider all sex offender cases at full panel meetings, pressure of numbers had caused others to discuss only those cases classified by the SACJ at a high level of risk. Indeed, this is likely to become the norm as numbers rise further. In these circumstances, the preliminary assessment process is clearly critical to the effectiveness of the system, and can have major consequences for whether and how offenders are eventually 'risk managed'. Even so, we found only one area which had recognised the importance of expert oversight at the initial assessment stage, and had placed a senior and experienced person in charge of this process. The latter was able both to 'filter out' cases classified as 'high risk' by the SACJ which he felt did not merit the label, or to 'filter in' cases in which there were special circumstances to which actuarial instruments were not sensitive. Elsewhere, the application of the SACJ tended to be delegated to junior staff with very little training, so the scope for the use of expert judgment to 'overrule' the actuarially-derived result was minimal.

An interesting variation on this theme was found in one area where high level public protection panels were set up only on ad hoc basis, to deal with individual cases referred by police or probation officers as posing a high risk to the public. In this area there was no standard method of initial assessment, the routine work of classification of registered sex offenders being left to the judgment of local detective inspectors (DIs) in consultation with the probation service. The SACJ was not used at all. This was found to produce considerable inconsistency, in that some DIs rarely categorised anyone at all as 'high risk', whereas others placed quite high proportions into this category and requested panel meetings much more frequently. From interviews with DIs about how they undertook their initial risk assessments, it became clear that they were influenced by a variety of factors beyond consideration of standard 'risk factors'. Some admitted to being 'pulled in two directions' in borderline cases. On the one hand, as a 'high risk' classification usually led to a significant commitment of local resources (in terms of surveillance, visits, etc – see below), it was tempting for those whose resources were already overstretched to plump for a lower categorisation. On the other hand, they felt that they were unfairly 'exposed', in that if someone they had failed (rightly or wrongly) to categorise as high risk committed a serious offence, it was they who were likely to be blamed: this might therefore cause them to 'play safe' and record a higher risk classification than they felt appropriate. DIs in this area were hence very receptive to a management plan to introduce routine use of the

SACJ, which they saw as relieving them of the burden of responsibility for these difficult decisions. The consequence of this, of course, would be a swing from a system vulnerable to individual vagaries and practical exigencies, to one over-reliant on the mechanical application of an actuarial instrument.

In summary, the research findings indicate that what is happening in terms of risk assessment is not simply a direct replacement of expert judgment by actuarial judgment, but new combinations and interactions between the two. It is also important not to underestimate the influence, at ground level, of both agency cultures and practical concerns and contingencies.

2 The consequences of risk classifications

A second set of empirical questions arise around the issue of 'risk management'. Most relevant for our discussion, to what extent are interventions by public protection panels into the lives of offenders actually 'risk driven'? More specifically – as one might expect under conditions of a fully-blown 'risk penality' – does the risk category to which an offender is assigned determine the level and nature of any intervention?

The broad answer is that there was a general expectation that partner agencies (and the police, in particular) would pay closer attention, and devote more resources, to 'high' risk than to 'medium' or 'low' risk offenders, although this did not follow in every case. It was also said by local DIs, who usually took a major share of the responsibility for police actions, that any case with a 'high risk' label would involve them in a considerable amount of work and would have resource implications. Some areas, indeed, specified a minimum level of intervention for each risk category, although this was usually limited to guidelines on the frequency of home visits or of formal reviews of the case.

At the same time, however, risk management activity in all cases tended to be at its greatest in the first few days or weeks after offenders arrived in an area, so at any one point of time there could be major variations in the amount of time and resources allocated to different cases, whatever their categorisation. More importantly, it was clear that actions tended to be very much tailored to the individual: a small number were felt to merit temporary covert surveillance or the systematic use of informants, others regular visits from police officers, others simply a general bulletin to patrol officers to 'keep an eye out', and so on. In summary, while the majority of the more intensive kinds of intervention were reserved for cases in the high risk category, there was significant individual variation within that category (and within the medium and low risk categories).

Another factor in the equation – reminiscent of the dilemma of local DIs, described above – is the problem of what might be called 'inflation of the currency of risk classification', combined with limitations on resources. As more and more people are categorised as 'high risk' (both because the overall number of registered sex offenders – who remain registered for many years – is mounting, and because of greater use of standard instruments rather than practitioner judgment),[5] even the senior agency managers who sit on high level public protection panels find it difficult to access all the resources they would wish for every such case. A consequence of this, we noted, was the creation in some areas of an informal category of 'exceptionally high risk' or 'highly dangerous' offenders, to whom very close attention was paid, while the remainder of the officially 'high risk' category were dealt with in more 'routine' fashion.

In summary, then, we are certainly not describing a mechanical system in which the risk classification determined the response. Indeed, in some cases it might even be argued that the anticipated response (which was limited by the resources available) helped to determine the risk categorisation. Moreover, 'risk management plans' for both high and medium risk offenders varied widely, depending upon individual circumstances. The one area in which actuarial risk assessment could be said to determine the response was in the case of offenders designated 'low risk'. Such cases were rarely looked at closely by panel members or other senior staff, and any actions taken tended to be routine: for example, visits or cursory panel reviews at long intervals.

3 Practitioner cultures and beliefs

It is important to emphasise that some of the core elements of the public protection system we have described are alien to the traditions and cultures of both its main partner agencies, the police and the probation services. The probation service (together with similar organisations in other countries) was perhaps the key agency in the so called 'modernist project' of understanding and reforming individual offenders, and the new approaches, which are built on more impersonal risk assessment and control strategies and in which there is an underlying assumption that most of the offenders dealt with cannot be 'changed', do not fit easily with its traditional working practices. Equally, despite periodic rhetoric about the importance of crime prevention, the basic police approach to crime control in most western democracies has been essentially reactive rather than proactive in character – that is, much more time has been spent in investigating past offences than in

---

5   It is estimated that around a quarter of all sex offenders to whom the SACJ is applied emerge with a 'high risk' rating. Police officers using only broad checklists of risk factors generally classified much smaller proportions than this as high risk.

anticipating and preventing future offences. Hence, the idea of systematically monitoring the movements of considerable numbers of individuals on a list, many of whom (despite their designation as 'risks') are not thought to be currently committing offences, is not one that fits easily with traditional working practices, particularly those of detectives. As Simon (1993, in relation to probation) and Ericson and Haggerty (1997, in relation to the police) have indicated, both types of organisation worldwide are experiencing rapid change, and in the UK, as elsewhere, managerial discourse and public statements of aims are often couched in terms consistent with the 'new penology'. However, empirical research by other writers such as Lemert (1993) and Lynch (1998, 2000) on probation and parole officers in the USA, and Maguire and John (1995) on detectives in England and Wales, has suggested that at 'ground level' there is a strong cultural resistance to these kinds of ideas and practices: so strong, indeed, that Lynch declares herself not certain who is eventually going to 'win the battle'.

In our own research, too, it was clear that organisational factors and cultural traditions played a big part in determining the character of public protection work in practice. For example, as already discussed, panels were loath to rely on actuarial assessment instruments and continued to view offenders as individuals. Another somewhat surprising finding was that within the police there was by no means strong agreement that public protection work should be regarded as a major priority. In most of the areas studied, police divisions had considerable autonomy in managing their budgets, and such work had to compete locally for limited resources against a plethora of other demands. The arrival in the area of an exceptionally and indisputably dangerous offender was always treated very seriously. On the other hand, while there were notable exceptions, it was clear from interviews that local commanders and senior detectives tended to regard more 'routine' public protection work (and particularly sex offender register work) as having lower priority in the competition for resources than initiatives against crimes such as burglary. A senior CID officer also noted that the systematic 'monitoring' of substantial numbers of potential offenders was still an unfamiliar form of work for police officers, and was regarded by some as a set of relatively unproductive administrative tasks rather than 'real police work'. It should be noted that these kinds of 'cultural resistance' to elements of the 'new penality' were not confined, in the case of the police, to the lower ranks, but were fairly widespread in the middle and senior ranks too.

On the other hand, there were clearly some elements of the 'new penality' which had penetrated quite deeply into the probation service, particularly among managers. While there were many local variations, the overall impression obtained from interviews and observation was that probation managers tended to accept the account of sex offenders as 'unlikely to change' and hence to focus firmly on the issue of control rather than on the possibilities of rehabilitation. Consistent with this view, they were content to pass on virtually any kind of information about individuals to the police and, in the case of prisoners released on licence, to recommend return to prison for even minor breaches of conditions or signs of 'risky' behaviour. In fact, relationships between police and probation services were in most areas extremely close and co-operative, and there were few hints of ideological disagreements at meetings. At least in this area of work, it might be argued that the probation service is undergoing a process which might be called (inelegantly) something like 'policification'. A similar convergence between police and parole officers' views of offenders in general has been noted in California by Lynch (1998), though in the case she describes, neither group's view is fully consistent with the 'new penality' paradigm: both tend to attribute volition to offenders, and hence the possibility of change through deterrence or other 'disciplinary' mechanisms.

Finally, returning to the culture of the police themselves – and following up on this last point – it was clear that many ordinary police officers had little faith in the idea that simply 'monitoring' sex offenders was sufficient to stop them re-offending. Not surprisingly, they also had little confidence in rehabilitative strategies. Instead, they tended to favour a conscious strategy of deterrence, based on conspicuous visits to offenders' homes which conveyed the unequivocal message that 'we are watching you': in other words, using the archetypal 'new penology' tool of surveillance to achieve an archetypically 'modernist' form of crime control.

4 Populist punitiveness, or leave it to the experts?

As outlined earlier, writers such as Pratt (2000) have argued that a strong sign of the collapse of the 'modernist project' and the advent of a new kind of penality is, somewhat ironically, the re-emergence of 'pre-modern' elements in ways of dealing with offenders. Key features of these include harsh punishment, and the direct involvement of the public rather than 'leaving it to penal experts'. In fact, the public protection systems we examined exhibited few if any such signs. On the contrary, they were run entirely by 'experts' and stringent efforts were made to maintain a low public profile for their activities. Quite unlike the situation in the USA, disclosure of the names or addresses of sexual or otherwise dangerous offenders even to other agencies outside the panels was unusual, and general disclosure to the public (in the manner of 'Megan's Law' notifications in the USA) was virtually unheard of. The press, too, was generally seen as a threat, and the leaking of information to journalists regarded as unacceptable behaviour. Another interesting issue was that certain local councillors tried to pressurise local authority staff who had attended risk management meetings (for example as housing department representatives) to reveal details of offenders to them, on the grounds that they were their 'employers' – their intention being to pass the information to the local press. Again, this type of incident was treated very seriously by panels, legal advice being taken and high level discussions held in order to prevent such disclosure.

This jealous guarding of secrecy might be interpreted as indicating concern for the rights of offenders, but the pragmatic reason is simply that disclosure is thought likely to result in them being 'hounded out' of their homes. This, in turn, may lead to offenders 'going underground' and hence becoming more difficult to monitor and control. There was also general distaste among panel members for the kinds of mob scene which had followed notorious paedophiles such as Sidney Cooke around the country after their release. At the time of the research, then, the advance of 'populist punitiveness' seemed largely to have been kept at bay from this particular 'expert-controlled' corner of the penal realm in the UK. However, subsequent events – in particular, the 'naming and shaming' by the *News of The World* of large numbers of convicted sex offenders, which resulted in a series of vigilante attacks on their homes,[6] together with a campaign for community notification which has already achieved some concessions from the government in this direction – have shown that this was a premature conclusion.

5 Managerialism and self-reference

As noted earlier, another set of characteristics that have frequently been associated with the concept of late (or post) modern penality revolve around a retreat into process rather than outcome, and a tendency towards organisational 'self-reference' rather than a focus on wider goals such as crime reduction. We found some evidence of this, especially in the general tendency of partnerships and panels to put more time, effort and resources into processes of risk assessment than into actions to actually manage the risks. Some panels, in fact, had begun by conscientiously considering every registered sex offender case coming to notice in their area (as well as many other 'PDO' cases). In the early months of the implementation of the Sex Offenders Act, this was a feasible task, but as time went on, the numbers grew to the extent that several senior members of local agencies were spending at least a whole day each month in systematically categorising large numbers of offenders into risk groups, despite the fact that, in reality, the limited resources available meant that little follow up action would be

---

6   There were also several cases of attacks on the basis of false rumour and mistaken identity, including one on the home of a female paediatrician.

undertaken in a considerable proportion of cases – and certainly not enough to justify the lengthy discussions over the issue of classification.

At the same time, 'managerialism' in the sense of a major focus on activity monitoring, performance indicators, audits, and so on, was not evident in many areas, perhaps because it had not yet had time to develop, though more likely because it develops less easily in a multi-agency context, where lines of accountability are more blurred (see later).

6 Other relevant findings

Finally, some brief miscellaneous points can be made in relation to others of the indicators of a 'new penality' listed earlier.

1 There was little evidence of a growing use and development of sophisticated technology in the system, either in the risk assessment or the risk management tasks. Assessment instruments were fairly crude in character and there was little computer analysis of databases. Equally, it was rare for the police to employ sophisticated 'bugging' or other electronic devices against sex offenders: in most cases, indeed, 'risk management' had something of an 'old-fashioned' feel about it, relying mainly on visits and conversations with offenders and people who knew them.

2 There was little evidence of the dispersal of state powers and responsibilities to private or voluntary agencies. This is clearly an area of crime control in which statutory agencies are continuing to maintain tight control of the agenda and of operational matters. (This is not to deny the important trend of dispersal of responsibility and accountability from the centre to the local and from single state agencies to partnerships of state agencies – which will be discussed in our final section.)

3 The notion of offenders' rights took low priority in the thinking of panel members: concern was rarely expressed about possible violations of rights to privacy, or of the fundamental distinction between those who are under statutory supervision or control (for example on probation or conditional release license) and those who are not (including those merely suspected of offending). Similarly, although police officers recognised that they had no right to enter the homes even of registered sex offenders, they often deliberately gave them the impression that they did have such rights. Both of these observations could be seen as features of the 'new penality', although of course they are by no means unusual in any system of crime control. Comment on broader issues of offenders' rights, accountability and regulation will be made below.

At this point we may pause to offer a preliminary answer, based on the evidence so far, to the question of where to locate the development of multi-agency risk management panels in terms of the debate about shifts in penality. The short answer seems to be that we are presented with a mixed and contradictory picture, in which the dominant discourse is increasingly in tune with the emergence of a risk penality, but there are numerous aspects of culture and practice which reflect the continuing strength of the 'modernist' project – for example, interest in the individual case, and the use of professional judgment to 'overrule' actuarial assessments. Similarly, signs of as yet unresolved struggles over the relative roles of 'experts' and the general public in determining crime control strategy are evident in, on the one hand, the desire of professionals (currently still supported by government) to confine both knowledge and decision-making within small groups of representatives of statutory agencies and, on the other hand, the growing media-supported public pressure for automatic community notification of sex offenders' names and addresses. Finally, however, as we shall see in the next section, there are areas in which the evidence for the emergence of something radically new is more substantial.

9.5 PARTNERSHIP AND ACCOUNTABILITY

The discussion in the previous section indicates that the location of multi-agency arrangements for the risk management of dangerous offenders within an overtly post-modern penal framework is far from clear-cut. Pratt's caveat that the 'old' and the 'new' will co-exist is reasonably well founded in this case. However, there are two aspects of these new arrangements in which multi-agency risk management work may be more clearly utilising the 'post-modern referent' and indeed challenging the boundaries of modern penality. These concern the nature of partnerships and accountability.

9.5.1 Partnership

Partnership in criminal justice is hardly new, and has been pursued both across the statutory sector and between the statutory and voluntary sectors (Cross, 1997). Such partnerships have been pursued for a variety of reasons, not least the political belief that they are economically more efficient and can achieve better targeting and more rational prioritising of scarce statutory resources (James and Bottomley, 1994). In business life, too, partnership has been seen as a source of enhanced flexibility and economic success, a mechanism for more appropriate responses in a changing world. According to Bergquist et al, 1995, pp x, xiv):

> The world is changing in ways that make partnerships more important, if not essential, to achieving success in virtually every kind of professional endeavour. Partnerships simply represent a better way to do things ... [They] offer a great potential as a humanising and ultimately liberating force in our society.

However, the question to be addressed here is whether present forms of partnership in public protection are simply another example of this general development of existing forms, or whether they can be regarded as an integral part of a shift towards a new, post-modern penality.

Hayward (1999), in an extensive unpublished review of multi-agency risk management panels in London, notes interesting reasons why current developments may be significantly different from previous concerns with partnership. He locates risk management partnerships within current penal policy concerns with public protection, and a growing public populism that has heightened public expectations of safety and risk avoidance. The 'core thread' for Hayward of such development is the acceptance by all the agencies concerned that risk is 'core business' (see also Kemshall, 1996).

Risk is both the rationale and the medium through which such partnerships are constituted. This typically frames the partnerships within a larger 'multi-agency' setting. For example, prison and probation work together to ensure smooth information exchange prior to prisoner release and in so doing service the risk knowledge needs of panels. The transactions between agencies are characterised by exchange rather than referral. These are not purchaser-provider relationships, and what is exchanged is knowledge, not a service or product. Such partnerships can be characterised as 'hybrid' organisational forms. They no longer represent individual agencies working in the multi-disciplinary format described by Prins (1995) with each agency contributing its own distinct knowledge base to the assessment process. Rather, they are characterised by knowledge passing through the agencies, perhaps best epitomised by the 'seamless join' between prison and probation. The panel itself operates as more than the sum of its constituent parts, a supra or hybrid institution with its own protocols, rules and procedures. Knowledge production and processing are the key activities of panel work, and the key objective of panel work is the constitution and reproduction of networks of surveillance. Such partnerships are radically different from their forerunners concerned with the exchange of goods and services.

Even so, the mutuality required for effective 'working together' is also a site of dissonance and conflict, and here some familiar themes of multi-agency work emerge. Whose language, whose criteria, and which agency's risk procedure should dominate the identification and classification process? Our research indicates that such conflicts are resolved in many ways, including the use of formal and informal power. Examples include control of resources (for example to monitor and carry out surveillance); control of the administrative processes which make panel business happen (clerical support, minutes, chairing); and expert knowledge on assessment tools and professional expertise, or access to precious resources (for example forensic health). As Ericson and Haggerty (1997, p 101) put it: 'Risk institutions also battle for institutional hegemony.'

Equally, it was clear that, in practice, agencies were often unwilling to move beyond a certain level of commitment to partnership work. As Davidson (1976) pointed out, as partnerships move up the ladder from communication, to co-operation, to co-ordinating services, to merger, each stage in the process requires greater commitment, resources and sacrifice of individual agency independence. The present public protection panels can be characterised by their high commitment to information exchange and emphasis upon risk assessment, but relatively low commitment to the outcome oriented work of risk management. Whilst such low risk strategies of information collaboration are not unusual (Gilling, 1994), the current arrangements are unusual in that they promise much higher levels of joint working. Inter-agency protocols, for example, promise close collaboration in the delivery of risk management plans and shared resources where appropriate. In reality this is not often delivered, and where it is, it tends to be in cases where agencies share a common statutory responsibility (for example, registered sex offenders subject to parole or probation supervision, where police and probation both have statutory duties). Whilst protocols state the common aim of 'public protection', in reality this has become an elastic concept, meaning almost anything to each agency involved, especially when its use facilitates the completion of internal agency tasks on risk.

Once again, then, we are presented with something of a mixed picture, in which agency cultures are clearly a strong factor in resisting change. However, there are elements of these partnerships which suggest that they represent the beginnings of a radical reconstitution of multi-agency forms and patterns of working. They are driven to some extent by the 'logic of risk', and they already transcend some of the traditional boundaries of inter-institutional operation, such as 'gate-keeping' via referrals, monetary exchange for services rendered, and distinct objectives and value-bases. In sum, if we are to focus attention on 'material forms' as well as expressed intent, then the operation of public protection partnerships may prove to be a fruitful arena for further investigations of new penal forms.

9.5.2 Accountability

It has been argued that the particular conditions of post-modernity raise significant issues for accountability and governance, not least that democratic accountability is dispersed and replaced by 'sub-political' forms like interest groups and NGOs (Beck 1992); and governance is 'privatised and dispersed across myriad fragmented institutions' (Ericson and Haggerty, 1997, p 6). In addition, the conditions of what Rose (1996, 2000) has termed 'advanced liberalism' have particular implications for relationships of trust and accountability, and upon the accountability of the self to the state.

Disputed knowledge claims and the lack of trust in experts seen as so characteristic of the risk society (Beck, 1992; Giddens, 1998a, b) have resulted in the increasing replacement of trust with formal, administrative procedures and risk tools. Decisions cannot be taken on trust, but must be subject to quality assurance and audit (Power, 1994; Kemshall *et al*, 1997). 'Risk work' is not only what practitioners do, it is also a key mechanism for holding them to account. This has been evident for several years in probation and is growing in the police service (Kemshall, 1998). Institutional rules, formats and technologies become both the site and the mechanism for such accountability, and where they do not exist they are quickly devised and implemented. In like manner, to avoid litigation and public discredit in the event of risk management failures, public protection panels are beginning to develop 'audit trails' of decision-making to demonstrate defensibility (see, for example, Leicestershire and Rutland Public Protection Panel, 2000).

In the multi-agency arena this gives rise to what have been characterised as peculiarly post-modern forms of accountability: dispersal of accountability away from the governmental centre (and with it dispersal of responsibility for risk management: Leiss and Chociolko, 1994); and self-perpetuating attempts to rationalise the uncertainty of risk to accountable and measurable forms, through formalised risk tools and procedures (Kemshall, 1998; Ericson and Haggerty, 1997). While, as noted earlier, the involvement of private or voluntary agencies was found to be minimal in the public protection panel system, dispersal of accountability within the public sector was evident in a number of ways. For example:

- The lack of statutory accountability for the development of multi-agency risk management panels into their present form. Home Office circulars and the interpretation of local risk management needs have driven much of the development.

- Dispersal of accountability from the centre through a lack of procedural guidance and lack of a national risk assessment tool (despite the gradual de facto accession of the SACJ to this status). This has resulted in the development of localised institutional forms, infrastructure, tools and practices. Structures of formal accountability (for example through management committees) vary extensively.

- The lack of corporate accountability for panel activities. Despite formal statements of protocol, accountability (as opposed to power) remains diffuse, with the police for example responsible for the sex offender register, monitoring and surveillance operations, and other agencies such as probation holding statutory responsibility for the case.

- The interface between each organisation's accountability structure and those of other agencies is a point of tension as they enter the multi-agency arena. The 'seamless join' is often more rhetoric than reality. This is not merely a matter of different cultural traditions and value bases; it is a matter of formal accountability systems and where they are located. This has implications for individual managers and staff. To whom are individual employees accountable, their own organisation or the collectivity of the panel? How binding are panel decisions upon frontline activities? Who is accountable for perceived risk management failures?

The panels also exhibit what Ericson and Haggerty (1997) have called the new 'infra-structure of risk communication' which transcends traditional territorial and organisational boundaries. This is exemplified by the very close working of agencies such as police and probation which have traditionally occupied very different locations in the criminal justice system and whose past working relations could be characterised as lukewarm at best. The 'logic of risk' has however presented a clear overarching rationale for their activities in which the efficient exchange of risk knowledge is perceived as essential for effective risk management (Maguire *et al*, 2001). However, as Ericson and Haggerty point out, the risk prevention justifications of risk knowledge exchange can be limitless, even in the face of Data Protection or Human Rights legislation (see also Maguire, 2000). The perceived 'dangers' are continually used to justify and legitimate disclosure. The possibilities of 'gate-keeping' and monitoring information exchange are also severely limited, not least because of the number of personnel and agencies involved, but also because of the anonymous and distanced nature of the process itself, often through computerised access:

> It is impossible to control such knowledge by using institutional border-guards because of the sheer volume of risk communications, the fact that knowledge can be taken but yet remain in its original place, and the fact that once known, knowledge can never be reclaimed. Remote control means that no one is in control [Ericson and Haggerty, 1997, p 107].

In sum, the inter-institutionalised nature of public protection panels marks them out as a potential exemplar of Ericson and Haggerty's risk knowledge/communication system, and gives them at least some of the key features of dispersed accountability noted as a growing characteristic of post-modern social forms (Rose, 2000).

9.5.3 Accountability and regulation

The broad conclusion from our research regarding the accountability of multi-agency panels is that management accountability is largely unclear, structures are variable, and public accountability is absent. The panels are their own referent, with some limited accountability in some areas to over-arching management committees comprising senior personnel of the key agencies (for example police, probation and social services). The potential threat to individual rights is substantial, particularly through the extension of such procedures to unconvicted persons and the lack of scrutiny to which panel decision-making is exposed. The promise of prevention is a very powerful rhetoric. The apparently value-neutral construction of public protection and the common sense acceptability of preventing dangerous offenders from harming others masks serious implications for individual rights. The process is self-justificatory and difficult to challenge without appearing to 'side with' a highly unpopular group of people.

To what extent can statutory rights provide an adequate safeguard against the potential for panel excesses? Whilst the European Convention on Human Rights is incorporated into United Kingdom law from October 2000 under the Human Rights Act 1998, the application of such legislation to public protection panels has been little discussed. The most relevant parts of the convention concern the right to liberty (Article 5), the right to a fair trial (Article 6), freedom from arbitrary punishment (Article 7) and the right to privacy and family life (Article 8). However, these can often be overridden in the interests of the prevention of disorder or crime. The Convention is also something of a balancing act of rights, in which protection of individuals from inhumane treatment and the fundamental right to life will naturally outweigh privacy if criminal behaviour is likely or threatened. Scott and Ward (1999, p 113) contend that this may mean that criminal justice agencies are held accountable for 'failures to protect the public from known and avoidable dangers by not enforcing court orders' and for 'denying the public information essential for the well-being of their families'. Victims may well also use the right to life clause to challenge the risk management failures of panels and the decisions of professionals involved. In short, the Convention, rather than providing a brake on any internal excesses, may inadvertently fuel the current predisposition to public protection at the expense of the individual rights of potential offenders.

Can the professionals involved provide adequate regulation of the process? Our research suggests that professionals are often a site of resistance to potential excesses, but this should not necessarily be interpreted as regulation. Resistance is variable, and is dependent upon degrees of power to operationalise it. It can be discredited very easily, and often it attracts further central government direction and 'interference' (Davies, 2000).

Professional self-regulation is highly dependent upon the maintenance of standards and codes of practice, for example those produced for doctors and regulated by the General Medical Council, or those for social workers produced by the National Institute of Social Work (NISW, 1997). As Davies (2000, p 279) states, the essential assumption of professional self-regulation is of independence and 'guardianship of the standards of the profession'. The central agencies concerned with public protection – police and probation – cannot make such claims. Neither is governed by independent regulatory bodies. In addition, both are dependent upon central government for funding, and are limited by both the policy and legal framework within which they must operate.

External inspection bodies often have a regulatory as well as an inspection and investigative function (for example the Health and Safety Executive). However, the inspection bodies in respect of police and probation (HM Inspectorates of Police and Probation respectively) have not traditionally carried out this task. Their function is increasingly one of audit, to carry out inspections to check compliance with policy statements, and to measure practice against pre-specified norms and expectations (Power, 1994). This is not the same as establishing and regulating codes of conduct. The latter involves establishing points of underlying principle and acceptable parameters for the remit of operation. The inspection process has largely avoided these areas.

In conclusion, the risk-driven character of public protection partnerships raises a number of major issues in relation to accountability and regulation, which may foreshadow future debates about the possibility of achieving effective systems of accountability under conditions of a more fully-blown 'risk penality'.

9.6 CONCLUDING REMARKS

The debates on whether we are witnessing a new form of ('post-modern') penality have continued for several years at a fairly abstract level, and it is our contention that what is needed to advance them further is the gathering of a significant body of relevant empirical evidence. Our own research, which echoes several of the findings of Lynch (1998, 2000), makes a modest contribution to this task by closely examining practice on the ground in an area of inter-institutional work which has at first sight many of the key features of a post-modern risk system. Our overall conclusion is that on closer inspection the transition is by no means clear-cut, especially because such risk imperatives are mediated and often resisted by practitioners on the ground. Organisational factors, institutional cultures and practices, and the choices of both managers and staff, militate against any smooth transition to a new risk penality. At the same time, there are perhaps clearer glimpses of the future in the emergence of new forms of partnership, driven by the 'logic of risk', and in the significant dispersal of accountability which has accompanied their development.

RISKINESS AND AT-RISK-NESS: SOME AMBIGUOUS FEATURES OF THE CURRENT PENAL LANDSCAPE

Vivian Leacock and Richard Sparks

10.1 INTRODUCTION

Much recent social theory, and no small amount of work in the social analysis of punishment and social control, educates us to take risk as key to current developmental tendencies of social institutions, techniques of governance and their associated varieties of politics. In a surprisingly short time (roughly during the 1990s) this foxy but evocative term has achieved a remarkable currency in criminological discussion. Of course the notion of risk is not itself new, even if this is sometimes overlooked. Indeed we will argue below (here following O'Malley, 2000a, b) that in forgetting the longer, messier and more embroiled prior history of risk and its associated ideas and practices we may sometimes be drawn into attributing a degree of novelty and revelatory power to this concept that can prove deceptive. Moreover, in so doing we may assume that developments in punishment and control that seem redolent of risk-calculation and risk management are likewise newer and more radically distinct from their precursors than is really justified.

Risk, in other words, is a fashionable idea – one whose moment would appear to have arrived. As can happen in the quite often rather modish world of social theory the wholesale and over-literal adoption of an apparently new and appealing vocabulary tends to produce a rather facile trend-spotting, and a preference for sighting novelties, transformations and departures rather than continuities or recurrences. In respect of the risk politics of criminal justice this can have some ironic consequences, not least in diverting attention away from the intractability of the very risks (dangers, problems and dilemmas) that crime policy addresses and hence also the *political* risks and temptations (scandals and embarrassments on the one hand, opportunities for the demagogic display of toughness on the other) that crime and punishment routinely generate for governments and other actors.

In our view, therefore, some versions of arguments about risk and criminal justice court either or both of two errors:

(1) reductionism (as though risk were only one thing or led only in one direction);

(2) totalisation (as if risk were the only issue).

The former envisions risk primarily in terms of changes in predictive practice and technique (what we here call the mode of calculation), and declines to theorise the involvement of risk in the generation of moral categories and the circulation of blame and censure, exposure and vulnerability. In other words it *confines* the question of risk to one primary kind of location, namely the development of new expert systems of risk management that allegedly erode or displace all other principles or modes of adjudicating and intervening. This is the tendency associated with the over-eager adoption of the notion of a 'new penology' (following Feeley and Simon's intervention (1992)), in which 'actuarial' reasoning allegedly elbows out all pre-existing (retributive, deterrent, clinical or social work based) approaches to offenders and offending. The latter tendency, this time flowing from the attractions of Beck's (1992) grand stylisation of a 'risk society', finds risk *everywhere* and (insofar as it is commonly referred to the global sway of free markets and the hegemony of neo-liberalism) nowhere in particular. Such placelessness effaces national histories, contingencies, events and local inflections of risk politics (what we term the mode of representation). Either way, when we speak of risk we seem prone to assume that 'it' is taking over. It is not just an ingredient in the cocktail of penal politics (not even the one that gives that heady mixture its intoxicating kick) but the spirit itself.

We see the matter somewhat otherwise, as we hope will become apparent. We suggest that the intrusions of risk into penal politics and practice assume more hybrid and arguably more loosely coupled forms than some accounts allow. Neither does risk figure only in respect of state liability for the containment, incapacitation and surveillance of dangerous or incorrigible groups, although there are abundant examples of such measures to be found in the field at present. The emergence of such phenomena as electronic monitoring, sex offender registration and notification measures, the revision of parole eligibility criteria, the ubiquity of the language of risk assessment and so forth are undoubtedly significant developments, with serious and as yet rather uncertain implications for the future roles and routine working practices of criminal justice professionals and associated trades such as psychiatry. But even if these are in some sense straws in the wind it is nevertheless a gusty and rather swirling one. It carries much other debris along with it; and neither does it simply blow away every existing obstacle in its path. Once we adopt the precautionary principles of not reading risk in a reductive or totalising fashion we also set aside the assumption that its influence on the penal field unrolls in an inevitable and one-directional manner. The result is that risk, like more or less any other significant force in human affairs, becomes impure. The thought experiment that begins by asking 'what if actuarial logic were to become the sole criterion for sentencing or releasing offenders?' over time cedes place to the recognition that the model does not survive its application in pristine form, unsullied by resistances and contingencies. The hiatus between the map and the territory remains unbridgeable; and, as O'Malley observes (2000b, p 159), changes in penal practice 'even if driven by some systematic pressure – are nevertheless implemented in the domain of politics'.

For this reason, rather than offering a further general overview of social theories of risk and their correlates in criminal justice, we propose to examine some of the twists and turns in the relations between discourse and practice in a certain field over a determinate period. Our field is the contentious one of British penal politics since 1990 and, more specifically, the shifting significance of youth justice controversies and legislation during this time. It is relatively easy to show that questions of risk and risk management did indeed become more prominent through the 1990s, albeit in a complex, uneven and sharply politicised way. At the same time, as the language of risk became increasingly central to political discourse so it also became messier and more plural. This was especially apparent in the arena of youth justice, which was taken as focal by the incoming New Labour government during and after the 1997 General Election. In differentiating its programme from that of the alleged failures of its Tory predecessor, Labour promised, *inter alia*, a vigorous renewal of activism and effectiveness in this sphere. In so doing it stretched the operative uses of 'risk' to encompass senses other than those which had hitherto been most prominent. In justifying, and popularising, its programme New Labour made equally free use of claims to superior technique and of appeals to common sense. At the same time it developed, or perhaps revived, an acknowledgment of the system's obligations for those 'at risk' or 'subject to risk'. In other words, one of the ways in which the risk vocabulary has been stretched lately is away from the strictly incapacitative/preventive domain and towards a series of more 'socialised' usage, some of them extending well beyond the bounds of the criminal justice system as such. We thus explore a series of developments in which the language of risk intersects variously and successively with neo-classical, new penological and, indeed, 'old' Labourist themes. Not all the 'moral inventions' (O'Malley, 1992) that emerge on the penal landscape are really produced entirely *de novo* therefore; the new configurations also involve the rearrangement (and sometimes the outright re-badging and re-cycling) of existing materials.

Such eclecticism leads some commentators, not unreasonably, to query not just the alleged dominance of risk-based reasoning in contemporary penality but also whether some measures that ostensibly claim justification in terms of their promise to reduce risk are really directed to this end at all. They may be gestures, whose real political or penological targets lie quite elsewhere. On this view we should attempt to preserve the notion of risk from such abuses: it has a proper sense and can only be used meaningfully when certain conditions obtain. We should point out the many misappropriations of the idea in order that we may return to a sensible debate in which risk, punishment and political obfuscation are each called by their right names. We share this scepticism about the transformative effects of the flourishing of risk. Moreover, it is difficult to resist pleas for greater lucidity in the interests of normative theorising. However, for present purposes it is really the stretchiness of the vocabulary that interests us. In our view risk has both gestural and programmatic uses; it is part of the tactics of politics and the technique of government. It has, moreover, taken on somewhat different inflections in the hands of different users.

The converse view to arguments for conceptual purity, therefore, is that none of this should surprise us unduly. In the big world beyond criminology and penology such arguments have raged for quite some time. The demand that risk be discussed in rationalist terms purged of emotivism and cultural baggage has been voiced and repudiated before. In countering the sociological naïveties of such attempts at purification students of risk perception and risk controversies have set out many ways in which risk, danger and dread can figure in our mental maps and political vocabularies, and the intransigence of the resulting disputes against attempts at closure. Hence we encounter an increasing number of acknowledgments (not least from the proponents of the 'new penology' thesis itself) that whereas developments redolent of new modes of risk calculation have indeed proliferated, and recourse to the terminology of risk assessment, prediction and anticipatory control has become commonplace, these have not colonised the field to the exclusion of other influences in quite the way originally predicted (Simon and Feeley, 1995; O'Malley, 2000b; Sparks, 2000). In this respect, Giddens (1991) may be correct in arguing that these days most political disputes are fought out 'on the terrain of' risk without its being assumed that this results in a diminution of political contention, nor that the heat can be drawn out of such disputes just by channelling them out into a specialist expert system. Rather, the converse result is equally characteristic, namely that disputes over risk among specialist practitioners spill out repeatedly into the larger domain of political discourse and media attention. Mary Douglas points out that the 'constitution' of particular political communities can be understood in part through their characteristic attributions of threat and blame. In Douglas's view risk thus becomes the contemporary vestment for societal conversations about morality and identity (1992, pp 15–16). In this process the notion of risk becomes 'prised away' from its more original and particular application to probability calculations properly so called and becomes a cultural key word with much wider reference within 'a debate about accountability':

> This dialogue, the cultural process itself, is a contest to muster support for one kind of action rather than another ... The cultural dialogue is therefore best studied in its forensic moments. The concept of risk emerges as a key resource in modern times because of its uses as a forensic resource [Douglas, 1992, p 24].

For Douglas and others the cognitive and affective formations that cultural theory terms 'political cultures' act as filters for risk – they select problems for attention, suggest images of threatening people and situations, propose diagnoses and so on. It is indeed the case that contemporary western societies increasingly think their crime and punishment problems in terms of risk but they think them in diverse and internally conflictual ways nevertheless (see Sparks, 2000 for a somewhat fuller exposition of Douglas's position and its implications for criminology). In the main body of this essay we review some of the ways in which key interventions in British penal politics in the 1990s can be seen as attempts to 'muster support' predicated on one depiction or another of risk. We begin with a brief exposition of developments under the Conservative government of John Major (a topic many of whose details have been rehearsed extensively already) before turning, at slightly greater length, to the mixed penological diction of New Labour.

10.2 RISK IN BRITISH PENAL POLITICS 1990–2001

One of us has argued elsewhere (Shapland and Sparks, 1999) that the twists and switchbacks of recent penal politics in Britain (or more especially those of England and Wales – a distinction of increasing importance in the post-devolutionary landscape) may be divided roughly but reasonably coherently into three main periods: (a) a phase of managerialist consolidation (1990–93); (b) a moment of vigorous retrenchment (1993–97); and (c) developments since the election of 1997. This periodisation makes sense only for key points of contention within the penal system as such. In the larger infrastructure of the governance of crime development has arguably been more gradual and continuous, albeit still substantially affected by the change of Government after 1997. Notwithstanding changes in resourcing, organisation and nomenclature under New Labour there has been a secular trend towards the formation of local alliances and inter-agency partnership arrangements in policing and crime prevention, latterly increasingly tied into strategies of urban 'boosterism' and regeneration initiatives; attempts to stimulate various forms of active citizenship and responsibilised uptake of security devices and practices; targeted, 'problem-solving' and performance-measured policing strategies. These developments, and the resulting complex of central and local government actions and voluntary and private sector investments, are central to any comprehensive account of contemporary crime control, but they intersect only tangentially with the story we wish to tell here.

10.2.1 Managerialist consolidation (1990–93)

It is quite intelligible that the moments of greatest politicisation of 'law and order' in recent times occurred at the beginning and ending of the Conservative supremacy in British politics. As Hall has argued (1988) it was crucial to Thatcher's success in 1979 that she secured the dominant interpretation of the 'winter of discontent' as a crisis of 'ungovernability'. The crisis favoured Thatcherism not merely electorally but ideologically: it was 'lived in its terms' (Hall, 1979, p 30). To roll back the boundaries of the state and to provide order and firm government were part and parcel of the same interpretation of 'freedom under law'. It is for this reason that Hall famously defines early Thatcherism as 'authoritarian populism' (Hall *et al*, 1978; Hall, 1979; Hall, 1988; Hay, 1996, pp 136–40; Brake and Hale, 1992).

Ironically, by contrast, the period of the mid- to late 1980s named by Hay as 'radical Thatcherism', during which the Thatcher project was most fully in possession of state power, saw markedly less open contention on criminal justice issues. Law and order figured much less prominently in the election manifestos and campaigns of 1987 and 1992 than in those of 1979 or 1983 (Downes and Morgan, 1997). Neither the Children Act 1989 nor the Criminal Justice Act 1991 betrayed obvious signs of authoritarian populism (even if they were consonant with the governing principles of neo-liberalism in their 'managerialist' and 'consumerist' dimensions) (Lacey, 1994). Indeed the Criminal Justice Act 1991 was far more centrally the product of cautiously progressive civil servants and Home Office ministers seeking to systematise a notoriously eclectic sentencing system and to restrain the seemingly inexorable expansion of the prison population than of any populist intuition. Curiously it seemed at the entree of the 1990s that a government born in a spirit of authoritarian populism was less concerned to refashion the Home Office than it was such other ministries as Health and Environment (where responsibility for local government lay).

Following the Criminal Justice Act 1991 the prison population in England and Wales fell significantly. In fact the prison population began to fall during the passage of the Act (and whilst magistrates and judges were being trained in its philosophy) and before the formal implementation of its sentencing provisions. Amongst the main relevant features of the 1991 Act were that it was substantially organised around 'justice model' principles; that it suggested a quite systematic tariff of penalties, ranged hierarchically according to the 'degree of loss of liberty' that they implied; that the White Paper which preceded it expressly denied deterrence as an independent sentencing objective and famously averred that prisons were often 'an expensive way of making bad people worse'; and that it introduced a unit-fine system which rapidly became extremely controversial – especially amongst its more affluent penal subjects – principally because the clumsiness of its attempt to tie the level of financial penalties to the offender's means allegedly led to seriously disproportionate results (see Windlesham, 1996, pp 11–17).

The 1991 Act did make reference to the assessment and reduction of risk – shortly to become a much more pivotal and publicly contentious term – but only in respect of the special and relatively technical arenas of extended sentencing on grounds of dangerousness (for those convicted of violent and/or sexual offences under s 2(2)(b) and the post-release supervision of prisoners. Acting on recommendations of the Carlisle Committee (Home Office, 1988) the 1991 Act made release from custody at the half-way point in sentence automatic for those serving less than 12 months; automatic but conditional for those serving between 12 months and four years and discretionary and conditional for all those serving four years or more. The element of conditionality meant that all prisoners serving sentences of more than 12 months would receive varying periods of post-release supervision (see Hood and Shute, 1994, 1995, 1996; Maguire *et al*, 1996). The 1991 Act also introduced changes in parole procedures, including more formal attempts at risk assessment for both determinate and life sentence prisoners (Copas *et al*, 1994; Hirschmann, 1996).

In sum, the period 1990–93 was largely one of managerialist modernisation on terms consonant with, even if not provided exclusively by, neo-liberal theory. However, this mood changed abruptly in 1993. When it did so sentencing and prison management were again both in the foreground of change, but now on terms once much more akin to 'authoritarian populism'. In that altered climate the official response to scandalous events in the prisons (especially two spectacular escapes in 1994 and 1995) were framed in quite different terms and 'managerialism' assumed another inflection altogether.

10.2.2 'Prison Works!' The return of authoritarian populism (1993–97)

The year 1993 proved to be an eventful and embattled one in British penal politics. At the outset the abduction and murder of two year old James Bulger dominated the media and became an unavoidable reference-point of anxious discussion, one whose near-unique circumstances did not prevent it from assuming potent indicative and symptomatic status in much commentary. Throughout the year the impunity of criminals, and especially of lawless youth, before impotent institutions was a recurring theme. The suggestion that the police – whose capacity not merely to uphold but virtually to embody a sense of order in their own persons has been such a cherished feature of English national self-understanding for most of the century – were no longer able to hold the line against ever-rising crime was voiced with some frequency. There were suggestions of incipient vigilantism, in broadsheet as well as tabloid newspapers (for example, *The Independent*, 31 August 1993). All of this is well known, and is beginning to be properly documented (especially Windlesham, 1996). It seems plausible to view this as one of those moments when the intractable presence of a high volume of crime, and the limitations of the state's capacity (or readiness) to act to reduce it (cf Garland, 1996), became politically visible and challenging.

Even before the provisions of the 1991 legislation had taken full effect the direction of penal policy underwent a quite marked reversal. Responding to widely reported judicial and magisterial criticism of restraints on sentencing discretion and of the operation of the unit fine system the Criminal Justice Act 1993 abruptly repealed the offending sections (see Windlesham, 1996, pp 3–36). At the Conservative Party Conference in September 1993 the new Home Secretary, Mr Howard, gave an unusually well received speech. To the rapture of his audience, and the delight of the next morning's press, he coined the expression 'Prison Works'. Inter alia, Mr Howard said:

Let's be clear, prison works. It ensures that we are protected from murderers, muggers and rapists and it makes many who are tempted to commit crime think twice. Today I make this announcement. We shall build six new prisons. They will be built ...

...CLAPPING...

... they will be built and managed by the private sector, and I can tell you one thing – Butlins won't be bidding for the contract.

...CLAPPING...

A rumour has gone out over the summer that I don't think prison should be a picnic. Well, I'll let you into a secret, I don't. And that's why I'm determined to ensure that conditions in our prisons should be decent but austere.

With rare determination and single-mindedness Mr Howard proceeded to legislate on these (and other related) premises. The Criminal Justice and Public Order Act 1994, in addition to an extensive and eclectic range of new police powers, created 39 new criminal offences and increased maximum penalties for a further 56 (Windlesham, 1996, pp 155–61). This was not all, however. In another major Conference performance in 1995 Mr Howard announced further plans for the protection of the public, including the abolition of parole for determinate sentence prisoners (on grounds of 'truth in sentencing'), mandatory minimum sentences for repeat burglars and drug dealers, and mandatory life sentences on second conviction for certain classes of serious violence and sexual offences (in effect a two-strikes provision). These proposals were brought forward in a White Paper, *Protecting the Public* (Home Office, 1996) and (with amendments accepted during horse-trading immediately prior to the 1997 General Election) formed the basis of the Crime (Sentences) Act 1997. The contention surrounding the latter measure, especially between Mr Howard and the higher judiciary – including most notably the late Lord Chief Justice, Lord Taylor – was acute and avidly covered in the media (see Henham, 1997).

The most obvious sequelae of this initiative have included a sharp increase in the numbers of people in prison. Reversing three years of decline (the first such period in more than a quarter of a century) the number of prisoners rose by more than 500 per month during the last quarter of 1993. Moreover, in a mirror image of the earlier fall the upturn *preceded* any legislative changes (see further Ashworth and Hough, 1996). The population rose by some 25% over the following two years. In February 1995 Home Office projections envisaged a prison population of 58,000 by 2002. In fact that figure was attained during 1996. The prison population in England and Wales topped 60,000 in the early summer of 1997. This rate of increase was sustained over most of the remainder of the decade, at least until it was reined back (or perhaps disguised) following the implementation of Home Detention Curfew provisions in 1999 which removed several thousand persons (those entering the closing months of their sentences) from the prison statistics by the simple expedient of placing them under electronic confinement in their homes.

But, and this too is indicative for the present discussion, 'Prison Works!' as a doctrine turned out to involve not just the quantity of punishment (its frequency and duration) but also a qualitative emphasis – in this case a change in the assumed appropriateness of the style and form of prison regimes. The phrase that recurs throughout the period is that prisons should be 'decent but austere'. Moreover, Mr Howard's 1993 Conference speech was slightly preceded by a leaked memorandum (reported by *The Observer* on 22 August 1993 – this is the 'rumour' to which the speech alludes) in which the Home Secretary affirmed that 'Prisoners enjoy a standard of material comfort which taxpayers find hard to understand' (see further Sparks, 1996). In sum, Mr Howard vigorously restated the case for incapacitation and deterrence, and was unabashed in arguing that for serious and persistent offenders more and longer prison sentences were the only certain means of ensuring the protection of the public. In the course of the debates he made frequent – albeit rhetorical – reference to academic research in support of his view (in respect both of incapacitation and deterrence) (see for example *Hansard* (HOC etc, April 1996)).

It is tempting to follow Garland (1996) in interpreting 'Prison Works' as a phenomenon of the 'denial' of the state's incapacity to deliver public security and reassurance in the face of chronically high crime rates and the bundles of anxieties characteristic of the lifeworld of late modernity. Yet caution is necessary here. Howard's emphasis on deterrence and incapacitation was entirely consistent with an ideological position which was bullish in stressing the centrality of incentive structures on human behaviour (for example, in the arenas of taxation and welfare benefits). Deterrence found a ready place among the motivational assumptions that Thatcherites, like their many historical predecessors especially in the latter decades of the 19th century, applied to governing the behaviour of rational economic actors. Mr Howard's proudest boast, both then and in his many subsequent apologias, was that he had 'changed the terms of trade' between the criminal justice system and the offender. There was no aberration here; no conceptual somersault; and no departure from the premises that Howard and his ideological ilk held dear. The refocusing of the aims of sentencing on the utilitarian instruments of deterrence and incapacitation was presented as a purism, a return to roots, a recovery of spirit, resolve and confidence (by express contrast with the immediately preceding period). From the point of view of neo-liberal minimal statists the array of penal powers that existed by 1997 (both in respect of sentencing and of institutional control) were ones with which they felt far more comfortable, and which seemed to them far more rationally defensible, than the complex of penal-welfare measures that they had inherited from the 1970s – naturally so, for they had to some considerable degree remade them in their own image. In promising to address offender risk through incapacitation and deterrence Howard centralised a certain set of motifs and targets – predatoriness, persistence and gravity in the iconography of offenders; burglary and drug dealing as primary in the litany of their offences.

In Britain in recent times the shifting fortunes and ideological dispositions of key political actors in respect of the penal realm have been quite complex. The assertive and somewhat authoritarian rhetoric characteristic of early Thatcherism gave way (especially during its years of greatest economic optimism and political dominance around the end of the 1980s) to a period during which the penal question was less overtly politicised. However, unsurprisingly since it also coincided with the stage that Hay (1996) has styled 'high Thatcherism', it was during the latter period that the Thatcher government began seriously to experiment with privatisation and other (broadly 'managerialist') innovations. Nevertheless, whilst these experiments in no way ceased, the conjunction between a number of unpropitious events (especially the Bulger murder and a series of controversies in the prisons) and a declining swing in the political-business cycle (Melossi, 1993) signalled a return to a crude politicisation of penal severity from 1993 onwards. If, however, there is any irony to be detected in the populist turn in penal politics after 1993 it lies not in any inconsistency with Thatcherite principles but only in the fact that as an electoral tactic it was an abject failure. It failed just because it was precisely a phenomenon of what John Gray has aptly called the 'Tory endgame' – the implosion of Conservative hegemony. The very promises that served the Tories so well in 1979 (the 'smack of firm government', the restoration of 'freedom under law') had become unredeemed debts against their political mortgage by

1993. Rising crime rates and rising measures of public insecurity (both peaking according to official measures in 1994) had themselves become – to reverse the polarity of Downes and Morgan's (1997) narrative of post-war penal politics – 'hostages to fortune'.

10.2.3 The moral inventiveness of New Labour (1997–)

Despite Mr Howard's best efforts, the Conservative Party were unable in the 1990s to wrest back political advantage from a resurgent Labour Party, in matters of law and order as on virtually every other political issue of consequence. The recessionary origins of the 'Prison Works' gambit, and its coincidence with the accumulation of assorted political scandals and embarrassments, rendered it largely ineffective in terms of electoral arithmetic – the very conditions that made it necessary also ensured that it would 'fail'. At the same time Blair moved coolly to reposition his party in such a way as to neutralise any lingering suspicion of 'softness' on law and order issues. His celebrated 1993 sound-bite 'tough on crime, tough on the causes of crime' (enunciated within a month of the Bulger murder) allowed him at one and the same time to adopt the new sentencing dispensation in every material particular whilst designedly accusing the Tories of having a narrow 'one-club' agenda, remote from voters' everyday concerns with youth offending, drugs, low-level public order problems and other incursions on their security and 'quality of life'.

The new configuration of rhetoric and practice that has begun to emerge since 1997 is thus more variegated and less obvious than its immediate precursors. On the one hand there is a determination not to resile in any way from toughness. The acceleration in the prison population did not slacken throughout the first two years of New Labour, and the incoming Home Secretary Jack Straw marked his departure from the stances of his (presumably 'old') Labour predecessors by declining to make the control of prison numbers a policy objective. Neither Straw nor Blair refrained from identifying categories of disreputable and marginal persons whom they considered worthy of condemnation, ineligible for public sympathy and ripe for stringent action by police and prosecuting authorities (cf Benyon and Edwards, 1997; Cohen, 1999). At the same time the New Labour dispensation is less flagrantly concerned with 'punitiveness' tout court than the Conservatives became after 1993, and the prison is to this extent dethroned from its position of solitary pre-eminence in penal politics. Rather the signature notion of the present period has become that of 'community safety', and the primary category of activity constituted under that heading (its principal 'moral invention' to borrow O'Malley's term(1992)) has been 'anti-social behaviour'. These terms assumed statutory form under the Crime and Disorder Act 1998, one of the new administration's first pieces of 'flagship' legislation and one energetically promoted as indicative of its novel approach to governance. Whilst this legislation has been exhaustively discussed already and numerous concise summaries of its main provisions exist (Brownlee, 1998), certain of its distinctive features merit further mention here. The New Labour programme differs from that of the Tories not on any tough-tender polarity but rather in point of its targets, means and rationales for intervention. Amongst the core topics on which New Labour focused its energies was that of young people at-risk – at risk of offending, at risk of being offended against, and at risk of 'social exclusion'. In other words it extended the application of risk language; it effected a different set of connections between criminal justice and other areas of social policy; and it increased the number and variety of instruments it envisaged using to achieve its ends.

The Crime and Disorder Act 1998 imposes new statutory duties on local authorities to form 'community safety partnerships' and to provide youth justice services in addition to establishing 'youth offending teams' (YOTs).[1] The Act states that the principal aim of youth justice is 'to prevent offending by children and young persons' (s 37(1) Crime and Disorder Act 1998). Partnerships are required to carry out 'community safety audits' and to develop strategies based upon their findings. Amongst the more significant and controversial of the measures at the disposal of local authorities are Anti-Social Behaviour Orders (ASBOs) – civil orders designed to constrain the conduct of any person whose behaviour is deemed likely to cause 'alarm, harassment or distress' to any person outside their own household. YOTs, meanwhile, are to have at their disposal a significant array of new powers and orders to intervene in the lives of young persons in trouble or 'at risk', including (in the case of the Child Safety Order and Local Child Curfew Schemes) those under 10. They may also impose Parenting Orders on the adult guardians of persistent young offenders. Amongst the more salient features of the new arrangements are: they include an evidence-based 'audit' component; they devolve substantial centrally-defined obligations upon localities; the responsible local bodies acquire significant discretionary powers; there is a preference for civil rather than criminal measures, but backed up by penal sanctions (Burney, 1999); there is a conscious targeting of high risk populations, defined both by location and age. The result is intended to be a more activist and more stringently managed system.[2]

---

1   The government connected the statutory obligation placed on the Local Authorities to provide youth justice services within the 1998 Act with provisions in the Children Act 1989 which place emphasis on the local authorities' role in preventing young people from offending (Crime and Disorder Act 1998, s 40(3)).

2   The creation of the Youth Justice Board for England and Wales in the 1998 Act is illustrative of the trend towards greater monitoring, the tighter management of and standardisation of youth justice services. Every Local Authority is required to submit an annual youth justice plan to the Board for approval. In addition to evaluating whether

Through the impositions it makes upon local authorities, the strictures it voices on criminal justice and social work professionals, the reporting and performance demands on which it insists, the central state repositions and re-arms itself. It 'responsibilises' others; it relays its desires via chains of actors organised in multi-agency 'partnerships' that straddle public, voluntary and commercial sectors. It makes available substantial sums of money, but these are commonly allocated on the basis of competitive tendering processes. This, like the creation of community safety auditing, stimulates the flowering of new professional cadres and their associated consultants, evaluators and other knowledge-workers. All of this has far-reaching and as yet largely uncharted implications for the reconfiguration of the criminal justice professions, for the ascending and declining influences of diverse think-tanks, lobbies and elites, and for the production, reception and differential support shown for certain varieties of criminological knowledge. However, whilst New Labour is in no degree less preoccupied with risk than were its Tory predecessors, it also extends the ambit of the risk rubric. Whereas Michael Howard's primary attention fell overwhelmingly on prolific offenders eligible for stringent deterrent and incapacitative punishment, New Labour penology also concerns itself with social and moral risks, especially to the young. Whereas Howard's instrumental utilitarianism largely precluded discussion of social causes of offending New Labour knows no such inhibition. In this sense it recovers and 'modernises' a series of erstwhile 'welfarist' concerns but in a way that stipulates much firmer and more controlling interventions than the 'excuse culture' purportedly associated with youth justice was wont to undertake.[3] New Labour thus emphasises not just riskiness but also at-risk-ness; and those at-risk of exclusion must be included, by compulsion where necessary. What is intriguing here is the fusion effected between a technical (indeed

---

2   [cont] the system succeeds in preventing young people from offending (through monitoring practice and commissioning research in this area), the Board has a specific remit to 'advise' the Secretary of State on the setting of National Standards for the provision of youth justice services and the provisions made for young people in custody (Crime and Disorder Act 1998, s 41(5)(b)(iii)).

3   Many of New Labour's social policies notoriously mark a departure from 'old' welfarism. The language of welfare-to-work focuses on the independence which work brings as opposed to the dependency of welfare. Frank Field, the Labour ex-Minister for Welfare Reform (1997) argued that a key aim of welfare reforms was to turn 'benefit offices into more *pro-active bodies* – by helping the young, lone parents and the disabled get into work' (Frank Field, in Hencke, 1997, p 2; emphasis added). Mikosz in discussing New Labour's 'Third Way' (cf Giddens, 1998) argues that underlying New Labour's welfare reforms is the view that individuals assume responsibility for protecting themselves and that society protects weak individuals (Mikosz, 1998, p 13; Buckby, 1998: 4). Mikosz explains, 'The state is seen less as a direct service provider than as an enabler of individual opportunity and of civic action' (Mikosz, 1998, p 13). New Labour's welfare-to-work policies and its social exclusion strategies have been targeted at specific groups, in particular, unemployed young people, single parents, the long-term unemployed and the 'underclass', and have overwhelmingly comprised incentives (both positive and negative) towards waged work.

often technocratic) language (the discourses associated with the diagnosis, measurement and reduction of risk) and a highly moralised one (the expression of tough love for society's wayward children).

Within this variant of risk discourse the notion of the 'risk factor' thus holds a key position. The 'new youth justice' focuses on 'risk-factors' in young people's lives, including risks to their moral welfare (and law-abidingness) resulting from 'social exclusion'.[4] Those forms of expertise that promise to identify sites of intervention by such means are most likely to receive official endorsement as constituting useful knowledge (Audit Commission, 1996). The perspectives on criminal careers that exercise influence on official policy have assumed a status of high certainty and authority, and the risk factors identified therein have become a checklist of triggers to action. The literature is read as a series of arguments for early and multiple interventions. Inhibitions against criminal justice system intervention of the kinds hitherto widespread amongst youth justice workers (on grounds of net-widening and other perverse consequences) are thus given short shrift, and the premise is established that tensions between care and control, welfare and punishment have been superseded. Action on drug use provides a case in point. New Labour's Drug Prevention Advisory Service's (DPAS) document *Drugs and Young Offenders: Guidance for Drug Action Teams and Youth Offending Teams* outlines the government's thinking on the links between drug use and youth offending and advocates an early interventionist approach to tackling drug use amongst young people.[5] The document indicates that intervention can occur at any stage of the youth justice system from early warnings, via arrests through to the sentencing stage. The argument is that contact with the youth justice system actually provides an opportunity to intervene and that under the Crime and Disorder Act 1998 the Local Authorities have a statutory obligation to provide youth justice services for young offenders aged between 10 and 17 years. Types of intervention can vary from information, advice, assessment, counselling, treatment and services relating to education, training and employment. Drug rehabilitation is also one possible provision available when a 'youth offender contract' is established by a Youth Offender Panel

---

4   Ruth Levitas (1998) suggests that in New Labour discourse the notion of social exclusion has shifted its sense. Having once been a term bearing some connection to social justice and redistribution it is increasingly one stressing normative integration in a morally inclusive 'community'.

5   See www.homeoffice.gov.uk/dpas/dyoff.pdf. New Labour introduced a new community order: 'Drug treatment and testing orders' (Crime and Disorder Act 1998, Part IV, s 61). Under the drug treatment and testing orders, sentencers can require drug misusing offenders (aged 16 years or over) to undergo treatment and regular mandatory drug testing. The minimum duration of the 'treatment and testing period' is six months and the maximum is three years (Crime and Disorder Act 1998, s 61(2)(a)). Treatment can be either in the form of inpatient or outpatient treatment (Crime and Disorder Act 1998, s 62(2)(a)–(b)).

(Youth Justice and Criminal Evidence Act 1999, para 8(2)(f)). The document often refers to the young person then being assessed by the YOT for a 'rehabilitative' programme. The aim of early intervention is to address the commonly identified 'risk factors' in order to prevent both drug use and other lawbreaking. High emphasis is placed on co-ordinated and multi-agency responses to young offenders with drug problems through Drug Action Teams and Youth Offending Teams comprised of a variety of agencies.

Similar fusions between 'safety', 'prevention' and 'control' abound in New Labour's youth justice policy. For example the Child Safety Order may be initiated (under s 11(5) of the 1998 Act):

in the interests of –

(a) securing that the child receives appropriate care, protection and support and is subject to proper control; or

(b) preventing any repetition of the kind of behaviour which led to the child safety order being made.

At the same time the conditions necessary for the imposition of the Order are essentially the same as those which would result in the imposition of an Anti-Social Behaviour Order on an older child: they relate, that is to say, primarily to the child as offender or potential offender rather than as victim. In other words there is a persistent ambiguity around the risks at issue: those faced by, or presented by, children and young people, especially in public space, and especially when under suspicion of being beyond parental control.

The Local Child Curfew Schemes provide another illustration of the ambiguity in New Labour's youth justice policies. There are protective and control aspects to the Child Curfew Schemes that make provision for early intervention in the interests/welfare of the child and simultaneously, place restrictions on the movement (within a specified area) of young people under the age of 10. However, the government has recently announced its intention to extend Local Child Curfew Orders to the age of 15 (Travis, 2001, p 8). Section 11(3)(c) of the 1998 Act indicates that the two orders – the Child Safety Order and the Local Child Curfew Order – lend weight to each other, that is, that the Child Safety Order could be issued following the contravention of the Local Child Curfew Order. Furthermore, contravention of the Child Safety Order can lead to greater intervention in the form of a care order under the Children Act 1989.

Many of the core elements of the New Labour dispensation, but arguably also those which introduce the greatest elements of ambiguity and instability, cluster around the terms 'responsibility' and 'safety' (or 'protection'). The notion of responsibility of course figures throughout the history of criminal jurisprudence, in youth justice as elsewhere. In New

Labour diction it is brought particularly closely into alignment with the arguments for early intervention. It does not, as in neo-classical discourse, include an argument for the exemption of children and youth from official sanction (as witness the symbolically central abolition of the common law doctrine of *doli incapax*). Rather the primary risk that 'at risk' youth run is precisely that of growing up without having adequately assimilated the principle of responsible self-government. In this respect the new youth justice stands in an interesting and complex relationship of both absorption and rejection to the 'old' welfarism. The idea of inculcating responsibilities has been active before, perhaps most distinctively in the Borstal system in its mid-20th century heyday. Similarly, the notion of 'at-risk-ness' expressly recalls the same usage in the 1970s when it was associated with the concept of 'pre-delinquency'. In that period, however, it presaged the invention of Intermediate Treatment and, latterly, the formation of a professional culture that was predominantly diversionary, anti-interventionist and sometimes outrightly abolitionist in its theoretical leanings and vocational commitments. In the face of an extended history of oscillations between intervening and diverting New Labour comes down squarely on the side of intervention. In this respect New Labour revisits an old social democratic preoccupation with at-risk youth but roundly repudiates what it depicts as the muddled and unduly indulgent effects of that tradition. Thus in its aptly-titled 1997 White Paper, *No More Excuses: New Approaches to Tackling Youth Crime*, Labour presents the youth justice system as having been compromised by an 'excuse culture':

> An excuse culture has developed within the youth justice system. *It excuses itself for its inefficiency and too often excuses the young offenders before it, implying that they cannot help their behaviour because of their social circumstances.* Rarely are they confronted with their behaviour and helped to take more personal responsibility for their actions. The system allows them to go on wrecking their own lives as well as disrupting their families and communities [Home Office, 1997].

In this vision no distinction is allowed between the language of helping and that of 'confronting' and 'responsibilising'. The old dichotomy between toughness and care is abolished as obsolete and, moreover, as contrary to 'common sense'. The resulting juxtaposition of toughness and love (with its implied critique of 'tolerance' – equated now with indifference, excuse and with 'walking away') is exemplified in the press release to *Tackling Youth Crime*, a government consultation paper.

> Young criminals damage themselves and damage their communities.

> There is no greater challenge than to stop this downward spiral in its tracks. For too long young criminals have been given the idea that they can get away with their crimes.

The youth justice system needs to be swift, consistent and effective. My top priority is to overhaul this system and to tackle youth crime. If we succeed we can make a real difference by preventing children falling into a life of crime.

We need to give hope and opportunity back to the lives of our young people, preventing them offending, bringing back stability and order to their lives and encouraging greater parental responsibility.

Protection of the public is of the utmost importance. Therefore we must ensure that punishments are effectively targeted to prevent children reoffending. [Home Office, September 1997.]

This passage makes clear the fusion effected in New Labour penology between responsibility, prevention and public protection. It also leaves little doubt (and any lingering doubt on this point is dispelled entirely by the most casual perusal of no end of other Ministerial statements) that protection trumps all other considerations – it is this that has the 'utmost importance'. But the 'safer and more responsible society' necessitates a sharing out of responsibilities; it requires the enlistment of young people, their parents (compulsorily if need be), local agencies and central initiative. In this sense, whereas the Conservatives' headlining of riskiness remained centred upon a rather traditional set of interactions between the offender and the courts, New Labour's reinvention of at-risk-ness envisions a wider array of networks and communications amongst co-operating agencies and their clients. It involves a chain of responsibilised actors, and reaches deeper and more ambitiously into the everyday operation of localities, communities and familial relationships.

10.3 CONCLUSIONS

There is ample material in the recent history of penal politics in Britain to vindicate O'Malley's (1999) observation that this arena has been, and continues to be both 'volatile and contradictory'. Here we have highlighted only a few indicative elements from a tortuous and contentious story; but these suffice to establish certain salient points.

For present purposes, including that of diagnosing the ideological identity of New Labour, what we chiefly observe is a clever rearrangement of the relations between the populist and technical, and between the 'penal' and the 'social' in crime control. As Ryan (1999) acutely observes, New Labour's key invention of 'crime and disorder' may be distinctly populist, but it is by no means merely gestural; rather it comes with a rigorous programme of interventions attached. The language of crime and disorder claims to speak over the heads of liberal élites, special interests and pressure groups to the needs of hard-pressed communities, especially those of inner urban high-crime localities. Thus, although involving some major reversals of traditional Labour home affairs policy, it posits as its prime beneficiaries some core Labour constituencies amongst respectable working- and lower-middle class voters. Its claim to privileged knowledge of and responsiveness to the concerns and aspirations of those communities serves to justify its impatience with its disreputable targets and their liberal apologists. There is little sign here of divestment or offloading on the part of the state, still less of 'defining deviance down'. Rather the programmatic and impatient nature of the policy agenda demands a repeated stress upon the immensity of the task; and the reforming zeal of those involved warrants a short way with dissenters, back-sliders, critics and sceptics. Neither is the current rediscovery of state capacity obviously well-described as an 'hysterical' or 'defensive' posture. To the contrary, the New Labour ideological apparatus is at pains to emphasise the integration between criminal justice and other social policy fields, especially housing, family policy and education. However distasteful to the legal guaranteeism espoused by its liberal critics (Ashworth *et al*, 1998), the New Labour position is a capacious and far from purely reactionary one – it relishes the doctrinally promiscuous and pragmatically inventive posture of 'third way' social policy (cf Rose, 2000; Stenson and Edwards, in press). Meanwhile, the repositioning of crime policy as social/community policy (as part-and-parcel of 'joined-up thinking', not to mention the prospects of research monies and jobs) tends to draw many former critics inside Mr Blair's 'big tent'.

The relation between New Labour's stance on 'crime and disorder' (so far) and those of its predecessor state regimes is complex, and will doubtless change further. Its key strategists have immersed themselves in the mores of Thatcherite neo-liberalism and, certainly at the level of technique and process, have adopted many of them (the focus on auditing and 'best value', the demand for evaluation, the responsibilising of local authorities, the creation of ad hoc 'partnerships' and so on). Yet those who foresaw a simple continuation of Michael Howard's hard-line classicism failed to anticipate either the modulation in ideological preferences and objectives that would ensue or the range, penetrativeness and commitment of the means used to pursue them. Indeed it is the very juxtaposition between familiar and novel sightings on the penal landscape that designedly disrupts existing political classifications and suggests the need for new thinking. If we wish to trace out a history of the present configuration of risk ideas in criminal justice we will have to acknowledge that they do not all originate in one place, either ideologically or temporally. For example, we have observed above the retrieval of some 'old' welfarist concerns in youth justice (and given greater space it would be possible to trace a long and complicated family tree of such resemblance) – but these no longer have only their former implications, nor do they now associate only with their old kin. What is important to note is that when certain conceptual threads 'braid with' others (O'Malley, 2000a, p 467) they create a new pattern that demands a contemporary response.

It is clearly the case that risk has come to occupy a pivotal position in penal politics and practice in recent times. It has moved from the margins (the question of what to do with certain people judged dangerous or incorrigible) to the centre (the question of how to organise the penal field so as to deliver maximum 'protection'). However, the questions of risk and protection have been differently inflected at different moments. They have occupied a distinct position in the rising and declining fortunes of political parties and in their tactical judgments; and they have also figured differently in the formation of programmes for governance and the selection of objects for intervention. Certain of the traditional dichotomies of social and political analysis (between 'populism' and 'technocracy', toughness and tenderness, modernisation and traditionalism, for instance) are thrown into some confusion here. Those who would claim to detect only continuity between the penal postures of the main political actors; or only abandonment in New Labour's attitude to social democracy; or only the workings-out of an historical destiny for a strictly actuarial 'new penology', are each equally likely to miss the ever-mobile target.

BIBLIOGRAPHY

Chapter 1

Beck, U, *Risk Society*, 1992, New York: Sage

Beck, U, 'Politics of risk society', in Franklin, J (ed), *The Politics of Risk Society*, 1998, Cambridge: Polity

Crawford, A, *The Local Governance of Crime: Appeals to Community and Partnerships*, 1997, Oxford: Clarendon

Crawford, MJ *et al*, 'Most psychiatrists oppose plans for new mental health act' (2001) 322 BMJ 866

Eastman, N, 'Public health psychiatry or crime prevention?' (1999) 318 BMJ 549

Ericson, R and Haggerty, K, *Policing the Risk Society*, 1997, Oxford: Clarendon

Feeley, M and Simon, J, 'The new penology: notes on the emerging strategy for corrections' (1992) 30(4) Criminology 449

Furedi, F, *Culture of Fear: Risk Taking and the Morality of Low Expectations*, 1997, London: Cassell

Garland, D, 'The limits of the Sovereign State' (1996) 34(4) Br J Crim 445

Gledhill, K, 'Managing dangerous people with severe personality disorder' (2000) 11(2) J Forensic Psychiatry 439

Home Office/Department of Health, *Managing Dangerous People with Severe Personality Disorder – Proposals for Policy Development*, 1999, London: HMSO

Home Office/Department of Health, *Reforming the Mental Health Act*, 2000, London: HMSO

Laing, J, 'An end to the lottery? The Fallon Report and personality disordered offenders' [1999] J Mental Health Law 87

Shearing, CD and Stenning, PC, 'Say cheese: the Disney order that is not so Mickey Mouse', in Shearing, CD and Stenning, PC, (eds), *Private Policing*, 1987, California: Sage

Sheptycki, J, 'Insecurity, risk suppression and segregation' (1997) 1(3) Theoretical Criminology 307

Chapter 2

Appelbaum, PS, Robbins, PC and Monahan, J, 'Violence and delusions: data from the MacArthur Violence Risk Assessment Study' (2000) 157 Am J Psychiatry 566

Blom-Cooper L, Hally H and Murphy E, 1995, *The Falling Shadow: One Patient's Mental Health Care, 1978–93*, 1995, London: Duckworth

Department of Health and Social Security, *Report of an Inquiry into the Care and Treatment of Sharon Campbell*, 1988, London: HMSO

Lidz, CW, Mulvey, EP and Gardner, W, 'The accuracy of prediction of violence to others' (1993) 269 J American Medical Association 1007

Monahan, J, Steadman, HJ, Appelbaum, PS, Robbins, PC, Mulvey, EP, Silver, E, Roth, LH and Grisso, T, 'Developing a clinical useful actuarial tool for assessing violence risk' (2000) 176 Br J Psychiatry 312

Petch, E and Bradley, C, 'Learning the lessons from homicide inquiries: adding insult to injury?' (1997) 8 Br J Forensic Psychiatry 161

Ritchie, J, Dick, D and Lingham, R, *The Report of the Inquiry into the Care and Treatment of Christopher Clunis*, 1994, London: HMSO

Royal College of Psychiatrists, *Good Medical Practice in the Aftercare of Potentially Violent and Vulnerable Patients Discharged from Inpatient Psychiatric Care*, 1991, London: Royal College of Psychiatrists

Swanson, GAW, Holzer, CE, Ganju, VK and Jonort, *Violence and Psychiatric Disorder in the Community: Evidence from the Epidemiologic Catchment Area Surveys*, 1990

Watkins, SJ, 'Conviction by mathematical error? Doctors and lawyers should get their probability theory right' (2000) 320 BMJ 2

Chapter 3

American Psychiatric Association, *Diagnostic and Statistical Manual of Mental Disorders*, 4th edn, 1994, Washington, DC

Babiak, P, 'When psychopaths go to work' (1995) 44 Int J Applied Psychology 171

Barbaree, H, Seto, M, Serin, R, Amos, N and Preston, D, 'Comparisons between sexual and nonsexual rapist subtypes' (1994) 21 Criminal Justice and Behaviour 95

Berrios, GE, *The History of Mental Symptoms: Descriptive Psychopathology Since the Nineteenth Century*, 1996, Cambridge: CUP

Brandt, JR, Kennedy, WA, Patrick, CL and Curtin, JJ, 'Assessment of psychopathy in a population of incarcerated adolescent offenders' (1997) 9 Psychological Assessment 429

Brown, SL and Forth, AE, 'Psychopathy and sexual assault: static risk factors, emotional precursors, and rapist subtypes' (1997) 65 J Consulting and Clinical Psychology 848

Cooke, DJ, 'Psychopathy across cultures', in Cooke, DJ, Forth, AE and Hare, RD (eds), *Psychopathy: Theory, Research, and Implications for Society*, 1998, Dordrecht, The Netherlands: Kluwer

Cooke, DJ, Forth, AE and Hare, RD (eds), *Psychopathy: Theory, Research, and Implications for Society*, 1998, Dordrecht, The Netherlands: Kluwer

Cooke, DJ and Michie, C, 'An item response theory analysis of the Hare Psychopathy Checklist' (1997) 9 Psychological Assessment 3

Cooke, DJ and Michie, C, 'Psychopathy across cultures: North America and Scotland compared' (1999a) 108 J Abnormal Psychology 58

Cooke, DJ and Michie, C, 'A hierarchical model of psychopathy: replication and implications for measurement' (1999b), paper presented at the APLS/EAPI/Psychology and Law International Conference, Dublin, Ireland, July 1999

Cooke, DJ, Michie, C, Hart, SD and Hare, RD, 'Evaluation of the screening version of the Hare Psychopathy Checklist Revised (PCL:SV): an item response theory analysis' (1999) 11 Psychological Assessment 3

Colé, G and Hodgins, S, *L'Echelle de psychopathie de Hare – Revisée: eléments de la validation de la version française*, 1996, Toronto, ON: Multi-Health Systems

Cruise, KR, Rogers, RR, Neumann, CS and Sewell, KW, 'Measurement of adolescent psychopathy: testing the two-factor model in juvenile offenders', paper presented at the American Psychology-Law Society Conference, New Orleans LA, March 2000

Dolan, B and Coid, J, *Psychopathic and Antisocial Personality Disorders: Treatment and Research Issues*, 1993, London: Gaskell

Douglas, KS, Ogloff, JRP and Nicholls, TL, 'Personality disorders and violence in civil psychiatric patients', paper presented at the 5th International Congress on the Disorders of Personality, Vancouver, British Columbia, June 1997

Dolan, M and Doyle, M, 'Violence risk prediction: clinical and actuarial measures and the role of the Psychotherapy Checklist' (2000) 177 Br J Psychiatry 303

Federal Bureau of Investigation, *Killed in the Line of Duty*, 1992, Washington, DC: United States Department of Justice

Firestone, P, Bradford, JM, Greenberg, DM and Larose, MR, 'Homicidal sex offenders: psychological, phallometric, and diagnostic features' (1998) 6 J American Academy of Psychiatry and Law 537

Forth, AE, *Psychopathy and Young Offenders: Prevalence, Family Background and Violence*, 1995, Programs Branch Users Report, Ottawa, Ontario: Ministry of the Solicitor General of Canada

Forth, AE and Burke, H, 'Psychopathy in adolescence: assessment, violence, and developmental precursors', in Cooke, DJ, Forth, AE and Hare, RD (eds), *Psychopathy: Theory, Research and Implications for Society*, 1998, Dordrecht, The Netherlands: Kluwer

Forth, AE, Hart, SD and Hare, RD 'Assessment of psychopathy in male young offenders' (1990) 2 Psychological Assessment 342

Forth, AE, Kosson, D and Hare, RD, *The Hare Psychopathy Checklist: Youth Version* (in press), Toronto, ON: Multi-Health Systems

Frick, PJ, 'Callous-emotional traits and conduct problems: applying the two-factor model of psychopathy to children', in Cooke, DJ, Forth, AE and Hare, RD (eds), *Psychopathy: Theory, Research, and Implications for Society*, 1998, Dordrecht, The Netherlands: Kluwer

Gonçalves, RA, 'Psychopathy and offender types: results from a Portuguese prison sample' (1999) 22 Int J Law and Psychiatry 337

Grann, M, Långström, N, Tengström, A and Kullgren, G, 'Psychopathy (PCL-R) predicts violent recidivism among criminal offenders with personality disorders in Sweden' (1999) 23 Law and Human Behaviour 205

Grann, M, Långström, N, Tengström, A and Stalenheim, EG, 'Reliability of file-based retrospective ratings of psychopathy with the PCL-R' (1998) 70 J Personality Assessment 416

Gretton, HM, 'Psychopathy and recidivism in adolescence: a ten-year retrospective follow-up', unpublished doctoral dissertation, 1998, University of British Columbia, Vancouver, Canada

Gretton, HM, McBride, M, O'Shaughnessy, R, Kumka G and Hare, RD, 'Psychopathy and recidivism in adolescent sex offenders' (2001) 28 Criminal Justice and Behaviour 427

Hanson, RK, 'The development of a brief actuarial risk scale for sexual offence recidivism' (User report No 1997-04), Ottawa, Canada: Department of the Solicitor General of Canada, 1997

Hanson, RK and Thornton, D, 'STATIC-2000 Unpublished report', Offending Behaviour Programmes Unit, Her Majesty's Prison Service, London

Hare, RD, *The Hare Psychopathy Checklist – Revised*, 1991, Toronto, ON: Multi-Health Systems

Hare, RD, 'Psychopathy, affect, and behaviour' (1998a), in Cooke, DJ, Forth, AE and Hare, RD (eds), *Psychopathy: Theory, Research, and Implications for Society*, Dordrecht, The Netherlands: Kluwer

Hare, RD, *Without Conscience: The Disturbing World of the Psychopaths Among Us*, 1998b, New York: Guilford Press

Hare, RD, Clark, D, Grann, M and Thornton, D, 'Psychopathy and the predictive validity of the PCL-R: an international perspective' (2000) 18 Behavioural Sciences and the Law 623

Hare, RD, Cooke, DL and Hart, SD, 'Psychopathy and sadistic personality disorder', in Millon, T, Blaney, P and Davis, R (eds), *Oxford Textbook of Psychopathology*, 1999, Oxford: OUP

Hare, RD and Hart, SD, 'A commentary on the Antisocial Personality Disorder Field Trial', in Livesley, WJ (ed), *The DSM-IV Personality Disorders*, 1995, New York: Guilford

Hare, RD and Hervé, H, *The Hare P-Scan*, 1999, Toronto, ON: Multi-Health Systems

Hare, RD, McPherson, LE and Forth, AE, 'Male psychopaths and their criminal careers' (1988) 56 J Consulting and Clinical Psychology 710

Harpur, TI, Hare, RD and Hakstian, R, 'A two-factor conceptualisation of psychopathy: construct validity and implications for assessment' (1989) 1 Psychological Assessment 6

Harris, AJR and Hanson, RK, 'Supervising the psychopathic sex deviant in the community' (1998) paper presented at the 17th Annual Research and Treatment Conference, The Association for the Treatment of Sexual Abusers, Vancouver, Canada, October 1998

Harris, GT, Rice, ME and Quinsey, VL, 'Violent recidivism of mentally disordered offenders: the development of a statistical prediction instrument' (1993) 20 Criminal Justice and Behaviour 315

Hart, SD, 'Psychopathy and risk for violence', in Cooke, DJ, Forth, AE and Hare, RD (eds), Psychopathy: Theory, Research, and Implications for Society, 1998, Dordrecht, The Netherlands: Kluwer

Hart, SD, Cox, DN and Hare, RD, The Hare Psychopathy Checklist: Screening Version, 1995, Toronto, ON: Multi-Health Systems

Hart, SD and Hare, RD, 'Discriminant validity of the Psychopathy Checklist in a forensic psychiatric population' (1989) 1 Psychological Assessment 211

Hart, SD, Kropp, PR and Hare, RD, 'Performance of psychopaths following conditional release from prison' (1988) 56 J Consulting and Clinical Psychology 227

Heilbrun, K, Hart, SD, Hare, RD, Gustafison, D, Nunez, C and White, A, 'Inpatient and post-discharge aggression in mentally disordered offenders: the role of psychopathy' (1998) 13 J Interpersonal Violence 514

Hemphill, JF, 'Psychopathy and recidivism following release from a therapeutic community treatment program', unpublished masters thesis, 1991, University of Saskatchewan, Saskatoon, Canada

Hemphill, JE and Hare, RD, 'The association between PCL-R scores and symptom counts for antisocial personality disorder', unpublished data, 2000, Department of Psychology, University of British Columbia

Hemphill, JF, Hare, RD and Wong, S, 'Psychopathy and recidivism: a review' (1998) 3 Legal and Criminological Psychology 141

Hemphill, JF, Newman, JP and Hare, RD, 'Psychopathy and recidivism in White and African-American offenders' (2000) as yet unpublished

Hemphill, JF, Strachan, C and Hare, RD, 'Psychopathy in female offenders' (1999) as yet unpublished

Hill, CD, Rogers, R and Bickford, ME, 'Predicting aggressive and socially disruptive behaviour in a maximum security forensic psychiatric hospital' (1996) 41 J Forensic Sciences 56

Hobson, L, Shine, L and Roberts, R, 'How do psychopaths behave in a prison therapeutic community?' (2000) Psychology, Crime, and the Law

Hodgins, S, Cote, G and Ross, D, 'Predictive validity of the French version of Hare's Psychopathy Checklist' (1992) 33 Canadian Psychology 301

Livesley, WJ, 'The phenotypic and genotypic structure of psychopathic traits', in Cooke, DJ, Forth, AE and Hare, RD (eds), *Psychopathy: Theory, Research, and Implications for Society,* 1998, Dordrecht, The Netherlands: Kluwer

Losel, F, 'Treatment and management of psychopaths', in Cooke, DJ, Forth, AE and Hare, RD (eds), *Psychopathy: Theory, Research, and Implications for Society,* 1998, Dordrecht, The Netherlands: Kluwer

Loucks, AD and Zamble, E, 'Predictors of criminal behaviour and prison misconduct in serious female offenders' (2000) 1 Empirical and Applied Criminal Justice Review 1

Lykken, DT, *The Antisocial Personalities,* 1995, Hillsdale, NJ: Erlbaum

Lynam, DR, 'Early identification of chronic offenders: who is the fledgling psychopath?' (1996) 120 Psychological Bulletin 209

McBride, M, 'Individual and familial risk factors for adolescent psychopathy', unpublished doctoral dissertation, 1998, University of British Columbia, Vancouver, Canada

McCord, W and McCord, J, *The Psychopath: An Essay on the Criminal Mind,* 1964, Princeton, NJ: Van Nostrand

McDermott, PA, Alterman, AI, Cacciola, JS, Rutherford, ML, Newman, JP and Mulholland, EM, 'Generality of Psychopathy Checklist – Revised factors over prisoners and substance-dependent patients' (2000) 68 J Consulting and Clinical Psychology 181

Mealey, L, 'The socio-biology of sociopathy: an integrated evolutionary model (1995) 18 Behavioural and Brain Sciences 523

Miller, MW, Geddings, VL, Levenston, GK and Patrick, CJ, 'The personality characteristics of psychopathic and non-psychopathic sex offenders' paper presented at the Biennial Meeting of the American Psychology-Law Society (Div 41 of the American Psychological Association), Santa Fe, New Mexico, March 1994

Millon, T, Simonsen, E, Birket-Smith, M and Davis, RD, *Psychopathy: Antisocial, Criminal, and Violent Behaviours*, 1998, New York: Guilford

Moltó, L, Poy, R and Torrubia, R, 'Standardization of the Hare Psychopathy Checklist Revised in a Spanish prison sample' (2000) 14 J Personality Disorders 84

Monahan, L and Steadman, H (eds), *Violence and Mental Disorder: Developments in Risk Assessment*, 1994, Chicago: University of Chicago Press

Newlove, T, Hart, SD, Dutton, DG and Hare, RD, 'Psychopathy and family violence' (1992) 33 Canadian Psychology 405

Ogloff, L, Wong, S and Greenwood, A, 'Treating criminal psychopaths in a therapeutic community program' (1990) 8 Behavioural Sciences and the Law 81

Pham, TH, 'Evaluation psychométrique du questionnaire de la psychopathie de Hare auprès d'une population carcerale belge' [Psychometric assessment of the Hare Psychopathy Checklist-Revised (PCL-R) in a Belgian prison sample] (1998) 24 Encephale 435

Pichot, P, 'Psychopathic behaviour: a historical overview' (1978), in Hare, RD and Schalling, D (eds), *Psychopathic Behaviour: Approaches to Research*, Chichester: John Wiley

Porter, S, Fairweather, D, Drugge, L, Heré, H, Birt, A and Boer, DP, 'Profiles of psychopathy in incarcerated sexual offenders' (2000) 27 Criminal Justice and Behaviour 216

Quinsey, VL, Harris, GE, Rice, ME and Cormier, C, *Violent Offenders: Appraising and Managing Risk*, 1998, Washington, DC: American Psychological Association

Quinsey, VL, Rice, ME and Harris, GT, 'Actuarial prediction of sexual recidivism' (1995) 10 J Interpersonal Violence 85

Rice, ME and Harris, GT, 'A comparison of criminal recidivism among schizophrenic and non-schizophrenic offenders' (1992) 15 Int J Law and Psychiatry 397

Rice, ME and Harris, GT, 'Cross-validation and extension of the Violence Risk Appraisal Guide for child molesters and rapists' (1997) 21 Law and Human Behaviour 231

Rice, ME, Harris, GT and Cormier, CA, 'An evaluation of a maximum security therapeutic community for psychopaths and other mentally disordered offenders' (1992) 16 Law and Human Behaviour 399

Robins, LN, 'Aetiological implications in studies of childhood histories relating to antisocial personality' (1978), in Hare, RD and Schalling, D (eds), Psychopathic behaviour: Approaches to Research, Chichester: Wiley

Rogers, R, Salekin, RT, Sewell, KW and Cruise, KR, 'Prototypical analysis of antisocial personality disorder: a study of inmate samples' (2000) 27 Criminal Justice and Behaviour 234

Salekin, R, Rogers, R and Sewell, K, 'A review and meta-analysis of the Psychopathy Checklist and Psychopathy Checklist-Revised: predictive validity of dangerousness' (1996) 3 Clinical Psychology: Science and Practice 203

Salekin, R, Rogers, R and Sewell, K, 'Construct validity of psychopathy in a female offender sample: a multitrait-multimethod evaluation' (1997) 106 J Abnormal Psychology 576

Salekin, RW, Rogers, R, Ustad, KL and Sewell, KM, 'Psychopathy and recidivism among female inmates' (1998) 22 Law and Human Behaviour 109

Serin, RC and Amos, NL, 'The role of psychopathy in the assessment of dangerousness' (1995) 18 Int J of Law and Psychiatry 231

Serin, RC, Malcolm, PB, Khanna, A and Barbaree, HE, 'Psychopathy and deviant sexual arousal in incarcerated sexual offenders' (1994) 9 J Interpersonal Violence 3

Serin, RC, Mailloux, DL and Malcolm, PB, 'Psychopathy, sexual arousal, and recidivism' (2001) 16 J Interpersonal Violence 234

Seto, MC and Barbaree, HE, 'Psychopathy, treatment behaviour, and sex offenders recidivism' (1999) 14 J Interpersonal Violence 1235

Silver, E, Mulvey, EP and Monahan, J, 'Assessing violence risk among discharged psychiatric patients: toward an ecological approach' (1999) 23 Law and Human Behaviour 237

Steadman, HL, Silver, E, Monahan, L, Appelbaum, PS, Robbins, PM, Mulvey, EP, Grisso, T, Roth, LH and Banks, SA, 'Classification tree approach to the development of actuarial violence risk assessment tools' (1999) 24 Law and Human Behaviour 83

Stone, MH, 'The personalities of murderers: the importance of psychopathy and sadism', in Skodol, AE (ed), *Psychopathology and Violent Crime*, 1998, Washington, DC: American Psychiatric Association

Suedfeld, P and Landon, PB, 'Approaches to treatment', in Hare, RD and Schalling, D (eds), *Psychopathic Behaviour: Approaches to Research*, 1978, Chichester: Wiley

Tengström, A, Grann, M, Långström, N, and Kullgren, G, 'Psychopathy (PCL-R) as a predictor of violent recidivism among criminal offenders with schizophrenia' (2000) 24 Law and Human Behaviour 45

Toch, H, 'Psychopathy or antisocial personality in forensic settings' (1998), in Millon, T, Simonsen, E, Birket-Smith, M and Davis, RD (eds), *Psychopathy: Antisocial, Criminal, and Violent Behaviours*, 1998, New York: Guilford

Toupin, L, Mercier, H, Déry, MC, Côté, G and Hodgins, S, 'Validity of the PCL-R for adolescents', in Cooke, DJ, Forth, AE, Newman, JP and Hare, RD (eds), *Issues in Criminological and Legal Psychology: No 24, International Perspectives on Psychopathy*, 1996, Leicester: British Psychological Society

Tucker, W, 'The "mad" vs the "bad" revisited: managing predatory behaviour' (1999) 70 Psychiatric Quarterly 221

Webster, C Douglas, Eaves, K and Hart, DS, *HRC-20: Assessing the Risk of Violence*, Version 2, 1997, Burnaby, BC, Canada: Simon Fraser University, Forensic Psychiatric Services Commission of British Columbia

Widiger, TA, 'Psychopathy and normal personality', in Cooke, DJ, Forth, AE and Hare, RD (eds), *Psychopathy: Theory, Research, and Implications for Society*, 1998, Dordrecht, The Netherlands: Kluwer

Widiger, TA, Cadoret, R, Hare, RD, Robins, L, Rutherford, M, Zanarini, M, Alterman, A, Apple, M, Corbitt, E, Forth, A, Hart, S, Kulterman, L and Woody, G, 'DSM-IV Antisocial Personality Disorder Field Trial' (1996) 105 J Abnormal Psychology 3

Windle, M and Dumenci, L, 'The factorial structure and construct validity of the Psychopathy Checklist-Revised (PCL-R) among alcoholic inpatients' (1999) 6 Structural Equation Modelling 372

Wintrup, A, 'The predictive validity of the PCL-R in high risk mentally disordered offenders', unpublished manuscript, 1994, Simon Fraser University, Burnaby, Canada

Wong, S and Hare, RD, *Program Guidelines for the Institutional Treatment of Violent Psychopaths*, in press, Toronto, ON: Multi-Health Systems

World Health Organisation, *International Classification of Diseases and Related Health Problems*, 10th edn, 1990, Geneva, Switzerland

Chapter 4

Papers

American Psychiatric Association, *Diagnostic and Statistical Manual*, 4th edn, 1994, Washington, DC: American Psychiatric Association

Bottoms, AE, 'Selected issues in the dangerousness debate', in Hamilton, JR and Freeman, H (eds), *Dangerousness: Psychiatric Assessment and Management*, 1982, London: Gaskell/Royal College of Psychiatrists

Butler, Lord, *Report of the Committee on Mentally Abnormal Offenders*, Cmnd 6244, 1975, London: HMSO

Coker, R, 'Public health, civil liberties and tuberculosis' (1999) 318 BMJ 14

Department of Health, *Reform of the Mental Health Act; Proposals for Consultation*, Green Paper (1999)

Department of Health, 'In-patients formally detained in hospitals under the Mental Health Act 1983 and other legislation, England: 1990–91 to 1995–96', Statistical Bulletin 1997/4

Eastman, NLG, 'Public health psychiatry or crime prevention?' (1999) 318 BMJ 549

Eastman, NLG, 'Ethical and policy implications of legal and administrative developments since enactment of the Mental Health Act 1983', unpublished MD thesis, 2000, University of London

Eastman, NLG and McInerny, T, 'Psychiatrists and the death penalty: ethical principals and analogies' (1997) 8(3) J Forensic Psychiatry 583

Eastman, NLG and Peay, J, 'Sentencing psychopaths: is the Hospital and Limitations Direction an ill-considered hybrid?' [1998] Crim LR 93

Fallon, P, Bluglass, R, Edwards, B and Daniels, G, *Report of the Committee of Inquiry into the Personality Disorder Unit, Ashworth Special Hospital*, 1998, London: HMSO

General Medical Council, *Duties of a doctor: guidance from the GMC – confidentiality*, 1995, London

Heginbotham, C and Elson, A, 'Public policy via law: practitioner's sword and politician's shield', in Eastman, N and Peay, J (eds), *Law Without Enforcement; Integrating Mental Health and Justice*, 1999, Oxford: Hart

Home Office, *Protecting the Public: the Government's Strategy on Crime in England and Wales*, Cm 3190, 1996, London: HMSO

Home Office, *Managing Dangerous People with Severe Personality Disorder, Proposals for Policy Development*, 1999, London: HMSO

House of Commons Select Committee on Home Affairs, *Managing Dangerous People with Personality Disorder: Report together with the Proceedings of the Committee, Minutes of Evidence and Appendices* (2000) HC 42

Hurwitz, B and Richardson, R, 'Swearing to care: the resurgence in medical oaths' (1997) 315 BMJ 1671

Kendall, R, 'Jack Straw and police under fire after Stone verdict' (1998) *The Times*, 29 October

King, M and Piper, C, *How the Law Thinks About Children*, 2nd edn, 1995, Aldershot: Arena

Lewis, A, 'Psychopathic personality: a most elusive category' (1974) 4 Psychological Medicine 133

Mackay, R, *Mental Condition Defences in the Criminal Law*, 1995, Oxford: Clarendon

Peay, J, *Tribunals on Trial*, 1989, Oxford: Clarendon

Pearson, G, 'Madness and moral panics', in Eastman, N and Peay, J (eds), *Law Without Enforcement; Integrating Mental Health and Justice*, 1999, Oxford: Hart

Rawls, J, *A Theory of Justice*, 1971, London: OUP

Ritchie, JH, QC, Dick, D and Lingham, R, *The Report of the Inquiry into the Care and Treatment of Christopher Clunis*, 1994, London: HMSO

Straw, J, 'Straw's riposte on mental treatment' (1998) *The Times*, 31 October

Straw J, *Hansard*, 5 February 1999, col 601-3

World Health Organisation, *International Classification of Diseases*, 10th edn, *Classification of Mental and Behavioural Disorders: Clinical Descriptions and Diagnostic Guidelines*, 1992, Geneva: WHO

Chapter 5

Beck, U, 'From industrial society to risk society: questions of survival, social structure and ecological enlightenment' (1992) 9 Theory, Culture and Society 91

Blom-Cooper, L, Grounds, A, Guinan, P, Parker, A and Taylor, M, *The Case of Jason Mitchell: Report of the Independent Inquiry*, 1996, London: Duckworth

Blom-Cooper, L, Hally, H and Murphy, E, *The Falling Shadow: One Patient's Mental Health Care 1978–93*, 1995, London: Duckworth

Castel, R, 'From dangerousness to risk', in Bruchell, G, Gordon, C and Miller, P (eds), *The Foucault Effect: Studies in Governmentality*, 1991, Hemel Hempstead: Harvester Wheatsheaf

Chesney, K, *The Victorian Underworld*, Pelican

Collins, P, 'The treatability of psychopaths' (1991) 2 J Forensic Psychiatry 103

Cope, R, 'A survey of forensic psychiatrists' views on psychopathic disorder' (1993) 4 J Forensic Psychiatry 227

Department of Health, 1990, *Care Programme Approach for People with a Mental Illness Referred to the Specialist Psychiatric Services*, HC (90)23/LASSL(90)11, London: HMSO

Department of Health, 1995, *Building Bridges: a Guide to Inter-agency Working for the Care and Protection of Severely Mentally Ill People*, London: HMSO

Department of Health, 1996, *Spectrum of Care: Audit Pack for Monitoring the Care Programme Approach – Background and Explanatory Notes*, NHS Executive HSG 96(6), London: HMSO

Department of Health, 1999a, *Effective Care Co-ordination in Mental Health Services: Modernising the Care Programme Approach: A Policy Booklet*, London: HMSO

Department of Health, 1999b, *Report of the Committee of Inquiry into the Personality Disorder Unit, Ashworth Special Hospital*, Cm 4194, London: HMSO

Department of Health, 1999c, *Review of the Mental Health Act 1983: Report of the Expert Committee*, London: HMSO

Department of Health, 2000, *In-Patients Formally Detained in Hospitals under the Mental Health Act 1983 and other Legislation, England: 1988–89 and 1994–95 to 1999–2000*, Statistical Bulletin 2000/19, London: HMSO

Foucault, M, *Discipline and Punish: The Birth of the Prison*, Sheridan, A (trans), 1977, New York: Pantheon

Grounds, A, 'The transfer of sentenced prisoners to hospital 1960–83: a study in one special hospital' (1991) 31 Br J Crim 54

Grounds, A, 'Transfers of sentenced prisoners to hospital' [1990] Crim L Rev 544

Gunn, J, Maden A and Sinton M, 'Treatment needs of prisoners with mental disorder' [1991] BMJ 303

Henham, R, 'Sentencing policy, appellate guidance and protective sentencing' [1996] J Crim Law 424

Home Office, *Report of the Committee of Inquiry into the Care and After-care of Miss Sharon Campbell* (The Spokes Report), Cmd 440, 1998, London: HMSO

Home Office, *Review of Health and Social Services for Mentally Disordered Offenders and Others Requiring Similar Services* (The Reed Report), Chairman Dr John Reed, Cm 2088, 1992, London: HMSO

Home Office, *Reform of the Mental Health Act 1983: Proposals for Consultation*, Cm 4480, 1999, London: HMSO

Home Office/Department of Health, Discussion Document: *Managing Dangerous People with a Severe Personality Disorder: Proposals for Policy Development*, 1999, London: HMSO

Home Office, *Reforming the Mental Health Act: Part I The New Legal Framework*, TSO 2000, Cm 5016-1, 2000a, London: HMSO

Home Office, *Reforming the Mental Health Act: Part II High Risk Patients*, TSO 2000, Cm 5016-2, 2000b, London: HMSO

Lewis, A, 'Psychopathic personality: a most elusive category' (1974) 4 Psychological Medicine 133

Pope, HMR, *A Treatise on the Law and Practice of Lunacy*, 1890, London: Sweet & Maxwell

Ritchie, JH, Dick, D and Lingham, R, *Report of the Inquiry into the Care and Treatment of Christopher Clunis*, 1994, London: HMSO

Rose, N, 'At risk of madness: law, politics and forensic psychiatry', paper delivered at the Cropwood Conference on The Future of Forensic Psychiatry, St John's College, Cambridge, 19–21 March 1997

Taylor, P and Gunn, J, 'Homicides by people with mental illness: myth and reality' (1999) 174 Br J Psychiatry 9

Wachenfeld, M, *The Human Rights of the Mentally Ill in Europe*, 1992, Copenhagen: Danish Centre for Human Rights

Chapter 6

Ashworth, A, 'Concepts of Criminal Justice' [1979] Crim LR 412

Ashworth, A, 'Criminal justice and criminal process' (1988) 28(2) Br J Crim 241

Ashworth, A, 'Principles, practice and criminal justice', in Birks, P (ed), *Pressing Problems in the Law*, Vol 1, *Criminal Justice and Human Rights*, 1995, Oxford: OUP

Ashworth, A, 'Crime, community and creeping consequentialism' [1996] Crim LR 220

Bauman, Z, *Modernity and the Holocaust*, 1989, Cambridge: Polity

Bauman, Z, *Postmodern Ethics*, 1993, Oxford: Blackwell

Beck, U, *Risk Society: Towards a New Modernity*, 1992, London: Sage

Benhabib, S, *Critique, Norm and Utopia*, 1986, New York: Columbia UP

Bottoms, A, 'The philosophy and politics of punishment and sentencing', in Clarkson, CMV and Morgan, R (eds), *The Politics of Sentencing Reform*, 1995, Oxford: Clarendon

Braithwaite, J, 'Restorative justice', in Tonry, M (ed), *The Handbook of Crime and Punishment*, 1998, New York: OUP

Braithwaite, J, 'Restorative justice: assessing optimistic and pessimistic accounts', in Tonry, M (ed), *Crime and Justice: A Review of Research*, Vol 25, 1999, Chicago; University of Chicago Press

Braithwaite, J and Pettit, P, *Not Just Deserts*, 1990, Oxford: OUP

Carlen, P, *Alternatives to Women's Imprisonment*, 1990, Milton Keynes: Open UP

Castel, R, 'From dangerousness to risk', in Burchell, G, Gordon, C and Miller, P (eds), *The Foucault Effect: Studies in Governmentality*, 1991, Chicago: University of Chicago Press

Clear, T, 'Risk and community practice', in Stenson, K and Sullivan, R (eds), *Crime Risk and Justice: The Politics of Crime Prevention in Liberal Democracies*, 2000, Collumpton: Willan

Cohen, S, *Visions of Social Control: Crime, Punishment and Classification*, 1985, Cambridge: Polity

Cohen, S, 'Social control and the politics of reconstruction', in Nelken, D (ed), *The Futures of Criminology*, 1994, London: Sage

Cohen, S, 'Intellectual scepticism and political commitment: the case of radical criminology', in Walton, P and Young, J (eds), *The New Criminology Revisited*, 1998, Basingstoke: Macmillan

Cornell, D, *The Philosophy of the Limit*, 1992, New York: Routledge

Crook, S, 'Ordering risks', in Lupton, D (ed), *Risk and Sociocultural Theory*, 1999, Cambridge: CUP

Derrida, J, 'Force of law: the 'mystical foundation of authority'' (1990) 11 Cardozo L Rev 971

Dershowitz, A, *Reasonable Doubts: The Criminal Justice System and the OJ Simpson Case*, 1997, New York: Touchstone

Douglas, M, *Purity and Danger: An Analysis of Conceptions of Purity and Taboo*, 1966, London: Routledge and Kegan Paul

Douglas, M, *Risk and Blame: Essays in Cultural Theory*, 1992, London: Routledge

Douglas, M, and Wildavsky, A, *Risk and Culture*, 1982, Berkeley, Ca: University of California Press

Duff, P, 'Crime control, due process and the 'case for the prosecution': a problem of terminology' (1998) 38(4) Br J Crim 611

Duff, RA, 'Penal communications: recent work in the philosophy of punishment', in Tonry, M (ed), *Crime and Justice: A Review of Research*, 1996, Chicago: University of Chicago Press

Duff, RA, 'Penal Communities', (1999) 1(1) Punishment and Society 23

Ericson, R and Carriere, K, 'The fragmentation of criminology', in Nelken, D (ed), *The Futures of Criminology*, 1994, London: Sage

Feeley, M and Simon, J, 'Actuarial justice: the emerging new criminal law', in Nelken, D (ed), *The Futures of Criminology*, 1994, London: Sage

Ferrara, A, *Justice and Judgement: The Rise and Prospect of the Judgement Model in Political Philosophy*, 1999, London: Sage

Garland, D, 'The limits of the Sovereign State: strategies of crime control in contemporary society' (1996) 36(4) Br J Crim 445

Garland, D, '"Governmentality" and the problem of crime: Foucault, criminology, sociology' (1997) 1(2) Theoretical Criminology 173

Garland, D, 'The culture of high crime societies: The social preconditions of the new politics of crime control', paper presented at the Conference on Crime, Neo-Liberalism and the Risk Society, John Jay College of Criminal Justice, New York, April 1999

Giddens, A, *The Consequences of Modernity*, 1990, Cambridge: Polity

Gordon, C, 'Governmental rationality: an introduction', in Burchell, G, Gordon, C and Miller, P (eds), *The Foucault Effect: Studies in Governmentality*, 1991, Chicago: University of Chicago Press

Habermas, J, *The Theory of Communicative Action*, Vols 1 and 2, 1984 and 1987, Boston, Mass: Beacon

Habermas, J, *Between Facts and Norms: Contribution to a Discourse Theory of Law and Democracy*, Rehg, W (trans), 1996, Cambridge: Polity

Hannah-Moffat, K, 'Moral agent or actuarial subject: risk and Canadian women's imprisonment' (1999) 3(1) Theoretical Criminology 71

Henham, R, 'Human rights, due process and sentencing' (1998) 38(4) Br J Crim 592

Home Office, 'Cautions, court proceedings and sentencing England and Wales' (1991) Statistical Bulletin 30/92, London: HMSO

Home Office, 'Cautions, court proceedings and sentencing England and Wales' (1997) Statistical Bulletin 18/98, London: HMSO

Home Office, *Protecting the Public: The Government's Strategy on Crime in England and Wales*, 1996, London: HMSO

Hudson, B, *Penal Policy and Social Justice*, 1993, Basingstoke: Macmillan

Hudson, B, 'Beyond proportionate punishment: difficult cases and the 1991 Criminal Justice Act' (1995) 22 Crime, Law and Social Change 59

Hudson, B, *Understanding Justice: An Introduction to Ideas, Perspectives and Controversies in Modern Penal Theory*, 1996, Buckingham: Open UP

Hudson, B, 'Punishment and governance' (1998a) 7(4) Social and Legal Studies 553

Hudson, B, 'Doing justice to difference', in Ashworth, A and Wasik, M (eds), *Fundamentals of Sentencing Theory*, 1998b, Oxford: Clarendon

Hudson, B, 'Restorative justice: the challenge of sexual and racial violence' (1998c) 25(2) J Law and Society 237

Hudson, B, 'Punishment, rights and difference: defending justice in the risk society', in Stenson, K and Sullivan, R (eds), *Crime, Risk and Justice: The Politics of Crime Prevention in Liberal Democracies*, 2000, Collumpton: Willan

Kelsen, H, 'What is justice', in Westphal, J (ed), *Justice*, 1996, Cambridge: Hackett

Kerruish, V, *Jurisprudence as Ideology*, 1991, London: Routledge

Lacey, N, 'Discretion and due process at the post-conviction stage', in Dennis, IH (ed), *Criminal Law and Justice*, 1987, London: Sweet & Maxwell

Lupton, D, 'Introduction: risk and sociocultural theory', in Lupton, D (ed), *Risk and Sociocultural Theory*, 1999, Cambridge: CUP

Lyotard, J-F, *The Post-Modern Condition: A Report on Knowledge*, Bennington, G and Massumi, B (trans), 1984, Manchester: Manchester UP

MacKinnon, CA, *Towards a Feminist Theory of the State*, 1989, Cambridge, Mass: CUP

McConville, M, Sanders, A and Leng, R, 'Descriptive or critical sociology: the choice is yours' (1997) 37(3) Br J Crim 347

Maffesoli, M, *The Time of the Tribes*, 1996, London: Sage

Marx, G, *Under Cover: Police Surveillance in America*, 1988, Berkeley: University of California Press

Mill, JS, 'On the connexion between justice and utility', in Westphal, J (ed), *Justice*, (1996), Cambridge: Hackett

Miller, P and Rose, N, 'Governing economic life' (1990) 19 Economy and Society 1

Minow, M, *Making All the Difference*, 1990, Ithaca, NY: Cornell UP

Morris, N, 'Dangerousness and incapacitation', in Duff, RA and Garland, D (eds), *A Reader in Punishment*, 1994, Oxford: OUP

O'Malley, P, 'Risk, power and crime prevention' (1992) 21(3) Economy and Society 252

O'Malley, P, 'Post-social criminologies: some implications of current political trends for criminological theory and practice' (1996) 8(1) Current Issues in Criminal Justice 26

O'Malley, P, 'Volatile and contradictory punishment' (1999) 3(2) Theoretical Criminology 175

Packer, H, *The Limits of the Criminal Sanction*, 1969, Stanford, Calif: Stanford UP

Pitch, T, *Limited Responsibilities: Social Movements and Criminal Justice*, English edn, 1995, London: Routledge

Pratt, J, 'Dangerousness, risk and technologies of power' (1995) 28(1) Australia and New Zealand J Crim 3

Rawls, J, *A Theory of Justice*, 1971, Oxford: OUP

Reiman, J, *Justice and Modern Moral Philosophy*, 1990, New Haven, Conn: Yale UP

Roberts, J and Domurad, F, 'Re-engineering probation: lessons from New York City' (1995) 1(1) Vista 59, Worcester: Association of Chief Officers of Probation

Rose, N, 'The death of the social? Refiguring the territory of government' (1996) 25(2) Economy and Society 327

Rose, N, and Miller, P, 'Political power beyond the state: problematics of government' (1992) 43 Br J of Sociology 173

Rutherford, A, 'Criminal policy and the eliminative ideal', unpublished inaugural lecture, 1996, University of Southampton

Sanders, A and Young, R, *Criminal Justice*, 1994, London: Butterworths

Sarat, A, 'Vengeance, victims and the identities of law' (1997) 6(2) Social and Legal Studies 163

Simon, J, 'The ideological effects of actuarial practice' (1988) 22(4) Law and Society Review 771

Simon, J, 'Criminology and the recidivist', in Schicor, D and Sechrest, DK (eds), *Three Strikes and You're Out: Vengeance as Public Policy*, 1996, Thousand Oaks, Calif: Sage

Smart, C, *Law, Crime and Sexuality: Essays in Feminism*, 1995, London: Sage

Van Swaaningen, R, *Critical Criminology: Visions from Europe*, 1997, London: Sage

Walzer, M, 'The politics of Michel Foucault', in Couzens Hoy, D (ed), *Foucault: A Critical Reader*, 1986, Oxford: Basil Blackwell

Williams, B, 'Bail bandits: the construction of a moral panic' (1993) 37 Critical Social Policy 104

Young, IM, *Justice and the Politics of Difference*, 1990, Princeton, NJ: Princeton UP

Von Hirsch, A, *Censure and Sanctions*, 1993, Oxford: OUP

Chapter 7

ABI, *Insurance Fraud Survey* – 1998, 1999, London: Association of British Insurers

Barnes, P and Sharp, D, *The Fraud Survey – 1998*, 1998, Leicester: Association of Certified Fraud Examiners

Blum, J, Levi, M, Naylor, T and Williams, P, *Financial Havens, Banking Secrecy and Money-Laundering*, Issue 8, UNDCP Technical Series, 1998, New York: United Nations (1998) UN document V 98-55024

British Retail Crime Survey, *Retail Crime*, 2000, London: British Retail Consortium

Clarke, M, *Business Crime*, 1990, Oxford: Polity

Computer Security, '1998 CSI/FBI computer crime and security survey' (1998) 4(1) Computer Security Issues and Trends 1

Customs and Excise, *Annual Report, 1998–99*, 1999, London: HMSO

European Commission, *Fight Against Fraud: Annual Report 1997*, 1998, Brussels, COM (98) 276

Goode Report, *Pension Law Reform, Report of the Pension Law Review Committee*, 1993, London: HMSO

Grabosky, P and Smith, R, *Crime in the Digital Age*, 1998, London: Transaction

Grabosky, P, Smith, R and Dempsey, G, *Electronic Theft*, 2001, Cambridge: CUP

Levi, M, *The Phantom Capitalists*, 1981, London: Heinemann

Levi, M, 'Sentencing white-collar crime in the dark: the case of the Guinness Four' (1991) 28(4) Howard Journal 257

Levi, M and Pithouse A, *White-Collar Crime and its Victims*, in press, Oxford: Clarendon

Levi, M and Sherwin, D, *Fraud '89: The Extent of Fraud against Large Companies and Executive Views on What Should be Done About It*, 1989, London: Ernst & Young

Levi, M and Sherwin, D, *Fraud: The Unmanaged Risk*, 1992, London: Ernst & Young

Levi, M and Sherwin, D, *Fraud: The Unmanaged Risk*, 1995, London: Ernst & Young

Levi, M and Sherwin, D, *Fraud – The Unmanaged Risk: An International Survey of the Effects of Fraud on Business*, 1996, London: Ernst & Young

Levi, M and Sherwin, D, *Fraud – The Unmanaged Risk: An International Survey of the Effect of Fraud on Business*, 1998, London: Ernst & Young

Levi, M and Sherwin, D, *Fraud – The Unmanaged Risk: An International Survey of the Effect of Fraud on Business*, 2000, London: Ernst & Young

McBarnet, D, 'Whiter than white collar crime: tax, fraud insurance and the management of stigma' (1991) 42(3) Br J of Sociology 324

McBarnet, D and Whelan, C, *Creative Accounting and the Cross-Eyed Javelin Thrower*, 1999, Chichester: John Wiley

Mann, D and Sutton, M, 'NetCrime: more change in the organisation of thieving' (1998) 38 Br J Crim 201

Mantle, J, *For Whom the Bell Tolls*, 1993, London: Mandarin

Mantle, J, *Fool's Gold: Tales from the Last Days of the Credit Culture*, 1995, London: Sinclair Stevenson

Mayhew, P and van Dijk, J, *Criminal Victimisation in Eleven Industrialised Countries*, 1997, The Hague: WODC, Ministry of Justice

Miller, T, Cohen, M and Wiersma, B, *Victim Costs and Consequences: A New Look*, 1996, Washington, DC: National Institute of Justice

Mirrlees-Black, C and Ross, A, *Crime against Retail and Manufacturing Premises: Findings from the 1994 Commercial Victimisation Survey*, 1995, London: HMSO

Pearce, F and Tombs, S, 'Realism and corporate crime', in Matthews, R and Young, J (eds), *Issues in Realist Criminology*, 1992, London: Sage

Pontell, H, Jesilow, P and Geis, G, 'Policing physicians: practitioner fraud and abuse in a government medical program' (1982) 30(1) Social Problems 117

Rebovich, D and Layne, J, *The 1999 National Public Survey on White-Collar Crime Completed*, 2000, Morgantown, West Virginia: National White-Collar Crime Centre

Royal Society, *Risk*, 1992, London: Royal Society

Schneider, S, 'Combating organised crime in (and by) the private sector: a normative role for Canada's forensic investigative firms' (1998) 14(4) J Contemporary Criminal Justice 351

Burrows, J, Hopkins, I, Bamfield, J, Hopkins, M and Ingram, D, *Crime against Business in Scotland*, 1999, Edinburgh: Scottish Executive Central Research Unit

Sen, A, 'On corruption and organised crime', in United Nations International Drug Control Programme (ed), *World Drug Report*, 1997, Oxford: OUP

Shapiro, S, *Thinking about White-Collar Crime: Matters of Conceptualisation and Research*, 1980, Washington, DC: Department of Justice, National Institute of Justice

Sterling, B, *The Hacker Crackdown: Law and Disorder on the Electronic Frontier*, 1993, London: Viking

Titus, R, 'Activity theory and the victim' (1995) 3(3) European Journal on Criminal Policy and Research 41

Titus, R, Heinzelmann, F and Boyle, J, 'Victimisation of persons by fraud' (1995) 41 Crime and Delinquency 54

US Coalition against Insurance Fraud, 'Insurance fraud: the hidden cost', 1998, internet document

Van Wyk, J and Benson, M, 'Fraud victimisation: risky business or just bad luck?' (1997) 21(2) Am J Criminal Justice 164

Chapter 8

Anderson, D and Mullen, P (eds), *Faking It: The Sentimentalisation of Modern Society*, 1998, Harmondsworth: Penguin

Anderson, R, Hughes, J and Sharrock, W, *Working for Profit: The Social Organisation of Calculation in an Entrepreneurial Firm*, 1989, Aldershot: Avebury

Beck, U, *Risk Society: Towards a New Modernity*, 1992, London: Sage

Berger, P and Luckman, T, *The Social Construction of Reality*, 1967, Harmondsworth: Penguin

Bittner, E, 'The police on skid-row: a study in peace keeping' (1967) 32(5) American Sociological Review 699

Bloor, M, *The Sociology of HIV Transmission*, 1995, London: Sage

Cantor, R, 'Rethinking risk management in the Federal Government' (1996) 545 Annals of the American Academy of Political and Social Science 135

Castel, R, 'From dangerousness to risk', in Burchell, G, Gordon, C and Miller, P, *The Foucault Effect: Studies in Governmentality*, 1991, London: Harvester Wheatsheaf

Cleaver, H, Wattam, C and Cawson, P, *Assessing Risk in Child Protection*, 1998, NSPCC Policy Practice Research Series, National Society for Prevention of Cruelty to Children, London

Cohen, S, *Folk Devils and Moral Panics: the Creation of the Mods and Rockers*, 1972, London: MacGibbon and Kee

Collins, H, *Changing Order: Replication and Induction in Scientific Practice*, 1985, London: Sage

Copas, J, 'The offender group reconviction scale: a statistical reconviction score for use by probation officers' (1999) 47(1) Applied Statistics 159

Dear, M and Taylor, S, *Not in Our Street: Community Attitudes to Mental Health Care*, 1982, London: Pion

Dingwall, R, '"Risk Society": the cult of theory and the Millennium?' (1999) 33(4) Social Policy and Administration 474

Dietz, T and Rycroft, R, *The Risk Professionals*, 1987, New York: Russell Sage Foundation

Douglas, M, 'Risk as a forensic resource', in Burger, E (ed), *Risk*, 1990, Ann Arbor: University of Michigan Press

Douglas, M, *Risk and Blame: Essays in Cultural Theory*, 1992, London: Routledge

Douglas, M and Wildavsky, A, *Risk and Culture*, 1982, Berkeley: University of California Press

Dreyfus, H and Rabinow, P, *Michel Foucault: Beyond Structuralism and Hermeneutics*, 1982, New York: Harvester Wheatsheaf

DTI, *Regulation in the Balance: A Guide to Risk Assessment*, 1993, London: Department of Trade and Industry

Duggan, C (ed), 'Assessing risk in the mentally disordered' (1997) Supplement 32 to Br J Psychiatry Vol 170, April

Ericson, R and Haggerty, K, *Policing the Risk Society*, 1997, Oxford: Clarendon

Ewald, F, 'Insurance and risk', in Burchell, G, Gordon, C and Miller, P (eds), *The Foucault Effect: Studies in Governmentality*, 1991, Chicago: University of Chicago Press

Feeley, M and Simon, J, 'The new penology: notes on the emerging strategy of corrections' (1992) 30(4) Criminology 449

Fischhoff, B, Watson, S and Hope, C, 'Defining risk' (1984) 17 Policy Sciences 123

Foucault, M, *The Archaeology of Knowledge*, 1972, London: Tavistock

Foucault, M, *Discipline and Punish: the Birth of the Prison*, Sheridan, A (trans), 1977, London: Allen Lane

Foucault, M, *The History of Sexuality, Vol One: An Introduction*, 1979, London: Allen Lane

Freudenberg, W, 'Perceived risk, real risk: social science and the art of probabilistic risk assessment' (1988) 242 Science 44

Funtowicz, S and Ravetz, J, 'Risk management as a post-normal science' (1992) 12(1) Risk Analysis 95

Garfinkel, H, *Studies in Ethnomethodology*, 1967, Englewood Cliffs, NJ: Prentice-Hall

Giddens, A, *The Consequences of Modernity*, 1990, Cambridge: Polity

Giddens, A, *Modernity and Self-Identity*, 1991, Cambridge: Polity

Goode, E and Ben-Yehuda, N, *Moral Panics: The Social Construction of Deviance*, 1994, Oxford: Blackwell

Gross, P and Levitt, N, *Higher Superstition: The Academic Left and its Quarrels with Science*, 1994, Baltimore: Johns Hopkins University

Hacking, I, *The Social Construction of What?*, 1999, Cambridge, Mass: Harvard UP

Hamilton, J and Bullard, H, 'Dangerousness: which patients should we worry about?', in Hawton, K and Cowen, P (eds), *Dilemmas and Difficulties in the Management of Psychiatric Patients*, 1990, Oxford: OUP

Her Majesty's Government, *Modernising Government*, Cm 4310, 1999, London: HMSO

Her Majesty's Government, *The Interim Response to the Report of the BSE Inquiry*, Cm 5049, 2001, London: HMSO

Hilgartner, S, 'The social construction of risk objects', in Short, J and Clark, L (eds), *Organizations, Uncertainties and Risks*, 1992, Boulder, Colo: Westview

Hinton, J (ed), *Dangerousness: Problems of Assessment and Prediction*, 1983, London: George Allen and Unwin

Home Office/Department of Health, *Managing Dangerous People with Severe Personality Disorder: Proposals for Policy Development*, 1999, London: HMSO

Horlick-Jones, T, 'The problem of blame', in Hood, C and Jones, D (eds) *Accident and Design: Contemporary Debates in Risk Management*, 1996, London: UCL Press

Horlick-Jones, T, 'Meaning and contextualisation in risk assessment' (1998) 59 Reliability Engineering and System Safety 79

Horlick-Jones, T, 'On taking the real world into account in risk research' (2000) Keynote presentation to the ESRC Risk and Human Behaviour Conference, September, London (edited version published in 'Towards a new risk analysis?' ESRC Risk and Human Behaviour Newsletter Issue 8)

Horlick-Jones, T, 'Urban disasters and megacities in a Risk Society', in Giddens, A (ed), *Sociology: Introductory Readings*, 2001, Polity, Cambridge: Polity

Horlick-Jones, T and De Marchi, B, 'The crisis of scientific expertise in *fin de siècle* Europe' (1995) 22(3) Science and Public Policy 139

Horlick-Jones, T and Peters, G, 'Measuring disaster trends; part one: some observations on the Bradford Fatality Scale' (1991) 3(3) Disaster Management 144

Horlick-Jones, T, Rosenhead, J, Ravetz, J, Löfstedt, R and Georgiou, I (in press) 'Decision support for organisational risk management by problem structuring' Health, Risk and Society

Ingleby, D, 'Understanding "mental illness"', in Ingleby, D (ed), *Critical Psychiatry: The Politics of Mental Health*, 1981, Harmondsworth: Penguin

Jasanoff, S, Markle, G, Petersen, J and Pinch, T (eds), *Handbook of Science and Technology Studies*, 1995, Thousand Oaks, CA: Sage

Kemshall, H, *Risk in Probation Practice*, 1998, Aldershot: Ashgate

Kemshall, H, 'Conflicting knowledges on risk: the case of risk knowledge in the probation service' (2000) 2(2) Health, Risk and Society 143

Lash, S, 'Reflexivity and its doubles: structure, aesthetics, community', in Beck, U, Giddens, A and Lash, S, *Reflexive Modernisation: Politics, Tradition and Aesthetics in the Modern Social Order*, 1994, Cambridge: Polity

Latour, B and Woolgar, S, *Laboratory Life: the Construction of Scientific Facts*, 2nd edn, 1986, Princeton, NJ: Princeton UP

Löfstedt, R and Horlick-Jones, T, 'Environmental regulation in the UK: politics, institutional change and public trust' (1999) in Cvetkovich, G and Löfstedt, R (eds), *Social Trust and the Management of Risk*, 1999, London: Earthscan

Lupton, D, *Risk*, 1999, London: Routledge

Mandel, M, *The High Risk Society*, 1996, New York: Times Business

Manning, P, 'Managing risk: managing uncertainty in the British nuclear installations inspectorate', in Short, J and Clarke, L (eds), *Organizations, Uncertainty and Risk*, 1992, Boulder: Westview

Marsh, D (ed), *Comparing Policy Networks*, 1998, Buckingham: Open UP

McQuaid, J, 'Improving the use of risk assessment in government' (1995) 73(B4) Transactions of the Institution of Chemical Engineers 539

O'Brien, M, Penna, S and Hay, C (eds), *Theorising Modernity*, 1999, Harlow: Addison-Wesley Longman

O'Riordan, T, Kemp, R and Purdue, H, 'On weighing gains and investments at the margin of risk regulation' (1987) 7(3) Risk Analysis 361

Osborne, D and Gaebler, T, *Reinventing Government*, 1992, Reading MA: Addison-Wesley

Parton, N, 'Risk, advanced liberalism and child welfare: the need to rediscover uncertainty and ambiguity' (1998) 28 Br J Social Work 5

Petts, J, Horlick-Jones, T and Murdock, G, *Social Amplification of Risk: The Media and the Public*, 2001, Contract Research Report 329/2001, Sudbury: HSE

Pfohl, S, *Predicting Dangerousness: The Social Construction of Psychiatric Reality*, 1978, Lexington, Mass: Lexington/DC Heath and Co

Polanyi, M, *Personal Knowledge*, 1958, London: Routledge and Kegan Paul

Porter, T, *Trust in Numbers: The Pursuit of Objectivity in Science and Public Life*, 1995, Princeton, NJ: Princeton UP

Power, M, *The Audit Explosion*, 1994, London: Demos

Reed, J, 'Risk assessment and clinical risk management: the lessons from recent inquiries', in Duggan, C (ed), *Assessing Risk in the Mentally Disordered* Supplement 32 to 170 Br J Psychiatry 4

Renn, O, 'Concepts of risk: a classification', in Krimsky, S and Golding, D (eds), *Social Theories of Risk*, 1992, Westport, Conn: Praeger

Rip, A, Misa, T and Schot, J (eds), *Managing Technology in Society: The Approach of Constructive Technology Assessment*, 1995, London: Pinter

Rose, N, 'Governing risky individuals: the role of psychiatry in new regimes of control' (1998) 5(2) Psychiatry, Psychology and Law 1

Rose, N, *Powers of Freedom*, 1999a, Cambridge: CUP

Rose, N, *Governing the Soul: The Shaping of the Private Self*, 2nd edn, 1999b, London: Routledge

Rosenhead, J and Thunhurst, C, 'Operational research and cost benefit analysis: whose science?', in Irvine, H, Miles, I and Evans, J (eds), *Demystifying Social Statistics*, 1979, London: Pluto

Sacks, H, *Lectures in Conversation*, 1992, Vols I and II (reprinted from notes on lectures delivered 1964–68 at the University of California), Oxford: Blackwell

Schön, D, *The Reflective Practitioner: How Professionals Think in Action*, 1983, New York: Basic, Schon

Sperber, D, *Rethinking Symbolism*, 1975, Cambridge: CUP

Snowden, P, 'Practical aspects of clinical risk assessment and management', in Duggen, C (ed) *Assessing risk in the mentally disordered* Supplement 32 to (1997) 170 Br J Psychiatry 32

Spector, M and Kitsuse, J, *Constructing Social Problems*, 1987, New York: Aldine De Gruyter

Stanko, E, 'Safety talk: conceptualising women's risk assessment as a "technology of the soul"' (1997) 1(4) Theoretical Criminology 479

UKOOA, *A Framework for Risk Related Decision Support*, 1999, London: UK Offshore Operators Association

Vaughan, D, *The Challenger Launch Decision: Risky Technology, Culture and Deviance at NASA*, 1996, Chicago: University of Chicago Press

Velody, I and Williams, R (eds), *The Politics of Constructionism*, 1998, London: Sage

Wolpert, L, *The Unnatural Nature of Science*, 1992, London: Faber and Faber

Woolgar, S, *Science: The Very Idea*, 1988, Chichester: Ellis Horwood/London: Tavistock

Wynne, B, 'Institutional mythologies and dual societies in the management of risk', in Kunreuther, H and Ley, E (eds), *The Risk Analysis Controversy*, 1982a, Berlin: Springer-Verlag

Wynne, B, *Rationality and Ritual*, 1982b, Chalfont St Giles: British Society for the History of Science

Wynne, B, 'Frameworks of rationality in risk management: towards the testing of näive sociology', in Brown, J (ed), *Environmental Threats: Perception, Analysis and Management*, 1989, London: Belhaven

Wynne, B, 'Knowledges in context' (1991) 16(1) Science, Technology and Human Values 111

Wynne, B, 'May the sheep safety graze? A reflexive view of the expert-lay knowledge divide', in Lash, S, Szerszynski, B and Wynne, B (eds), *Risk, Environment and Modernity: Towards a New Ecology*, 1996, London: Sage

Zonabend, F, *The Nuclear Peninsula*, 1993, Cambridge: CUP/Paris: Editions de la Maison des Sciences de l'Homme

Chapter 9

Ashworth, A, Gardner, J, Morgan, R, Smith, A, Von Hirsch, A and Wasik, M, 'Neighbouring on the oppressive: the Government's "Anti-Social Behaviour Order" proposals' (1998) 16(1) Criminal Justice 7

Beck, U, *The Risk Society: Towards a New Modernity*, 1992, London: Sage

Bergquist, W, Betwee, J and Meuel, D, *Building Strategic Relationships*, 1995, San Francisco: Jossey-Bass

Bottoms, A, 'Reflections on the renaissance of dangerousness' (1977) 16(2) Howard Journal 70

Bottoms, A, 'The philosophy and politics of punishment and sentencing', in Clarkson, C and Morgan, R (eds), *The Politics of Sentencing Reform*, 1995, Oxford: OUP

Bottoms, A and Brownsword, R, 'Dangerousness and Rights', in Hinton, J (ed), *Dangerousness: Problems of Assessment and Prediction*, 1983, London: Allen and Unwin

Butler Committee, *Report of the Committee on Mentally Abnormal Offenders*, Cmnd 6244, 1975, London: HMSO

Christie, N, *Crime Control as Industry: Towards Gulags, Western Style*, 1994, London: Routledge

Clarke, J and Langan, M, 'Restructuring welfare: the British welfare regime in the 1980s', in Cochrane, A and Clarke, J (eds), *Comparing Welfare States: Britain in International Context*, 1993, London: Sage/Open UP

Cobley, C, 'Keeping track of sex offenders: Part 1 of the Sex Offenders Act 1997' (1999) 60 MLR 690

Cross, B, 'Partnership in practice: the experience of two probation services' (1997) 36(1) Howard Journal 62

Davidson, S, 'Planning and co-ordination of social services in multi-organisational contexts' (1976) 50 Social Services Review 117

Davies, C, 'The demise of professional self-regulation: a moment to mourn?' in Lewis, G, Gewortz, S and Clarke, J (eds), *Rethinking Social Policy*, 2000, London: Sage

Douglas, M, *Risk and Blame: Essays in Cultural Theory*, 1992, London: Routledge

Ericson, RV and Haggerty, KD, *Policing and the Risk Society*, Clarendon Studies in Criminology, 1997, Oxford: OUP

Feeley, M and Simon, J, 'The new penology: notes on the emerging strategy for corrections' (1992) 30(4) Criminology 449

Feeley, M and Simon, J, 'Actuarial justice: the emerging new criminal law', in Nelken, D (ed), *The Futures of Criminology*, 1994, London: Sage

Floud, J and Young, W, *Dangerousness and Criminal Justice*, 1981, London: Heinemann

Foucault, M, *The Archaeology of Knowledge*, Sheridan, A (trans), 1971, London: Tavistock

Garland, A, 'Penal modernism and postmodernism', in Blomberg, T and Cohen, S (eds), *Punishment and Social Control: Essays in Honor of Sheldon Messinger*, 1995, New York: Aldine De Gruyter

Garland, D, 'The limits of the Sovereign State: strategies of crime control in contemporary society' (1996) 36(4) Br J Crim 445

Giddens, A, *The Third Way: The Renewal of Social Democracy*, 1998a, Cambridge: Polity

Giddens, A, 'Risk society: the context of British politics', in Franklin, J (ed), *The Politics of Risk Society*, 1998b, Cambridge: Polity in association with the IPPR

Giddens, A, *The Consequences of Modernity*, 1990, Cambridge: Polity

Gilling, DJ, 'Multi-agency crime prevention: some barriers to collaboration', (1994) 33(3) Howard Journal 246

Grubin, D, *Sex Offending Against Children: Understanding the Risk*, Police Research Series Paper 99, 1998, London: Home Office

Hacking, I, *The Taming of Chance*, 1991, Cambridge: CUP

Hanson, R and Thornton, D, 'Improving risk assessments for sex offenders: a comparison of three actuarial scales' (2000) 24(1) Law and Human Behaviour 119

Hebenton, B and Thomas, T, 'Tracking sex offenders' (1996) 35(2) Howard Journal 97

Hebenton, B and Thomas, T, *Keeping Track? Observations on Sex Offender Registrations in the US*, Crime Detection and Prevention Series Paper 83, 1997, London: HMSO

Hayward, C, 'Managing risk together: a template for inter-agency collaboration to protect the public', unpublished MBA Dissertation, 1999, Kingston Business School

Home Office, *Partnership in Dealing with Offenders in the Community*, 1992, London: HMSO

Home Office, *Managing Dangerous People with Severe Personality Disorder: Proposals for Policy Developments*, 1999, London: HMSO

Hughes, B, Parker, H and Gallagher, B, *Policing Child Sexual Abuse: The View from Police Practitioners*, 1996, London: HMSO

James, A and Bottomley, K, 'Probation partnerships revisited' (1994) 33(2) Howard Journal 158

Kellner, D, 'Theorizing the present moments: debates between modern and postmodern theory' (1999) 28 Theory and Society 639

Kemshall, H, *Reviewing Risk: A Review of Research on the Assessment and Management of Risk and Dangerousness: Implications for Policy and Practice in the Probation Service*, 1996, London: Home Office

Kemshall, H, *Risk in Probation Practice*, 1998, Aldershot: Ashgate

Kemshall, H, *Risk Assessment and Management of Known Sexual and Violent Offenders: A Review of Current Issues*, 2000, London: Home Office

Kemshall, H, Parton, N, Walsh, M and Waterson, J, 'Concepts of risk in relation to organisational structure and functioning within the personal social services and probation' (1997) 31(3) Social Policy and Administration 213

Kemshall, H and Ross, E, 'Value for money in probation partnerships', (2000) Social Policy and Administration, December, forthcoming

Leicestershire and Rutland Public Protection Panel, *Specification for Evaluation and Monitoring: Consultancy Briefing Notes*, 2000

Leiss, W and Chociolko, C, *Risk and Responsibility*, 1994, London: McGill-Queen's UP

Lemert, E, 'Visions of social control: probation considered' (1993) 39 Crime and Delinquency 447

Leonard, P, *Postmodern Welfare: Reconstructing an Emancipatory Project*, 1997, London: Sage

Lynch, M, 'Waste managers? The new penology, crime fighting and the parole agent identity' (1998) 32(4) Law and Society Review 839

Lynch, M, 'Rehabilitation and rhetoric: the ideal of reformation in contemporary parole discourse and practices' (2000) 2(1) Punishment and Society 40

National Institute of Social Work, *GSCC Implementation Group General Social Services Council: Principles and Concepts*, 1997, London: NISW

Maguire, M, 'Parole', in Stockdale, E and Casale, S (ed), *Criminal Justice Under Stress*, 1992, London: Blackstone

Maguire, M, 'POP, ILP and partnership' (1998) 32 Criminal Justice Matters 22

Maguire, M, 'Policing by risks and targets: some dimensions and implications of intelligence-led crime control' (2000) 9 Policing and Society 315

Maguire, M and John, T, *Intelligence, Surveillance and Informants: Integrated Approaches*, 1995, Crime Detection and Prevention Paper 64, London: Home Office

Maguire, M, Kemshall, H, Noaks, L, Sharpe, K and Wincup, E, *Risk Management of Sexual and Violent Offenders: The Work of Public Protection Panels*, 2001, London: Home Office

Monahan, J, *Predicting Violent Behaviour*, 1981, Beverly Hills: Sage

Monahan, J, 'Clinical and actuarial predictions of violence', in Faigman, D, Kaye, D, Saks, M and Sanders, J (eds), *West's Companion to Scientific Evidence*, 1997, St Pauls, Minn: West

O'Malley, P, *Crime and the Risk Society*, 1998, Aldershot: Ashgate

Parton, N, 'Social work under conditions of (post) modernity' (1994) 5(2) Social Work and Social Sciences Review 92

Plotnikoff, J and Woolfson, R, *Where Are They Now? An Evaluation of Sex Offender Registration in England and Wales*, 2000, London: Home Office

Power, M, *The Audit Explosion*, 1994, London: Demos

Power, H, 'The Crime and Disorder Act 1998: sex offenders, privacy and the Police' [1999] Crim LR 3

Pratt, J, 'Dangerousness, risk and technologies of power' (1995) 29 Australian and New Zealand J Crim 236

Pratt, J, 'The return of the wheelbarrow men: or, the arrival of postmodern penality?' (2000) 40 Br J Crim 127

Prins, H, 'Risk assessment: seven sins of omission' (1995) 42(4) Probation Journal 199

Radzinowicz, L and Hood, R, 'A dangerous direction for sentencing reform' [1981] Crim LR 756

Reichman, N, 'Managing crime risks: toward an insurance based model of crime control' (1986) 8 Research in Law, Deviance and Social Control 151

Rose, N, 'Governing "advanced" liberal democracies', in Barry, A, Osbourne, T and Rose, N (eds), Foucault and Political Reason, 1996, London: UCL Press

Rose, N, 'Government and control', (2000) 40 Br J Crim 321

Scott, J and Ward, D, 'Human rights and the probation service' (1999) 5(2) Vista106

Simon, J, 'The ideological effects of actuarial practices' (1988) 22 Law and Society Review 772

Simon, J, Poor Discipline: Parole and the Social Control of the Underclass, 1993, Chicago: University of Chicago Press

Simon, J and Feeley, M, 'True crime: the new penology and public discourse on crime', in Blomberg, T and Cohen, S (eds), Punishment and Social Control: Essays in Honor of Sheldon Messinger, 1995, New York: Aldine De Gruyter

Sparks, R, 'Recent social theory and the study of crime and punishment', in Maguire, M, Morgan, R and Reiner, R (eds), The Oxford Handbook of Criminology, 1997, Oxford: OUP

Chapter 10

Ashworth, A and Hough, M, 'Sentencing and the climate of opinion' [1996] Crim LR 776

Ashworth, A, Gardner, J, Morgan, R, Smith, ATH, von Hirsch, A and Wasik, M, 'Neighbouring on the oppressive' (1998) 16(1) Criminal Justice 7

Audit Commission, Misspent Youth: Young People and Crime, 1996, London: Audit Commission

Beck, U, Risk Society, 1992, London: Sage

Benyon, J and Edwards, A, 'Crime and public order', in Dunleavy, P, Gamble, A, Holliday, I and Peele, G (eds) Developments in British Politics 5, 1997, Basingstoke: Macmillan

Brake, M and Hale, C, Public Order and Private Lives: The Politics of Law and Order, 1992, London: Routledge

Brownlee, I, 'New Labour-new penology? Punitive rhetoric and the limits of managerialism in criminal justice policy' (1998) 25(3) J Law and Society 313

Buckby, S, 'Reforming the Welfare State: a new social contract' (1998) 110(1) Fabian Review

Burney, E, *Crime and Banishment: Nuisance and Exclusion in Social Housing*, 1999, Winchester: Waterside

Copas, J, Ditchfield, J and Marshall, P, 'Development of a new reconviction score' (1994) 36 Home Office Research Bulletin 30

Douglas, M, *Risk and Blame: Essays in Cultural Theory*, 1992, London: Routledge

Downes, D and Morgan, R, 'Dumping the hostages to fortune: the politics of law and order in post-war Britain', in Maguire, M, Morgan, R and Reiner, R (eds), *The Oxford Handbook of Criminology*, 2nd edn, 1996, Oxford: OUP

Feeley, M and Simon, J, 'The new penology: notes on the emerging strategy of corrections and its implications' (1992) 30(4) Criminology 449

Garland, D, 'The limits of the Sovereign State' (1996) 36(4) Br J Crim 445

Giddens, A, *Modernity and Self-Identity*, 1991, Cambridge: Polity

Giddens, A, *The Third Way*, 1998, Cambridge: Polity

Gray, J, *Endgames: Questions in Late Modern Political Thought*, 1997, Cambridge: Polity

Hall, S, 'Drifting into a law and order society', The Cobden Lecture, 1979, London: Cobden Trust

Hall, S, *The Hard Road to Renewal: Thatcherism and the Crisis of the Left*, 1988, London: Lawrence and Wishart

Hall, S, Clarke, J, Critcher, C, Jefferson, T and Roberts, B, *Policing the Crisis*, 1978, London: Macmillan

Hay, C, *Re-Stating Social and Political Change*, 1996, Buckingham: Open UP

Hencke, D, 'Field "victory" in welfare revolution' (1997) *The Guardian*, 21 October

Henham, R, 'Anglo-American approaches to cumulative sentencing and the implications for UK sentencing policy' (1997) 36(3) Howard Journal 263

Hirschmann, D, 'Parole and the dangerous offender', in Walker, N (ed), *Dangerous People*, 1996, London: Blackstone

Home Office, *No More Excuses*, Cm 3809, 1997, London: HMSO

Hood, R and Shute, S, *Parole in Transition*, 1994, Oxford: Centre for Criminological Research

Hood, R and Shute, S, *Paroling With New Criteria*, 1995, Oxford: Centre for Criminological Research

Hood, R and Shute, S, 'Parole criteria, parole decisions and the prison population: evaluating the impact of the Criminal Justice Act 1991' [1996] Crim LR 77

Levitas, R, *The Inclusive Society? Social Exclusion and New Labour*, 1998, Basingstoke: Macmillan

Maguire, M, Peroud, B and Raynor, P, *Automatic Conditional Release: The First Two Years*, Home Office Research Study 156, 1996, London: Home Office

Melossi, D, 'Gazette of morality and social whip' (1993) 2 Social and Legal Studies 259

Mikosz, D, 'The Third Way' (1998) 110(1) Fabian Review

O'Malley, P, 'Risk, power and crime prevention' (1992) 21(3) Economy and Society 252

O'Malley, P, 'Volatile and contradictory punishment' (1999) 3(2) Theoretical Criminology 175

O'Malley, P, 'Uncertain subjects: risks, liberalism and contract' (2000a) 29(4) Economy and Society 460

O'Malley, P, 'Criminologies of catastrophe: understanding criminal justice on the edge of the new millennium' (2000b) 33(2) Australian and New Zealand J of Crim 153

Rose, N, 'Government and control', in Garland, D and Sparks, R (eds), *Criminology and Social Theory*, 2000, Oxford: OUP

Ryan, M, 'Penal policy making towards the millennium: elites and populists; New Labour and the new criminology' (1999) 27 Int J Sociology of Law 1

Shapland, J and Sparks, R, 'Les politiques penales et la politique', in Van Outrive, L and Robert, P (eds), *Crime et Justice en Europe Depuis 1990*, 1999, Paris: Harmattan

Sparks, R, 'Penal austerity: the doctrine of less eligibility reborn?', in Francis, F and Matthews, R (eds), *Prisons 2000*, 1996, London: Macmillan

Sparks, R, 'Perspectives on risk and penal politics', in Hope, T and Sparks, R (eds), *Crime, Risk and Insecurity*, 2000, London: Routledge

Sparks, R, 'Penal austerity and social anxiety at the century's turn: governmental rationalities, legitimation deficits and populism in British penal politics in the 1990s', in Loic Wacquant (ed), *From Social State to Penal State*, in press, University of Minnesota Press

Stenson, K and Edwards, A, 'Crime control and liberal government: the Third Way and the return to the local', in Stenson, K and Sullivan, R (eds), *Crime, Risk and Justice*, 2000, Devon: Willan

Travis, A, 'Straw ups the stakes on crime' (2001) *The Guardian*, 20 January

Windlesham, Lord, *Responses to Crime, Vol 3: Legislating with the Tide*, 1996, Oxford: OUP

INDEX

Printed in the United Kingdom
by Lightning Source UK Ltd.
114939UKS00001B/52